W9-ABH-979

EUCHARISTIC RESERVATION IN THE WESTERN CHURCH

Eucharistic Reservation in the Western Church

By
ARCHDALE A. KING

SHEED AND WARD : NEW YORK

Nihil obstat: Ricardus Roche, s.t.d., *censor deputatus*

Imprimatur: ✠ Franciscus, *Archiepiscopus Birmingamiensis*

datum Birmingamiae, 17*a Augusti*, 1964

The *Nihil obstat* and *Imprimatur* are a declaration that a book or pamphlet is considered to be free from doctrinal or moral error. It is not implied that those who have granted the *Nihil obstat* and *Imprimatur* agree with the contents, opinions or statements expressed. The *Nihil obstat* and *Imprimatur* in this book, *Eucharistic Reservation in the Western Church*, refer to the main section.

Library of Congress Catalog Card Number 65-20722

PRINTED IN GREAT BRITAIN

PREFACE

BY THE REV. CANON J. B. O'CONNELL

Member of the Liturgical Commission of the Second Vatican Council

THE story of Eucharistic Reservation in the Western Church is not only of great interest to liturgiologists, but it is important for the light that it throws on the theology of the Blessed Eucharist: for example, the evidence that it affords of the constant, firm belief in the Real Presence from the earliest centuries of the Church.

Mr. King divides the story into three clear periods: reservation before the twelfth century; from that century to the Reformation (which introduced drastic changes into the theology of the Eucharist); and from the Reformation until the codification of the Canon Law (1918), which summarizes the existing legislation on Reservation.

He deals not only with the manner of reservation, so varied over the centuries (the place, mode, marks of honour gradually introduced to the Sacrament and so on), but also with the development of the worship of the Reserved Sacrament—including its ceremonial manifestation—which was not prominent for the first thousand years of the Church's history, but blossomed forth so abundantly from the later middle ages: exposition of the Sacred Host, processions in Its honour, Benediction with the Blessed Sacrament, and the rest. The exuberance of devotion to the Sacrament since the thirteenth and subsequent centuries needed no encouragement, but rather control by the Church, and so this book gives an account of the development of legislation on this point.

For full measure Mr. King treats of such questions as the time and manner of the distribution of Holy Communion and its frequency.

One outstanding value of this book is the writer's diligent study of documents dealing with Eucharistic piety. His statements all through are well documented, not merely from the works of liturgical scholars, but by exact references to original sources. These are frequently cited textually.

The excellent illustrations of Eucharistic vessels, etc., are a valuable addition to the text.

Eucharistic Reservation in the Western Church should be of great interest to readers of all Christian denominations.

J. B. O'Connell.

Westminster
Corpus Christi, 1964.

AUTHOR'S PREFACE

It is not always realized how primitive was the practice of reserving the Blessed Sacrament, although in the early centuries it would not have been in the church. Similarly, it may seem strange to many that for a thousand years there was little or no idea of any worship of the reserved Eucharist. Tabernacles, also, as we know them today, were virtually unknown before the sixteenth century.

A number of books have appeared in England on the subject of reservation, but they have been mainly written from a propaganda standpoint: the legality or otherwise of the practice in the Church of England. Here, however, an attempt has been made to give a succinct and factual history of reservation in the Western Church from the earliest times to the codification of Canon Law in 1918. Contemporary references have been given, whenever possible, with descriptions of the various places and modes of reserving the Sacrament over the centuries.

A full account has been given also of the ceremonies connected with the Easter sepulchre on the concluding days of Holy Week, with special mention of the eucharistic processions of 'burial' and 'resurrection,' still to be witnessed in the primatial church of Braga.

It is indeed an undeserved honour that a member of the Liturgical Commission of the Second Vatican Council has been kind enough to supply a foreword.

Much valuable advice was given by Canon Pilkington of Westminster Cathedral, who corrected and improved the manuscript, as it was being written.

I would also like to thank Mr. Martin Gillett for bringing to my notice a mode of reservation popular in many of the churches of Aragon.

It would be impossible to name all those who have helped me in my researches, but I am by no means ungrateful for their kindly assistance.

Similar feelings pertain to those who have supplied the illustrations, and in particular I would like to thank Bishop Colin Dunlop for so generously making it possible for me to obtain a photograph of the Easter sepulchre in Lincoln Cathedral, where he was formerly dean.

A reproduction of the engraving of the thirteenth-century high altar of Arras Cathedral was supplied by the well-known Cistercian historian, Fr. Anselme Dimier, who, over the years, has helped me in so many and various ways.

Dr. Eric Segelberg, a priest of the Lutheran Church of Sweden and professor of Uppsala University, sent me a photograph of the sacrament house in the cathedral church of Linköping, and provided information as to modes of reservation in the medieval churches of his country. Fr. Duin of Hamar has greatly helped also respecting Norwegian churches.

In conclusion, a word of thanks to a law student of Louvain University, M. Frederick Maes, for all the trouble he has taken to obtain illustrations of some of the magnificent sacrament houses to be found in Belgium.

ARCHDALE A. KING.

Westminster
Corpus Christi, 1964.

CONTENTS

Part I

RESERVATION BEFORE THE TWELFTH CENTURY

Part II

RESERVATION FROM THE TWELFTH CENTURY TO THE REFORMATION

Part III

RESERVATION FROM THE REFORMATION TO THE CODIFICATION OF CANON LAW

SUPPLEMENT

By Cyril E. Pocknee

LIST OF ILLUSTRATIONS

ACKNOWLEDGEMENTS

THANKS are due to the following for the use of copyright photographs, in addition to those acknowledged elsewhere:

Institut Royal du Patrimoine Artistique, 1 Parc du Cinquantenaire, Bruxelles, for Plates 13, 14, 15.

Victoria and Albert Museum, South Kensington, London, for Plates 3, 6, 8.

Plates 23 and 24 are reproduced by permission of the Dean and Chapter of Gloucester Cathedral.

The photograph for Plate 21 was kindly supplied by the Rev. C. E. Pocknee, who has kindly given much help with the choice of illustrations for this book.

PART I

RESERVATION BEFORE THE TWELFTH CENTURY

1: PURPOSE OF THE RESERVED SACRAMENT

For the Communion of the Faithful

THE earliest reference to a reservation of the Blessed Sacrament after the conclusion of the liturgy dates from about the middle of the second century. It is found in the *Apologia* of St. Justin Martyr (*c.* 155), where we read that the Eucharist was taken by deacons to those who had been unable to attend the service: 'When the president has given thanks, and all the people have expressed their assent ["Amen"], then those whom we call deacons give to each of those present to partake of bread and wine mixed with water over which the thanksgiving has been pronounced; and they carry away [a portion] to those who are absent.'[1] And again in another place: 'The distribution and partaking of those things over which the thanksgiving has been pronounced is made to each one, and [they] are sent to the absent by the hands of the deacons.'[2]

This would seem to have been the practice at Rome and, probably, elsewhere, especially in Palestine and Ephesus, where the saint had previously lived.[3]

In the next century, Pope St. Damasus (366–84) composed a poem in honour of the martyred acolyte Tarcisius, who had been beaten and stoned to death while carrying the Sacrament to one of the faithful:[4]

> Tharcisium sanctum Christi Sacramenta gerentem
> Cum malesana manus peteret vulgare prophanis,

[1] Just. Mart., *Apol.* I, 65; *Pat. Graec.*, t. IV, col. 428 (Gk.), 427 (Lat.); Blunt, *Apol. of Justin Martyr* (Cambridge, 1911), p. 98.
[2] *Ibid.*, *Apol.* I, 67; *ibid.*, t. IV, col. 429 (Gk.), 430 (Lat.), Blunt, p. 101.
[3] Köster, *De Custodia Sanctissimae Eucharistiae*, p. 8.
[4] *Damasus*, carmen XXXV; *Pat. Lat.*, t. CXXIII, col. 331–32.

Ipse animam potius voluit dimittere caesus
Prodere quam canibus rabidis caelestia membra.

Tarcisius had refused to show the pagans what he was carrying, and had evidently consumed the sacred species, since there was no trace of it when his body was recovered. In these circumstances it would have been difficult for him to do so, if the Eucharist had not been either in one kind or intincted in the precious blood. The death is chronicled on August 15th in the Martyrology of Ado (ninth century).

For Viaticum

The first and primary purpose of reserving the Blessed Sacrament has always been to have it in readiness for those who were in danger of death, and from the earliest times Viaticum has been regarded as indispensable for those in a position to obtain it. The first text extant in which there is an express mention of Viaticum comes from the East. Dionysius, bishop of Alexandria (247–64), speaks of a certain Serapion, who, conscious of approaching death, sent his nephew to ask the priest to bring him the Blessed Sacrament. The priest himself was ill, and entrusted the Eucharist to the boy.[1]

The first council of Nicea (325) was silent on the subject of reservation, despite the assertion of the council of Trent,[2] but, unless it had been a general practice of the Church, it would have been impossible to administer the Viaticum. 'With respect to the dying,' says Nicea, 'the ancient and canonical rule of the Church should continue to be observed, which forbids that anyone who is on the point of death should be deprived of the last and most necessary Viaticum

[1] Eusebius, *Hist. Eccl.*, lib. VI, cap. XLIV.

[2] 'The custom of reserving the holy Eucharist in the *secretarium* is so ancient, that even the century of the Nicene Council knew of it.' Trent, sess. XIII (2 October 1551), cap. VI, can. 6; Denzinger-Schönmetzer (1963), p. 388.

(ἐφοδίν) . . . And let the bishop give the Eucharist with due investigation, to everyone who asks to receive it at the end.'[1]

Later in the century, we read in the life of St. Ambrose, written by his secretary Paulinus almost immediately after the death of the saint (397), that he asked Honoratus, bishop of Vercelli, to give him the Eucharist, and that he died in the act of consuming it.[2]

References to the administration of Viaticum become increasingly frequent after the sixth century, and in the so-called Statutes of St. Boniface (ninth century) there is a first hint of the obligation of reserving the Eucharist: priests are reminded that it is incumbent upon them to take the sacred chrism, holy oil and life-giving Eucharist when on a journey.[3] The Excerpts, to which the name of Egbert, archbishop of York (748), has been attached, although they are probably no earlier than the middle of the ninth century, say that every priest should mercifully give the Viaticum and communion of the body of Christ to all the sick before they pass from this world.[4] And again in another place: that the priest should always have the Eucharist at hand to administer it to the sick, lest they should die without communion.[5]

In the following century, a number of episcopal decrees expressed a similar obligation, and often in more or less the same words.[6] One of the canons enacted under the Anglo-Saxon King Edgar (959–75) enjoined that 'a priest have the housel always ready for those who need it.'[7] Full directions

[1] I Nicea, 325, can. 13; Labbe, *Concil.*, t. II, p. 36.
[2] *Sancti Ambrosii opera omnia*, edit. Ballerini, t. VI (Milan, 1883), cap. XLVII, pp. 902–03.
[3] *Stat. S. Bonif.*, can. 4; Mansi, *Concil.*, t. XII, col. 383–84; cf. can. 18, *ibid.*, col. 385.
[4] *Excerpt. Ecgberti*, XX; Thorpe, *Ancient Laws and Institutes of England*, vol. 2 (London, 1840), p. 100.
[5] *Excerpt. Ecgberti*, XII; *ibid.*
[6] Köster, *op. cit.*, p. 12.
[7] Can. 38; Thorpe, *op. cit.*, vol. 2, p. 253.

for administering unction and communion to sick monks are also found in the *Concordia Regularis*, a tenth-century work ascribed to St. Ethelwold (d. 984) or St. Dunstan (d. 988). The monks were bidden to receive the Sacrament daily from the morrow-mass of the convent, to be brought with some considerable ceremony, and in the presence of the brethren.[1] Odo of Cluny, in his life of Gerald of Aurillac (d. *c.* 950) records the celebration of Mass, in order to provide Viaticum after compline.[2] When the first abbot of Bec, St. Herluin, was dying (1078), monks were sent to the church for the Sacrament, but found on arrival that the pyx was empty. It so happened, however, that a priest was saying Mass at the time, and was holding in his hand the host that he had just consecrated. It was possible therefore for a portion of this host to be taken to the dying abbot.[3]

The paramount importance of receiving the Viaticum before death is shown in the ninth-century life of the Alsatian abbess, St. Odilia (d. 720), recording how her companions, fearing that the saint had died without communion, restored her to life through their prayers. Then she asked for a chalice wherein the Sacrament—Body and Blood of the Lord—was kept, and so made her communion.[4] There is no hint in the narrative, says Freestone, that the saint sent at Mass time for the Eucharist, and the natural sense of the passage is that the sacrament was reserved conjointly in both kinds in a chalice.[5] It would probably have been an intincted host, which, as Andrieu says, was for long everywhere widespread.[6] Evidence of this usage

[1] *Pat. Lat.*, t. CXXXVII, col. 50. [2] *Pat. Lat.*, t. CXXXIII, col. 694.
[3] *Pat. Lat.*, t. CXXXIII, col. 711.
[4] *Vita*, p. 22; Freestone, *The Sacrament Reserved* (London, 1917), p. 138.
[5] Freestone, *op. cit.*, p. 138.
[6] Andrieu, *Immixtio et Consecratio* (Paris, 1924), pp. 114–41.

is also given by Dom Lambot in the *North Italian Services of the Eleventh Century*.[1]

Later, about the twelfth century, inspired by the Presanctified rite of Good Friday, the host, for practical reasons, was dipped in ordinary wine, which was thought at the time to be consecrated by contact.[2]

Ritual Reservation signifying Unity of Faith and Sacrifice

The doctrinal origin of this ritual reservation in the early centuries of the Church is to be found in the First Epistle of St. Paul to the Corinthians: 'Is not the bread we break a participation in Christ's body? The one bread makes us one body, though we are many in number; the same bread is shared by all.'[3]

St. Ignatius of Antioch (*c.* 107) in his epistles strongly emphasized the note of unity in celebrating the one Eucharist in the one church or diocese. Writing to the Philadelphians, he says: 'Take great care to keep one Eucharist.[4] For there is one flesh of our Lord Jesus Christ and one cup to unite us by His blood; one sanctuary, as there is one bishop, together with the presbytery and the deacons, my fellow-servants. Thus all your acts may be done according to God's will.'[5]

The inestimable value of this one Eucharist has been well expressed by the seventeenth-century Anglican bishop of Durham, John Cosin: The virtue of the Eucharistic sacrifice 'doth not only extend itself to the living and those that are present, but likewise to them that are absent, and

[1] Lambot, *North Italian Services of the 11th century*; *Henry Bradshaw Society* (1931), pp. XLI, 47.
[2] Andrieu, *op. cit.*, pp. 141–44. [3] 1 Cor. x. 16–17, Knox version.
[4] The first use of this word for the Sacrament.
[5] Ignat., *Epist. to the Philadelphians*, IV; Bettenson, *Early Christian Fathers* (London, 1963), p. 64.

them that be already departed, or shall in time to come live and die in the faith of Christ.'[1]

Fermentum

The rite of fermentum comprised a transmission of a particle of the consecrated bread to the bishop of another church, who, as a token of unity, consumed it at his own Liturgy. No bread other than leavened would have been used at this early period, but it is unlikely that the term *fermentum* would have indicated this. It was rather that the leaven of unity permeates and transforms Christians, so that they become one in Christ.

Already in the second century, popes sent the Eucharist to other bishops as a pledge of unity of faith, as we learn from Eusebius, who in his *Ecclesiastical History* recalled the letter of St. Irenaeus of Lyons (*c.* 195) to Pope Victor I, in which he protested against the pontiff's excommunication of those who followed the Asiatic reckoning of Easter (Quartodecimans). The relevant passage runs: 'Your predecessors before Soter who presided over the church of which you are now the head, I mean Anicetus and Pius, Hyginus and Telesphorus and Sixtus, never kept [the Asiatic custom] nor would they permit those with them to do so. And none the less, though they did not keep it themselves, they were at peace with those who came to them from the "parishes"[2] in which it was kept . . . and never was anyone excommunicated for this reason. But though they did not keep [this custom] your predecessors sent the Eucharist to those from the "parishes" which observed it.'[3]

[1] John Cosin, *Works*, vol. V (Oxford, 1855), pp. 352 seq.
[2] Parishes, *paroikiai*, is the usual pre-Nicene word for a church with its own bishop.
[3] Eusebius, *Eccles. Hist.*, bk. V, 24.

It seems improbable that the Eucharist would have been sent across the sea to Asia Minor, and in later times the *fermentum* was expressly forbidden to be sent outside the confines of the diocese or even of the city. These *paroikiai* would most likely have been groups of Asiatic Christians living in Rome with clergy of their own and following their own customs. In second-century Rome, their union with its bishop was symbolized by sending to them the *fermentum* reserved from the papal Eucharist.[1] Irenaeus, as a Christian from Smyrna, would himself have been at one time a member of one of these 'parishes' in Rome.[2] It is noteworthy that Irenaeus recalled the sending of the *fermentum* at Rome uninterruptedly for the past thirty years, which would have carried the practice back to about the year 120. Other bishops followed a similar custom, as we learn from the council of Laodicea (*c.* 363).[3]

The kindred ceremonies of the *fermentum* and *sancta* are sometimes confused, but they are quite distinct both in origin and intention, although they both demonstrate the teaching of the Church that the faithful offer the sacrifice as the one mystical body of Christ, a united body at one with itself. The *fermentum* expressed unity in point of place; the *sancta* in point of time.[4]

When the pope was unable to celebrate the solemn Mass in person, he sent a fragment of the loaves consecrated by him at a previous Mass by the hands of a subdeacon, and a similar custom obtained at the Masses celebrated in the titular churches. The fragment was put into the chalice by the celebrant, in place of the *sancta*, and at the same liturgical moment: 'The peace of the Lord be with you always.'[5] The *Liber Pontificalis*, a not altogether reliable

[1] Dix, *A Detection of Aumbries*, p. 17. [2] *Ibid.*, p. 18. [3] Can. 14.
[4] Atchley, *Ordo Romanus Primus*, p. 108. [5] *Ibid.*, p. 107.

work for the early popes, claimed Zephyrinus (199–217) as the originator of the usage,[1] to which further details were added by Melchiades[2] (311–14) and Siricius (384–99).[3]

The purpose of the *fermentum* for absent clergy is discussed in a letter of Pope Innocent I to Decentius, bishop of Gubbio, in 416: 'But concerning the *fermentum*, which we send on Sundays to the titular churches, you wished to consult us superfluously, since all our churches are situated within the city, the presbyters of which being unable to meet together with us on that day, because of the people committed to their care, therefore receive by the hands of acolytes *fermentum* consecrated by us, so that they may not appear to be separated from communion with us, specially on that day. I do not, however, think that this should be done for country chapels, because the sacraments should not be carried about far (we do not send to the presbyters attached to the different cemetery-oratories) and their presbyters have the power and licence to consecrate.'[4]

In the Ordo of St. Amand, a manuscript dating from about the year 800, the *mansionarii*[5] of the titular churches were bidden to go to the Lateran on Easter Eve in order to get the *fermentum* consecrated by the pope, which they carried back wrapped in a corporal.[6] The ceremony of the *fermentum* persisted until the ninth century, and it was found not only in Rome and Italy, but also in Gaul and Germany, although its use in those countries was by no means general.[7]

[1] *Lib. Pontif.*, edit. Duchesne, t. I (Paris, 1955), p. 139.
[2] *Ibid.*, p. 168. [3] *Ibid.*, p. 216.
[4] Innoc. I, *epist. XXV ad Decentium ep. Eugubinum*; *Pat. Lat.* t. XX, col. 553.
[5] 'Guardians of the sacred building, and the prebend assigned to it; perpetual chaplains.' Du Cange, *Glossarium Manuale*, t. IV, p. 534.
[6] Atchley, *op. cit.*, p. 54; Andrieu, *Les Ordines Romani du Haut Moyen Age*, t. II (Louvain, 1948), *ordo* IV, n. 95, p. 168. [7] Köster, *op. cit.*, p. 29.

Sancta

The St. Amand manuscript made no mention of the *sancta*, which had figured in the *Ordo Romanus Primus*, in which two acolytes, holding open caskets (*capsae*) containing the sacred species reserved from the last Mass, were directed to approach the pope as he went to the altar. The subdeacon showed the particles to the pontiff, who saluted them with bowed head and, if he considered that there were too many for the liturgy, ordered the residuc to be taken back to the *conditorium* (*secretarium*).[1] The *sancta* were put into the chalice at the words: 'The peace of the Lord be with you always.'[2] In sixth-century Gaul, there is considerable doubt as to whether it was the *sancta* or the offertory breads that were carried in a tower by the deacon at the offertory.[3] The ceremony of the *sancta* had everywhere disappeared by the eleventh century.[4]

Liturgy of the Presanctified

The Presanctified Liturgy, which by its very nature demanded a reservation of the sacred species, would seem to have been introduced into Syria in the early years of the sixth century by Severus, bishop of Antioch (d. 538), and later adopted at Constantinople and elsewhere.[5] The alleged evidence for the Presanctified rite in the forty-ninth canon of the council of Laodicea (*c.* 363), had the support of Hefele-Leclercq in their work on the Councils, but it has been described by Köster as 'merely negative'[6]: 'During Lent one ought not to offer the bread, unless it is a Saturday or Sunday.'[7]

[1] *O.R.I.*, 8; *Pat. Lat.*, t. LXXVIII, col. 941. Cf. Andrieu, *ordo* I, n. 48, pp. 82–83.
[2] *O.R.I.*, 18; *Pat. Lat.*, t. LXXVIII, col. 945; Andrieu, *ordo* I, n. 95, p. 98.
[3] Köster, *op. cit.*, p. 30. Cf. Righetti, *Manuale di Storia Liturgica*, vol. I, part 2, cap. III, p. 120.
[4] Köster, *op. cit.*, p. 31. [5] *Ibid.*, pp. 13–14. [6] *Ibid.*, p. 14, n. 33.
[7] Hef.-Lerc., *Histoire des Conciles*, t. I, part 2 (Paris, 1907), book 6, pp. 1021–22.

The earliest explicit mention of it appears in the *Chronicon Paschale* of Sergius of Constantinople under the year 615: 'In this year, under Sergius, Patriarch of Constantinople, . . . there began to be sung from the first week of the Fasts, after the saying of Psalm 140. 2, at the time when the presanctified gifts are being brought into the sanctuary, after the priest has said "According to the free gift of thy Christ"; the people straightway begin (to sing the hymn) "Now the powers".'[1]

Its use in Lent was formally prescribed by the council of Trullo in 692.[2] The Liturgy of the Presanctified probably appeared in the West for use on Good Friday in the following century.

Ordo Romanus Primus, in describing the ceremonies of Holy Thursday, said: *servat de sancta usque in cratismum*[3] (sic), and for Good Friday: *Presbyteri . . . mox ut salutaverint, intrant secretarium, vel ubi positum fuerat corpus Domini, quod pridie remansit. . . .*[4] The Presanctified liturgy figured also in the Gelasian sacramentary (*c.* 700).

When, as a result of the heresy of Berengarius (d. 1088), a cultus of the reserved Sacrament appeared in the Church, we find an enhanced ceremonial prescribed in the customary of Bec for the Eucharist reserved for the liturgy on Good Friday. The customs of the Norman abbey were partially adopted by Lanfranc, when archbishop of Canterbury (d. 1089), and introduced into the larger Benedictine abbeys. On Holy Thursday during vespers which followed

[1] J. W. Tyrer, *Historical Survey of Holy Week: Its Services and Ceremonial, Alcuin Club*, no. 29 (1932), p. 134.

[2] Counc. Trullo, 692, can. 52; Mansi, *op. cit.*, t. XI, col. 967.

[3] *O.R.I.*, 31; *Pat. Lat.*, t. LXVIII, col. 952. Cf. Andrieu, III; p. 396, Ordo XXVIII § 24: . . . pontifex venit ante altare et communie et omnis populus ordine suo et servat de Sancta usque in crastinum.

[4] *O.R.I.* 35; *ibid.*, col. 954. Cf. Andrieu III: p. 400, Ordo XXVIII, § 41: Presbiteri vero duo priores, mox ut salutaverint, intrant in Sacrarium, vel ubi positum fuerit corpus domini, quod pridie remansit.

the Mass, a priest with assistants carried the body of the Lord to a place suitably prepared for its reception. Incense was offered, and a light was kept burning before the reserved Sacrament. On Good Friday afternoon, after the adoration of the Cross, the priest and his assistants went to the place of repose, where, on both knees, they adored the body of the Lord. The Eucharist was then taken to the high altar, where in the Presanctified rite all communicated.[1] Directions for a fitting reservation of the Sacrament from Holy Thursday to Good Friday were given also by John of Avranches, brother of Richard, Duke of Normandy and archbishop of Rouen (d. 1079). It was prescribed that a light should be kept burning until the extinction of the last taper in the office of Tenebrae on Thursday night.[2]

For the Ordination of Bishops and Priests

In about the eighth century, the Roman rite, as exemplified in *Ordo Romanus* VIII, directed a bishop at his consecration to take sufficient particles of the sacred species to serve him for forty consecutive days at his own Mass, so that it might serve as a token of unity between consecrator and consecrated.[3] Like the *fermentum*, a particle would have been put into the chalice after the embolism of the *Pater noster* on each of the days, and for the same reason: that the sacred species was too hard and dry to be

[1] Lanfranc, *Decreta pro Ord. S. Benedicti*, I, 4; *Pat. Lat.*, t. CL.

[2] Bridgett, *History of the Holy Eucharist in Great Britain*, vol. 2, pp. 246–47.

[3] At the time of Communion, the apostolic lord offered him the sacred oblation; and, having received it, the bishop communicated from it at the altar, reserving what was left, in order to serve for Communion for the following forty days. *O.R.* VIII, 9; *Pat. Lat.*, t. LXXVIII, col. 1004. But cf. Andrieu, IV p. 46, Ordo XXXV, § 73: p. 110, Ordo XXXVB, § 48: But when he comes to receive communion, the lord bishop offers him the whole sacred oblation, and the [newly consecrated] bishop, receiving it, communicates himself from it at the altar. And what of it remains, he keeps for himself, so that he may communicate himself afresh every day, until forty days are completed.

swallowed unless moistened.[1] The term of forty days was chosen, according to Fulbert of Chartres (1007), because during that space of time our Lord at intervals showed himself to the disciples after his resurrection and 'refreshed them as with the sweetness of the bread of heaven.'[2] However, Fulbert himself, moved by the accidental loss of the sacred species by another, had, when recently ordained, asked this bishop whether it would not be advisable to shorten the term. The bishop was adverse to this.[3] Yet, as we shall see, it was sometimes done.

The practice seems to have 'originated somewhere in Italy,'[4] and to have lasted about four hundred years. It was also common in France, and there is evidence for its observance in the provinces of Toulouse, Rouen and Rheims, where the forty days were maintained.[5] Fulbert, bishop of Chartres (d. 1028), who directed the particles to be reserved in a little bag of parchment,[6] 'had thought this certainly to be so much the custom of all churches as not to seem new or useless to anyone.' 'For the bishops of our province,' he added, 'all concur in using a ceremony of this kind.'[7] A similar practice was found in a twelfth-century pontifical of Sarum.[8]

The exact number of days, however, was not always fixed at forty. *Ordo Romanus* IX, which is probably of the ninth century, prescribed no more than eight days.[9] A pontifical of Salzburg had a rule of forty days for bishops, but said of priests: 'The bishop gives whole oblates to each

[1] Mabillon, *Comment. in Ord. Rom. Mus. Ital.*, t. II, p. 39; Scudamore, *Notitia Eucharistica* (London, 1876), p. 907.

[2] Scudamore, *op. cit.*, p. 907. [3] *Ibid.*, pp. 907–08.

[4] Morin, *De Ordin.*, p. 131; Scudamore, *op. cit.*, p. 907.

[5] Scudamore, *op. cit.*, p. 908. [6] *Ibid.*, p. 907.

[7] Fulbert, *epist.* III; *Pat. Lat.*, t. CXLI, col. 193. [8] Köster, *op. cit.*, p. 15.

[9] 'And gives the Eucharist to each of the newly ordained priests, who communicate from it for the ensuing eight days.' *O.R.* IX, 2; *Pat. Lat.*, t. LXXVIII, col. 1005.

newly-made presbyter, and they are communicated therefrom for seven days.'[1] The Mainz pontifical had thirty days for a bishop, but does not provide for the case of presbyters.[2]

A scandalous procedure, which a synod of Ravenna (998) has described as 'most reprehensible' (*valde reprehensibilem*), existed in some places: subdeacons sold consecrated particles to the bishops at the time of their consecration.[3]

This ordination rite virtually ceased after the thirteenth century, probably because of the introduction of concelebration, but, despite the assurance of Fulbert to the contrary, it had never been a universal practice.[4]

For the Consecration of Virgins

Some churches, in imitation of the ordination of bishops and priests, directed that virgins, for eight consecutive days after their consecration, should give themselves Holy Communion from the hosts that they had brought from the church. The usage, according to Mabillon,[5] was especially favoured from the tenth to the twelfth century, but it was still to be found in the fifteenth century. An Ordo of St. Gatien at Toulouse (tenth century) says: 'The girl . . . communicates and from that Communion reserves sufficient to communicate herself on the following eight days.' Similar directions are found in the pontificals of Sarum, Savigny, Cambrai, Arles and Mende.[6] The practice may have been a quasi-continuation of the reception of Holy Communion in private houses.[7]

[1] Scudamore, *op. cit.*, p. 908. [2] *Ibid.*
[3] Syn. Ravenna, 998; Mansi, *op. cit.*, t. XIX, col. 219.
[4] Köster, *op. cit.*, p. 16.
[5] Mabillon, *Annal. Bened.*, t. IV, 118.
[6] Martène, *Ant. Eccl. Rit.*, t. II, pp. 524–51; t. I, pp. 695–96.
[7] Köster, *op. cit.*, pp. 16–17.

For the Consecration of a Church or Altar

A curious and reprehensible custom grew up about the ninth century in the West: the reservation of the Eucharist in the sepulchre of the altar, either with or without the addition of relics, at the consecration of a church or altar. The first document extant to prescribe the usage as a distinctive rite is the collection of canons of the English council of Celichyth (Chelsea) in 816, in which, having directed that 'all be performed in order as in the service book,' it was added: 'afterwards, let the Eucharist, which has been consecrated by the bishop at the same service, be enclosed with other relics in a casket (*capsula*), and kept in the same basilica. And, if he cannot find any other relics, then will the Eucharist most of all serve, as it is the body and blood of our Lord Jesus Christ.'[1] It would seem to have been customary to reserve three particles for this purpose. The 'Pontifical of Egbert' for the consecration of an altar also says: 'Then he places three particles of the Body of the Lord within the confession, and three of incense, and they are enclosed with the relics.'[2] Similarly in the 'Pontifical of St. Dunstan,' now in the Bibliothèque Nationale in Paris: 'If there are relics they are placed fittingly under the confession of the altar, or in some suitable place with three particles of the body of the Lord.'[3] The three particles are prescribed also in the Sacramentary of Ratoldus (*c.* end tenth century).[4] The practice was by no means universal, but it is found in many pontificals from the ninth to the thirteenth century in England, France, Germany and Spain.

[1] Counc. Celichyth, 816, can. 2; Mansi, *op. cit.*, t. XIV, col. 356.
[2] '*Pontif. Egbert*,' 45, 46. Manuscript dating from the tenth-eleventh century, now in Paris; *Pontif. Egbert*, *Surtees Society*, Vol. 27 (1853), p. 46.
[3] Rock, *Church of our Fathers* (London, 1905), vol. I, p. 36, n. 36.
[4] *Sacram. Ratoldus*; *Pat. Lat.*, t. LXXVIII, col. 424.

It is noteworthy that a number of the manuscripts have the essentially Roman word '*confessio*' in place of '*sepulchrum*,' and it is used again in a letter of Pope Benedict VIII (1017–24).[1]

The usage was condemned by Guido de Baysio, an Italian canonist (d. 1313), who said that the body of Christ was the food of the soul, and that it ought only to be reserved for the sick: 'Take and eat' was the command, not 'take and bury.'[2] Other voices also were raised against the practice, and there was no reference to it in the majority of the liturgical texts of the fourteenth and fifteenth centuries, although the great English canonist, William Lyndwood, says that where relics are wanting it is sometimes customary to put the body of Christ,[3] and the practice is found as late as the first decades of the sixteenth century.

Buried with the Dead

This abuse may possibly be an extension of the use of the Sacrament as a charm or amulet. The Dialogues of St. Gregory tell us that St. Benedict, in order to secure the repose of the body of a monk who would not remain buried, forthwith (*protinus*) produced a consecrated host, and gave it to the dead man's parents, commanding them to lay it with all reverence upon the breast of the corpse, and to proceed with burial. This expedient, we are assured, had the desired effect.[4]

The custom of burying the host with the dead was never officially approved by the Church, and it was, in fact, repeatedly condemned. The synod of Hippo (393) said: 'The Eucharist is not given to the bodies of the dead,'[5]

[1] Bened. VIII. *epist.* XXXV; *Pat. Lat.*, t. CXXXIX, col. 1633.
[2] Köster, *op. cit.*, p. 18.
[3] Lyndwood, *Provinc.* III, 26, note m (Oxford, 1679), p. 249.
[4] *Greg. Dialog.*, II, 24; *Pat. Lat.*, t. LXVI, col. 180–81.
[5] Syn. Hippo, 393, can. 4.

and the reason was supplied by the third council of Carthage (397) four years later: 'The Lord said: take and eat, and dead bodies can neither take nor eat.'[1] Similar prohibitions are found in the council of Auxerre[2] (*c.* 583–603), council of Trullo[3] (692) and the statutes of pseudo-Boniface.[4]

The reasons alleged for this strange practice were that the Eucharist given to the dead was a substitute for not having received it before death, a payment of the debt due to sin, or a talisman against demons. The sacred species was either put on the breast of the dead man or buried with him in a casket, as we find reported in the lives of St. Basil and St. Cuthbert and in the book of the finding or translation of the body of St. Udalric (eleventh century). The whole proceeding, however, had a somewhat pagan flavour, reminiscent of the *obolus* placed in the mouth of the corpse in payment to Charon for ferrying him across the Styx.

[1] Counc. III Carthage, 397, can. 5.
[2] Counc. Auxerre, *c.* 583–603, can. 12.
[3] Counc. Trullo, 692, can. 58.
[4] Stat. pseudo-Bonif., can. 18; Mansi, *op. cit.*, t. XII, col. 385.

2: PLACE OF RESERVATION

(*a*) Outside a Church

In Private Houses

THE first witness to the custom of keeping the Eucharist in a private house for the purpose of Communion is found in Tertullian (*c.* 160–220). Rigorists had mistakenly believed that the faithful ought to refrain from Communion on fast days (Wednesday and Friday), and Tertullian pointed out that those who feared that Holy Communion would break the fast could reserve the Eucharist in their own homes until such time as the station was ended: 'They take the body of the Lord, and reserve it, and thus participate of the sacrifice, as well as comply with the obligation of fasting.'[1] It is worthy of note that Tertullian used the actual word *reservare*.

In his exhortations to a Christian woman not to marry a pagan, Tertullian says in another place: 'Will not your husband know what it is you take in secret before eating any other food? If he recognizes it as bread, will he not believe it to be what it is rumoured to be? Even if he has not heard these rumours, will he be so ingenuous as to accept the explanation which you give, without protest, without wondering whether it is really bread and not some magic charm?'[2] The 'rumour' was that Christians dipped their food in the blood of a baby that had been murdered.

A clearer reference to reservation in a private house was given by St. Cyprian in the middle of the third century

[1] *Accepto corpore Domini, et reservato, utrumque salvum est, et participatio sacrificii, et executio officii.* Tertull. *De Oratione*, cap. XIX; *Pat. Lat.*, t. I, col. 1182–83; *Corpus Scriptorum Ecclesiasticorum*, vol. XX, p. 192. Vienna, 1890.

[2] Tertull., *Ad Uxorem,* lib. 2, cap. V; *Pat. Lat.*, t. I, col. 1296.

(249–58), when a eucharistic 'miracle' was recorded. A certain woman, who had been guilty of an act of idolatry at a pagan altar, immediately afterwards presumed 'to take in her unhallowed hands, and endeavour to open her casket (*arca*) or little box which contained the sacrament of the Lord, but was so terrified by a burst of fire flashing from within, that she dare not lay hold on it.'[1] About the same time, an unknown author, who was once considered to be St. Cyprian, but may very possibly have been Novatian (*c.* 250), spoke in his work on the public games (*De Spectaculis*) of a 'lax Christian, who, after his dismissal from the Lord's sacrifice, hastened to the circus, and still bearing with him, as is usual (*ut assolet*), the Eucharist, this unfaithful communicant carried around the holy body of Christ amidst the vile bodies of harlots.'[2]

The Apostolic Tradition of Hippolytus was 'long known under the name of the "Egyptian Church Order",' said Anton Baumstark,[3] with the inference that scholars had disavowed an African origin for the document, and seen fit to ascribe it to the antipope Hippolytus (*c.* 200). Jungmann cites it as 'the most important source for the life of the Roman Church in the third century.'[4] A similar view was held also by Gregory Dix,[5] J. H. Srawley[6] and Laurence Köster.[7] Srawley, while agreeing that the document was Roman in origin, went on to say that 'the later Latin rite developed on lines independent of it, and its subsequent history lies in the East,'[8] thereby unconsciously raising the doubts of some future scholar as to whether it was in fact

[1] Cyprian, *Liber de Lapsis*, 26; *Pat. Lat.*, t. IV, col. 486.
[2] *De Spectaculis*, cap. V.
[3] Baumstark, *Comparative Liturgy* (London, 1958), p. 9.
[4] Jungmann, *Missarum Sollemnia* (Paris, 1950), p. 55.
[5] Dix, *Treatise on the Apostolical Tradition of St. Hippolytus of Rome* (London, 1937).
[6] Srawley, *Early History of the Liturgy* (Cambridge, 1949), p. 68.
[7] Köster, *op. cit.*, pp. 21–22.
[8] Srawley, *op. cit.*, p. 68.

a Roman document. It would seem, however, that the question has been settled in a recent work by a professor of the *Gregorianum* in Rome,[1] in which he proves conclusively that Hippolytus was an Alexandrian both by turn of mind and intellectual formation,[2] although resident in Rome for some years. His liturgy, says Fr. Hanssens, makes no appeal to the authority of a particular Church, and no liturgical observance described in it is exclusively Roman,[3] while the doxologies are Alexandrine, and of a type that was unknown at Rome.[4] The whole tenor of the document is a harking back to the institutions of apostolic origin.[5] The following further reference to a reservation of the Eucharist in private houses is consequently more directly concerned with Alexandria: 'Let everyone of the faithful be careful to receive the Eucharist before he eats anything else . . . and let them be careful that no one not of the faithful eat of the Eucharist, nor a mouse nor any other animal, and that none of it fall or be lost.' A token cup of wine blessed by the communicant himself was directed to be drunk after receiving the sacred species.[6] The precaution regarding non-Christians as well as mice and other animals makes it clear that the author had in mind the practice of reservation in private houses.

St. Zeno, bishop of Verona (d. 380), also referred to the custom in two of his tracts[7] and St. Jerome (d. 420) in his epistle to Pammachius appealed to the conscience of people who do not go to church and yet have no fear to receive the Eucharist in their own houses.[8] The last Western document to speak of the usage would seem to be the *Liber*

[1] Hanssens, *La Liturgie d'Hippolyte*, Rome, 1959.
[2] *Ibid.*, p. 508. [3] *Ibid.*, pp. 507–08. [4] *Ibid.*, p. 510.
[5] *Ibid.*, p. 509. [6] Hippol., *Apostolic Tradition*, XXXII, 1–4.
[7] Zeno, *De Continentia*, V, 8; *Pat. Lat.*, t. XI, col. 309 and *De Spirituali Aedificatione Domus Dei*, XIV, 3; *ibid.*, t. XI, col. 358–61.
[8] Jerome, *epist.* XLVIII *ad Pammach.*; *Pat. Lat.*, t. XXII, col. 506.

contra Julianum of St. Augustine (d. 430).[1] The reasons for its continuance had ceased to exist.

The persecution of Christians by the State was a thing of the past and the Empire itself was now nominally Christian. In addition to this, spiritual fervour had waned and the reception of Communion was less frequent. In 506 it had been found necessary for the council of Agde in southern Gaul to exhort the faithful to receive Holy Communion at least three times a year.[2] The Spanish councils of Saragossa[3] (380) and I Toledo[4] (400) may have hastened a discontinuance of the practice by directing the sacred species to be consumed at the time of the Communion in church, since the Priscillianists, not to appear heretics, frequented Catholic churches and took the Eucharist, without receiving it either there or elsewhere.

Private reservation had also become increasingly dangerous, and it was not unknown for the sacred species to be used for magical and other improper purposes. St. Augustine mentions the case of a poultice made from the Eucharist.[5] Baronius gave it as his opinion that the custom of reserving in private houses lasted at Rome until the time of Pope Hormisdas (514–23).[6]

The consecrated bread was either wrapped in linen or kept in a little casket, as St. Cyprian indicated. In the sixth century, a certain Mosco (d. 620) speaks of a young servant who, 'according to the custom of the province, wrapped the Communion she had received on Holy Thursday into the cleanest linen and kept it in a chest.'[7]

[1] August., *Lib. contra Julian.*, lib. III, 162; *Pat. Lat.*, t. XLV, col. 1315.
[2] Counc. Agde, 506, can. 18; Labbe, *Concil.*, t. IV, col. 1390.
[3] Counc. Saragossa, 380, can .3; Mansi, *op. cit.*, t. III, col. 634.
[4] Counc. I Toledo, 400, can. 14; *ibid.*, t. III, col. 1000.
[5] August., *contra Julian.*, III, 162.
[6] Baronius, *Annal. Eccles.*, t. I (Antwerp, 1597), p. 598.
[7] *Vitae Patrum sive Pratum spirituale*, X, 79.

On a Journey

The custom for priests and monks to carry the Eucharist with them on their journeys persisted for many centuries. St. Ambrose recorded in his sermon *De Excessu Fratris sui Satyri* (375) how his brother Satyrus, who was still a catechumen, feared for his life in a shipwreck, and asked a companion who was carrying the Sacrament to give it to him. On receiving it, he wrapped it round his neck in a piece of linen, and threw himself into the sea: 'not fearing death, but rather that he should die without the mystery . . .'[1] On reaching safety he desired Baptism and Communion, 'for having found the heavenly Mystery wrapped in a napkin such a protection, he knew not what blessing he might not expect, if he were to receive it with his mouth and absorb it into his innermost being.'[2]

A letter of St. Jerome (d. 420) to a monk of Gaul by the name of Rusticus (398), after praising the bishop of Toulouse, St. Exuperius (d. *post* 410), for his Christian poverty and endurance, added that no one has greater riches than he who carries the Lord's body in a wicker basket (*canistrum vimineum*) and his blood in a glass vessel (*vitrum*).[3] It was apparently the custom of the bishop to take Communion to the sick in this fashion.

St. Gregory the Great in the third book of the Dialogues (*c.* 593) tells how St. Maximinian, later bishop of Syracuse, was shipwrecked, and how that he and his fellow passengers were saved after they had received Holy Communion.[4]

In the following century, we read of St. Birinus, first bishop of Dorchester (d. *c.* 650), always carrying the

[1] Ambr., *De Excessu . . . Satyri*, I, 43; *Pat. Lat.*, t. XVI, col. 1304; Dudden, *Life and Times of St. Ambrose* (1935), vol. I, p. 178.

[2] *Ibid.*, I, 46; *ibid.*; Dudden, p. 179.

[3] Jer., *epist.* CXXV *ad Rusticum*, 20; *Pat. Lat.*, t. XXII, col. 1085.

[4] Greg., *Dialog.*, III, cap. XXXVI; *Pat. Lat.*, t. LXXVII, col. 304.

Eucharist about with him, suspended round his neck and wrapped in a pall that Pope Honorius had given him.[1]

Travel in those far-off centuries was fraught with danger, and penalties were imposed for negligence respecting the Sacrament. A canon of Gildas (d. 570) said that 'if anyone by negligence let fall and lose a sacrifice, leaving it to be devoured by birds or beasts,' he incurred a penance of three Quarantains or Lents.[2] Similar penalties for carelessness were imposed by the Anglo-Saxon Church, for, as St. Bede says in his Penitential, priests 'when they go among the people far from a church should always take the holy Eucharist with them.'[3] For allowing a chrismal to fall to the ground, St. Egbert (d. 729) imposed a day's fast, and for losing it, either forty days or three forties, according to the degree of negligence.[4] Decisions of the same kind were made also by St. Theodore of Canterbury[5] (d. 690) and St. Oswald of York (d. 992). Weighty penances were prescribed in the *Regula Coenobialis* of St. Colomban for dropping the Eucharist accidentally or leaving it behind through negligence: anything up to a year on bread and water.[6] Elsewhere we find a penance of forty days inflicted on anyone who should fall into the water while carrying the Eucharist. The traveller was ordered to drink the water that had seeped into the chrismal and reverently to consume the particle.[7]

Celtic monks, when working in the fields or going on a voyage, invariably carried the Eucharist with them, either

[1] Martène, *Ant. Eccl. Rit.*, t. I (1700), lib. I, cap. V, art. 4, p. 651.
[2] Bridgett, *History of the Holy Eucharist in Great Britain*, vol. I, pp. 22–23.
[3] Hadden and Stubbs, *Councils and Eccles. Documents relating to Great Britain and Ireland*, t. III, p. 329.
[4] *Ibid.*, t. III, p. 428.
[5] Theodore, *Penitent.*, 12; *ibid.*, vol. III, p. 187.
[6] Columb. *Reg. Coenob.*, cap. XV, Gaudemart, *Les Aspects Canoniques de la Règle de S. Colomban, Mélanges Colombaniens*, p. 171.
[7] Cumean, *Lib. de Mensura Paenit.*, XIII; *Pat. Lat.*, t. LXXXVII, col. 996.

in a small receptacle (*chrismal*) worn bandolier-fashion, or in a little bag (*perula*) hung round the neck under their clothes. Irish and British texts make frequent mention of the practice.[1] It was not, however, only for the purpose of giving Communion, but also to ensure safety in battle and to serve as a talisman against the attacks of brigands.

The life of St. Comgall (d. *c.* 601) tells how on one occasion the Saint was attacked by heathen Picts while working in a field, but, on seeing the chrismal on his cloak, the pagans did not dare to touch it, under the belief that it was Comgall's god. The Saint was much moved, and exclaimed: 'Lord, thou art my strength, my refuge and my redeemer.' So late as 1150, we hear of four priests in Ireland who were attacked by brigands while carrying the Eucharist. The Sacrament was profaned, but misfortune overtook the assailants, who ended by hanging themselves.[2] In the time of St. Laurence O'Toole (d. 1180), when brigandage was rife, priests, with the protection of the sacred species, were accustomed to escort parties of travellers along the roads.[3]

In Dwellings of Religious

Solitaries frequently reserved the Eucharist in their cells, in order to give themselves Holy Communion, but such private reservation tended to disappear when they became members of a community.[4] From about the middle of the third century it was very general for hermits in the East, especially in Palestine and Egypt, to reserve the Sacrament in their cells, but in the West there were comparatively few hermits, and evidence is lacking.

[1] e.g. *Paenitent. Cummeani*, XI, 3.
[2] Blouet, *Le Chrismale de Mortain*, chap. II, p. 21.
[3] *Ibid.* [4] Freestone, *op. cit.*, p. 55.

(*b*) Inside a Church

The council of Nicea (325) makes it clear that the Eucharist was reserved for the sick and dying, and later in the century for the ceremony of the fermentum, but there is no indication as to where it was kept. St. Ambrose (d. 397), writing to Felix, bishop of Como, after the consecration of a basilica, seems to suggest that the Eucharist was reserved there.[1] St. Optatus of Milevis (*c.* 365) also appears to indicate reservation in the churches of North Africa, when, in describing the outrages committed by the Donatists, he says that they threw 'the holy body' to the dogs.[2] The reserved Sacrament under the species of wine was found in Constantinople in the time of St. John Chrysostom (d. 407), if we may judge from a letter written by the Saint to Pope Innocent I (d. 417), in which he says that while administering Baptism on Holy Saturday soldiers invaded the church, and in the course of the tumult the most holy blood of Christ was spilt over the clothing of the soldiers.[3] It is impossible to say whether such reservation was habitual or occasional, but from the tenor of the letter it would not seem that reservation of the Eucharist was anything exceptional to either Chrysostom or Innocent.[4] Possibly the Sacrament had been reserved expressly for the occasion, as it was customary to give infants a drop of the precious Blood after Baptism.

Sacristy or some similar place

Before the Peace of the Church (313) the Eucharist for the Viaticum would have been reserved in the houses of the

[1] 'There a golden jar (*dolium*), containing manna, the receptacle indeed of spiritual and divine nourishment, the repository (*promptuarium*) of knowledge.' Ambr., *epist.* IV *ad Felicianum*, 4; *Pat. Lat.*, t. XVI, col. 890.

[2] Optat., *De Schismate Donat.*, II, 19; *ibid.*, t. XI, col. 972.

[3] Jn. Chrysos, *epist. to Innocent*, 3; *Pat. Graec.*, t. LII, col. 533.

[4] Köster, *op. cit.*, p. 30.

priests, but a cessation of persecution led in course of time to a more suitable place, adjoining the church and answering to our sacristy, known as the '*pastoforium*' or '*secretarium*.'

Churches of the Byzantine rite usually have a small 'room' on either side of the *bema* or sanctuary: the *prothesis* on the left, serving for the preparation of the matter for the sacrament and the *diakonicon* on the right, used as a vesting chamber. This arrangement was found also in some few Western churches in countries influenced by the East. The church of St. Pierre in Vienne, now a museum, has retained its '*prothesis*,' but the '*diakonicon*' has disappeared. The sixth-century basilica of S. Maria delle Grazie at Grado had a small square 'room' at the end of each aisle. It would have been the *diakonicon* to which the fourth-century Apostolic Constitutions were referring, when they directed the deacons to carry 'into a suitable place, called "*pastoforium*," what remained of the bread consecrated in the liturgy.'[1]

St. Paulinus of Nola (d. 431), in describing his church of St. Felix, said that the chief apse was flanked by two subsidiary apses, and went on to describe their purpose: the *secretarium* to the right was known as the *diakonicon*, housing the Eucharist and the sacred vessels: 'Here is the place where the reserved Sacrament is kept and the accessories which go to the splendour of worship.' The *secretarium* to the left, which is called the *prothesis*, contains the holy books: 'If one should desire to meditate on the law, he can do so here in consulting the sacred books.'[2]

[1] *Apost. Constit.*, VIII, 13; *Pat. Graec.*, t. I, col. 1109; Brightman, *Liturgies Eastern and Western*, p. 25.

[2] *Paulin. Nolen.*, *epist.* XII *ad Severum*; *Pat. Lat.*, t. LXI, col. 337.

The *secretarium* in the Roman basilicas, however, was situated at the lower end of the nave, on the men's side of the church.[1]

In Anglo-Saxon churches, also, the sacristy was used for reservation, as one of its names indicates: *husel-portic* or 'sacrament-porch.' Bede says in his Ecclesiastical History that St. Gregory was buried at the entrance to the sacristy (*secretarium*), which King Alfred translates: '*his lichama waes bebyriged on Sce Petres cyricean beforan pam husulportice*.'[2] 'If by 900 this translation was understandable to Alfred's subjects,' say van Dijk and Walker, 'there must have been a common practice of reserving the Sacrament in the sacristy.'[3]

A marginal note interpolated in some of the texts of St. Jerome's Commentary on Ezekiel gives '*thalami*' as the Latin equivalent for '*pastoforia*': 'Wherefore the sacristy in which lies the body of Christ who is the true bridegroom of the Church and of our souls is rightly called the bridal chamber or *pastoforium*.'[4]

The key of the *pastoforium* was committed to the deacon, to whom allusion is made by Aurelius Prudentius, a Spanish poet of the fourth century (d. after 405), who in his poem to the martyrs glorified St. Laurence in these words:[5]

> Claustris sacrorum praeerat,
> Caelestis arcanum domus
> Fidis gubernans clavibus,
> Votasque dispensans opes.

Reservation in fifth and sixth-century Gaul was in the sacristy, where Communion would also have been given,

[1] Atchley, *Ordo Romanus Primus*, p. 23.
[2] Edit. T. Miller, *Early English Text Society*, vol. 95 (Oxford, 1890), 94 f.; Bede, *Eccles. Hist.*, book 2, chap. I.
[3] Van Dijk and Hazelden Walker, *The Myth of the Aumbry*, p. 44.
[4] Jer. *In Ezech.*, 40.
Aurel. Prudent., *Peristephanon*, hymn 2; *Pat. Lat.*, t. LXX, col. 302.

in accordance with the second council of Mâcon (585): 'Whatever remnants of the sacrifices are left over in the sacristy after the completion of Mass on Wednesday and Friday, let innocent boys be brought to church by him whose business it is, and a fast having been imposed on them, let them receive the same remnants sprinkled with wine.'[1] Mabillon, however, in his work on the Gallican liturgy, states specifically that the Sacrament was reserved for the sick, and that Communion out of Mass was rarely given.[2]

It was from the sacristy that the deacon at the offertory of the Mass brought a small 'tower' to the altar, containing the sacred species reserved from the day before.[3] The particle was placed in the chalice and consumed by the celebrant at his Communion, while a new particle was put in the 'tower' to serve for another liturgy. The practice was seemingly indicated in a somewhat laconic canon of the council of Orange (441).[4] St. Gregory of Tours (d. 594) relates a miracle respecting this use of the *sancta*: how that when an unworthy deacon of Riom picked up the 'tower' in the sacristy, the Eucharist flew out of it and landed on the altar.[5] This is the explanation given by Köster in *De Custodia Sanctissimae Eucharistiae*;[6] but Righetti inclines to the view that the 'tower' contained the bread to be consecrated in the Mass that was in progress.[7] The terms 'body and blood' were therefore in the nature of a prolepsis, as we find in the Byzantine liturgy. The fact that a chalice

[1] Counc. Mâcon, 585, can. 6; Labbe, *op. cit.*, t. V, col. 982.

[2] Mabillon, *De Lit. Gall.*, lib. I, cap. IX; *Pat. Lat.*, t. LXXII, col. 166.

[3] The deacon having received the tower, in which the mystery of the Lord's body was contained. Mabillon, *ibid.*; *Pat. Lat.*, *ibid.*

[4] Counc. Orange. 441, can. 17; Hefele, *Concil.*, vol. II, part i, p. 444.

[5] *Greg. Turon.*, *Lib. Mirac.*, lib. I, *De Gloria Martyrum*, cap. LXXXVI; *Pat. Lat.*, t. LXXI, col. 781.

[6] Köster, *op. cit.*, p. 30.

[7] Righetti, *Manuale di Storia Liturgica*, vol. I, part 2, cap. III, p. 120.

of wine was carried at the same time, with both 'tower' and chalice covered by a precious veil, would seem to point to this explanation, rather than that of Köster.

The Sacrament reserved for the Mass of the Presanctified on Good Friday was kept in the sacristy, as directed in the Gelasian sacramentary for Holy Thursday: 'They communicate and reserve of this sacrifice until the morrow; and thence let them communicate.'[1] (Good Friday): 'The prayers written above being finished, the deacons go into the sacristy. They proceed with the body and blood of the Lord which remained the day before, and place it on the altar.'[2] The *Regularis Concordia* for the guidance of Benedictine houses in England in the time of King Edgar (959–75) required the Eucharist to be reserved on Holy Thursday for the Presanctified rite on the following day. The document directed that the antiphon *Sepulto Domino* should be sung on Good Friday, after the cross had been laid in the sepulchre (*monumentum*) and before the Sacrament was taken by the deacon and subdeacon to the altar.[3] A somewhat similar injunction is found in the Leofric missal (*c.* 1070), which, in describing the ceremonial for Good Friday said: 'The deacons go into the sacristy and proceed with the body of the Lord, which has remained from the previous day, but without the consecrated wine, and place it upon the altar.'[4]

The decree of the sixteenth council of Toledo (694) certainly considered that the Sacrament should be reserved in the sacristy: 'Whatever remains over (from the liturgy) may be kept for reservation in a small receptacle (*ad conservandum modico loculo . . . conserventur*) without risk or harm; or else, in case it seems necessary, may be consumed.'[5]

[1] *Lib. Sac. Rom. Eccles.* (Gelasian sacramentary), edit. Wilson, p. 72.
[2] *Ibid.*, p. 77. [3] *Reg. Concord.*; *Pat. Lat.*, t. CXXXVII, col. 494.
[4] Warren, *Leofric Missal*, p. 96. [5] Counc. XVI Toledo, can. 6.

On or Over the Altar

The sacristy would seem to have been the earliest place for the reserved sacrament, if we except the primitive usage in private houses, but about the end of the ninth century there were regulations in some churches directing the Eucharist to be reserved within the church itself, in close proximity to the altar. It has been considered by a number of writers, including Bona[1] and Mabillon,[2] that a hanging pyx was prescribed by the second council of Tours (567): 'That the body of the Lord on the altar should be placed in the form of a cross, not in some imaginary fashion.'[3] A recent work has endorsed this opinion,[4] but it is almost certainly erroneous, and the reference is rather to the arrangement of the particles on the paten at the time of the fraction. The decree was a condemnation of superstitious practices, such as arranging the particles to represent a human form—a practice which had been specifically proscribed in a letter of Pope Pelagius to Sabaudus, bishop of Arles (558).[5] The Treatise appended to the Stowe missal (eighth-ninth century) gives seven different dispositions of the particles, according to the day. At Christmas and Easter the pattern is in the nature of a wheel cross, so frequently to be found in Celtic art.[6] The Gallican rite, no less than the Celtic, had a complicated fraction of the kind, although details are wanting.[7] Still to-day in a chapel of the cathedral church of Toledo, where the Mozarabic rite is celebrated, the Host is divided into nine particles and arranged symbolically on the paten in the form of a cross.[8]

[1] Bona, *Rer. Lit.*, lib. 2, cap. XVII, 6, p. 439.
[2] Mabillon, *De Azymo*, cap. VIII; *De Lit. Gallic.*, lib. i, cap. IX, 24.
[3] Counc. II Tours, 567, can. 3; Labbe, *op. cit.*, t. V, col. 853.
[4] Maffei, *op. cit.*, p. 59. [5] Righetti, *op. cit.*, t. I, part 2, cap. III, p. 122.
[6] *Stowe Missal, Henry Bradshaw Society*, vol. 32 (1906), pp. 38–39 (Irish), 41–42 (English); King, *Liturgies of the Past*, chap. IV, pp. 268–69.
[7] King, *op. cit.*, chap. III, p. 178.
[8] King, *Liturgies of the Primatial Sees*, chap. IV, pp. 615–16.

It is evident that the Eucharist was reserved in the chapel of St. Guthlac (d. 714) at Croyland, as we read in his life that he 'sat throughout the night in his oratory. . . . He stretched out his hand to the altar, and strengthened himself with the communion of the body and blood of Christ and, raising his eyes to heaven and stretching out his arms, he breathed forth his soul into the joys of everlasting beatitude.'[1]

The 'first instance of reservation at a high altar' is said by Gregory Dix to be inferred from Ethelwold's poem on Lindisfarne (802):[2]

> Cui compacta nitet perpulchris mensa tabellis,
> Porticus in medio, sancti quam fronde coronant,
> Dum buxis claudunt pretiosae munere vitae.

The pyx (*buxis*) in question had been given to the church by the abbot Sigbald.[3] If, however, Dix is correct in his assumption, such a manner of reservation was altogether at variance with general Anglo-Saxon practice.

It was not before the end of the ninth century that we find a definite regulation to reserve the Eucharist on or over the altar. This is found in the *Admonitio Synodalis*, an anonymous document, although a number of names have been suggested for the authorship: 'The altar should be covered with clean linen; nothing should be placed on the altar except reliquaries and relics and (*al.* or possibly) the four gospel-books, and a pyx with the body of the Lord for the viaticum of the sick; other things should be kept in some seemly place.'[4] The *Admonitio* was received by Ratherius, bishop of Verona, in the synod of 966.[5] Habitual

[1] *Vita S. Guthlaci*, *Acta SS.*, April 12, t. II; Bridget, *op. cit.*, vol. 2, p. 187.
[2] Dix, *op. cit.*, p. 28.
[3] Ethelwold, *Carmen de abbatibus S. Petri in insula Lindisfarnensi*, cap. XIV; *Pat. Lat.*, t. XCVI, col. 1338.
[4] *Admonit. Synod.*, 6; *Pat. Lat.*, t. CXXXVI, col. 456 and t. CXV, col. 677–78.
[5] Syn. Verona, 966, 6; *Pat. Lat.*, t. CXXXVI, col. 559.

reservation was clearly contemplated, as the text says: '*ad viaticum infirmis*,' but the wording of the decree would seem to exclude an enclosing of the pyx in a casket or aumbry, although there must surely have been some means of security. Freestone, however, without, seemingly, any justification, says that '*super altare*' in the synodical decrees infers that an aumbry was built into the wall at the back or or in the reredos behind the altar. '*Super altare*' will consequently mean *above* the altar, and not upon it.[1]

Regulations prescribing the reservation of the Eucharist in the church now become traditional in collections of canons, visitation inquiries, etc. Those ascribed to Regino, abbot of Prüm (d. 915), and Burchard, bishop of Worms (d. 1025), are among the best known. The inquiry of Regino in *De Ecclesiasticis Disciplinis et Religione Christiana* says: *Inquirendum si pyxis semper sit cum sacra oblatione ad viaticum infirmis.*[2] A canon preserved by Regino, which Burchard of Worms and Ivo of Chartres (d. 1116) have attributed to a council of Tours, directed that 'the pyx or other vessel should always be kept locked (*obseratum*) *super altare*, on account of mice or impious men (*propter mures et nefarios homines*),' which seems to suggest that the eucharistic vessel was out of the reach of sacrilegious hands, and therefore suspended above the altar.[3]

According to the rubrics of *Ordo Romanus* II, which is a tenth-century amendment of *Ordo Romanus Primus*, for the use of certain churches in Gaul and Germany, the *sancta* was no longer brought in solemn procession from the *sacrarium* at the beginning of Mass, but was already on the altar when the ministers entered.[4] It was not stated

[1] Freestone, *op. cit.*, pp. 193–94.
[2] Regino, *Notitiae*, I, 9; *Pat. Lat.*, t. CXXXII, col. 187.
[3] *Ibid.*, I, 70; *ibid.*, CXXXII, col. 205–06.
[4] *O.R.* II, 4; *Pat. Lat.*, t. LXXVIII, col. 970.

whether it was habitually there or whether it was placed on the altar just before the liturgy. Probably the former, in accordance with the more or less contemporary regulations of Regino and others. The *Eclogae de Officio Missae* of the same period inferred also that the *sancta* should be found on the altar.[1]

[1] *Eclog. de Offic. Missae*; *ibid.*, t. CV, col. 1317.

3: DILIGENCE IN RESERVING THE EUCHARIST

THE possibility of negligence called for definite regulations, and so early as the second decade of the third century we find the Constitutions of the Egyptian Church directing the faithful to take the greatest care of the Eucharist reserved in their homes.[1] The Celtic and Anglo-Saxon churches, as we have seen, provided a scale of penances for monks and priests who failed to observe due care of the Sacrament which they were carrying on their persons. Profanation was unlikely when the Eucharist was reserved in a locked sacristy, of which the priest or deacon held the key, but in the era of Carolingian reform, when synods and councils began to enjoin reservation *super altare*, it became necessary to issue warnings against 'mice and impious men.'[2]

The decree promulgated by Regino is of especial interest, as it contains the one definite statement as to the use at this period of an intincted host for reservation.[3] The practice of intincting the host with the precious blood would never seem to have been customary in Rome, but it was at one time much in favour in northern countries as a means of giving communion to the sick under two kinds. It was prescribed in the regulations of Regino,[4] Burchard of Worms[5] and Ivo of Chartres.[6] Its wide diffusion is confirmed also by the frequency with which, in the eleventh

[1] *Constit. Eccles. Aegypt.*, c. 220, can. 29; Funk, *Didascalia et Constitutiones Apostolicae*, t. II, p. 116.

[2] Regino, *Notitiae*, 70; *Pat. Lat.*, CXXXII, col. 205–06.

[3] 'The sacred oblation ought to be intincted in the blood of Christ, so that the priest may be truly able to say to the sick man: the body *and* blood of the Lord preserve thee, etc.' *Ibid.*

[4] Regino, *De Synod. causis*, I, 70; *Pat. Lat.*, t. CXXXII, col. 206.

[5] Burchard, *Decretum*, V, 9; *Pat. Lat.*, t. CXL, col. 754.

[6] Yves, *Decretum*, II, 19; *Pat. Lat.*, t. CLXI, col. 165.

and twelfth centuries, the formula of administration alludes to intinction: '*Corpus D.N.J.C. sanguine suo tinctum conservet.*'[1] It was not, however, universally accepted as a legitimate usage, and the first time we hear of disapproval was in the seventh-century third council of Braga (675), in which it was likened to the 'sop of Judas.'[2] The council of Clermont (1096) also saw fit to condemn the practice.[3] In England, it was advocated by Ernulf, bishop of Rochester (d. 1124), in a letter to a monk of St. Bertin (St. Omer),[4] but formally forbidden in the same century by the council of Westminster (1175).[5]

The carrying of the Eucharist to the sick in two separate kinds would seem to have been unusual, but we do hear of St. Jerome (d. 420) commending the bishop of Toulouse for taking the Lord's body in a wicker basket and his blood in a glass vessel.[6]

[1] Jungmann, *op. cit.*, (Paris, 1954), t. III, p. 317, n. 76; Andrieu, *Immixtio et consecratio*, pp. 136 seq.
[2] Counc. III Braga, 675, can. 2; Labbe, *op. cit.*, t. VI, col. 564.
[3] Syn. Clermont, 1096, can. 28; Mansi, *op. cit.*, can. 28, t. XX, col. 818.
[4] Ernulf, *epist.* II; Achéry, *Spicilegium*, t. III, pp. 471–72.
[5] Counc. Westminster, 1175, can. 16; Labbe, *op. cit.*, t. X, col. 1466.
[6] Jer., *epist.* CXXV *ad Rusticum*, 20; *Pat. Lat.*, t. XXII, col. 1085.

4: EUCHARISTIC VESSELS AND MODE OF RESERVATION

Arca or small box

THE Eucharist, when taken to private houses for communion by the faithful in the primitive Church, would normally have been reserved in *arcae* (*arculae*): little boxes, such as have been found in sarcophagi in the Vatican catacombs, lying on the breasts of the deceased. They open in front, and have, fastened at the top, a ring through which a cord or string might be passed, so that they could be easily carried round the neck. These *arculae*, which appear to be of the second or third century, are engraved with symbols.[1] A fresco of the first half of the third century in the Roman catacombs of St. Peter and St. Marcellinus shows a eucharistic box of the kind.[2] St. Cyprian, as we have seen, speaks of a woman daring to open her *arca*, containing the Sacrament of the Lord, when she had been guilty of an act of idolatry.[3] The Vatican examples were of gold, but they were more generally of wood or ivory. A fine ivory *arca* of the fourth century, with representations of Christ and the apostles and the sacrifice of Abraham, may be seen in the architectural museum (*Kuntstkammer*) in Berlin.[4]

Ivory boxes from Alexandria were a feature of Merovingian France in the sixth and seventh centuries, many of them elegantly carved with Christian subjects. Some of them would in all probability have been used for the

[1] Rock, *Hierugia*, pp. 194–95.

[2] Wilpert, *Le pitture recentemente scoperte nel cimiterio dei SS. Pietro e Marcellino*; *Nuovo bollettino di archeologia cristiana*, vol. 6, 1900, pp. 90 seq.

[3] Cyprian, *De Lapsis*, 26; *Pat. Lat.*, t. IV, col. 500–01.

[4] Maffei, *op. cit.*, p. 37.

Eucharist, while others served equally for relics and profane purposes, such as jewel boxes. The supply would have ceased with the conquest of Alexandria by the Moslems in 640.[1]

Canistrum Vimineum or Wicker Basket

Wicker baskets, which figured in both Jewish and pagan cults, were admitted also by the Christian Church for carrying the Eucharist and, very possibly, for private reservation. It has been noted elsewhere how the fourth-fifth-century bishop of Toulouse carried the Lord's body in a wicker basket.[2] Baskets of the kind figure in two second-century frescoes in the Catacombs of St. Callixtus outside Rome and also in the mosaics of a fourth-century pavement in the basilica of Aquileia.

Chrismal

The term 'chrismal' has a variety of meanings, but here we are only concerned with the vessel in which the sacred species was reserved, whether in church, or carried by Celtic and Anglo-Saxon priests and monks on their journeys. A *prefatio chrismatis* is found in the Rheims codex of the Gregorian sacramentary, to which a note is appended: *Ubi chrismalis seu chrismal, sive chrismale sumitur pro vase in quo Christi corpus servatur.*[3] The Leofric missal[4] (*c.* 1050) and the *Missale Francorum*[5] (eighth century) have forms for the blessing of the chrismal.

[1] Mâle, *La Fin du Paganisme en Gaule et les plus anciennes Basiliques Chretiennes*, chap. XI, pp. 285–88.
[2] Jer., *epist CXXV ad Rusticum*, 20; *Pat. Lat.*, t. XXII, col. 1085.
[3] *Pat. Lat.*, t. LXXVIII, col. 421.
[4] Leofric missal, edit. Warren, p. 222.
[5] *Missale Franc.*; *Pat. Lat.*, t. LXXII, col. 330.

A poem was addressed to this eucharistic vessel by St. Aldhelm, bishop of Sherborne (d. 709):[1]

> Alma domus veneror divino munere plena;
> Valvas sed nullus reserat, nec limina pandit,
> Culmina in fuerint aulis sublata quaternis,
> Et licet exterius rutilent de corpore gemmae,
> Aurea dum fulvis flavescit bulla metallis:
> Sed tamen uberius ditantur viscera, crassa
> Potis qua species flagrat pulcherrima Christi.
> Candida sanctarum sic floret gloria rerum
> Nec trabes in templo surgunt, nec tecta columnis.

The treasury of the cathedral church of Chur in Switzerland has a leather chrismal overlaid with gold, dating from the seventh-eighth century. The most perfect example of a chrismal extant is probably that of Mortain in Normandy: a beechwood coffer with figures of Christ Pantocrator, St. Michael and St. Gabriel on the outside; and a seraphim with outstretched wings surrounded by birds on the lid. The back of the lid has a runic inscription: 'May God help Eado who made this chrismal.' The iconography is said to be partly reminiscent of Coptic art and partly of Celtic.[2] The provenance is unquestionably Northumbria, 'between 660 and 700, but perhaps rather 725.'[3] The donor was in all probability Robert, Count of Mortain and brother of William the Conqueror, who founded the collegiate church of St. Evroult at Mortain in 1082.[4] A reference to this same chrismal is found in an *ordo* of 1741, now in the archives of the church, in respect to a curious liturgical custom on the feast of St. Mark (April 25th), when a subdeacon went

[1] Aldhelm, *epist. ad Acircium*; *Opera*, edit. Giles, p. 264.
[2] Blouet, *op. cit.*, chap. IV, p. 33.
[3] *Ibid.*, chap. II, pp. 16, 19.
[4] René Herval, *En Normandie, de la Dives au Mont-Saint-Michel* (Grenoble, 1951), pp. 119–20.

in procession to the church of Notre-Dame du Rocher, vested in an alb, and carrying a tenth-century book of the gospels[1] and 'a little golden coffer' (*parvam capsam aureatam*), which was suspended from his neck.[2]

Tower

A number of 'towers' and 'doves' in precious metals, offered as gifts to the Roman basilicas, are recorded in the *Liber Pontificalis*. In some few instances they are said to be destined for relics, but, in general, there is nothing to suggest their ultimate purpose, although it is possible that some of them may have been used for the Eucharist. In the time of St. Sylvester (314–35), we read that the emperor Constantine gave the basilica of St. Peter: 'a golden paten with a tower, from the purest gold a dove, adorned with grass-coloured (*prasinis*) gems and jacinths; pearls to the number of two hundred and fifteen.'[3] A silver tower with paten and a gilded dove were among the gifts received at the consecration of St. Gervase and St. Protase by Innocent I (401–417);[4] while in the pontificate of St. Hilary (461–68) the baptistery at the church of the Lateran had a silver tower with dolphins and a silver dove. The tower was said to weigh sixty pounds and the dove no more than two.[5]

We are on more realiable ground in sixth-century Gaul, where towers were in general use in the liturgy. At the time of the offertory, the deacon brought the bread to the altar, in a tower-shaped vessel, while the wine was carried in a chalice.[6] A chant, known as the *sonus* or *sonum* was sung

[1] The codex, which was of the Winchester school, was destroyed by enemy action in June 1944.

[2] Blouet, *op. cit.*, chap. III, p. 30.

[3] *Lib. Pontif.*, edit. Duchesne, t. I (Paris, 1955), p. 176.

[4] *Ibid.*, p. 220. [5] *Ibid.*, p. 243.

[6] Pseud.-Germ., Duchesne, *Christian Worship* (London, 1904), p. 203; *Pat. Lat.*, t. LXXII, col. 93.

meanwhile. An alternative explanation for the use of this tower has been given elsewhere.[1] From the earliest days, the deacon administered the Eucharist to the sick, and in Gaul the tower became one of his distinctive attributes. A somewhat fanciful reason for the use of a 'tower' is found in Pseudo-Germanus in the '*Explanation of the Mass*' (*c.* end of seventh century): 'The body of the Lord[2] is carried in a tower because the tomb of the Lord was cut out of the rock in the shape of a tower, and within it was the bed where rested the Lord's body, whence also the king of glory rose triumphantly.'[3] The Leofric missal describes the tower as a 'new sepulchre for the Lord's body.'[4]

Flodoard (d. 966) in his 'History of the Church of Rheims' quotes the Testament of St. Remigius (436–533): that the bishop enjoined his successor to have tabernacles made in the form of towers, as the golden vase which had been offered by Clovis.[5] A later bishop of Rheims, Landunus, ordered a golden tower to be made, which he placed (*posuit*) on the altar of the church of St. Mary in his cathedral city in the time of King Sigebert.[6] It was said of a predecessor of St. Gregory in the see of Tours, by the name of Leo, that he had been a skilful carpenter, especially in the construction of wooden eucharistic towers, which he overlaid with gold.[7]

[1] Pp. 29–30.

[2] A prolepsis, unless Köster was correct in assuming that the tower contained the sancta. Similar terminology appears in Gregory of Tours.

[3] Pseud.-Germ., *Exposit. brevis antiq. liturg. gallic.*; *Pat. Lat.* t. LXXII, col. 93.

[4] 'That through our blessing this vessel may be sanctified, and a new sepulchre of the body of Christ may be completed by the grace of his spirit.' *Leofric missal*, edit. Warren, p. 222.

[5] Flodoard, *Hist. Eccles. Remen.*, lib. I, cap. XVIII; *Pat. Lat.*, t. CXXXV, col. 62.

[6] *Ibid.*, lib. II, cap. VI; *Ibid.*, col. 107.

[7] *Greg. Turon, Hist. Eccles. Franc.*, lib. X, cap. XXXI; *Pat. Lat.*, t. LXXI, col. 569.

Venantius Fortunatus has left a poem commemorating the tower, which Felix, bishop of Bourges (d. soon after 573), had obtained for his church:[1]

> Quam bene juncta decent, sacrati ut corporis agni
> Margaritam ingens aurea dona ferant.
> Cedant chrysolitis Salomonia vasa metallis,
> Ista placere magis ars (arx) facit, atque fides.
> Quae data, Christe, tibi Felicis munera sic sint.
> Qualia tunc tribuit de grege pastor Abel.
> Et cujus tu corde vides, pietate coaeques
> Siraptae merito, quae dedit aera duo.

The tower figures also in a collect for the hallowing of the sacred vessels in the Bobbio missal.[2]

In recent times, a tower has been hung in the chapel of the Dominican friars in the church of St. Vincent Ferrer, New York, but the Eucharist is not reserved in it, and it serves merely as an ornament.[3]

Hanging Pyx: Dove

The earliest indication of a vessel in the form of a dove is found in Tertullian (*c.* 200), but, despite the assurance of Dom Leclercq,[4] there is absolutely nothing to suggest a eucharistic purpose. It is, as the quotation says, a figure of Christ.[5] As we have seen, doves of gold and silver are recorded in the *Liber Pontificalis* as gifts to the Roman

[1] Venant. Fortun. *Carm.* XX, *Miscellanea,* lib. III, cap. XXV; *Pat. Lat.*, t. LXXXVIII, col. 144–45; *Monum. Germ. Hist.*, t. IV, part 1 (Berlin, 1881), p. 71.

[2] Bobbio Missal, *Henry Bradshaw Society*, vol. LVIII, p. 169, no. 554; *Pat. Lat.*, t. LXXI, col. 1185.

[3] *St. Vincent Ferrer's Church, 66th Street and Lexington Avenue, New York, N.Y.*, New York City, 1944, p. 210.

[4] Leclercq, *Dict. d'Archéol. Chrét. et de Lit.*, t. III, part 2, col. 2231.

[5] *Nostrae columbae etiam domus simplex, in editis semper et apertis ad lucem. Amat figura spiritus sancti Orientem, Christi figuram.* Tertullian, *Lib. adv. Valent.*, cap. III; *Pat. Lat.*, t. II, col. 545; *Corpus Script. Eccles. Latin.*, vol. XLVII (Vienna, 1906), p. 179.

basilicas in the fourth and fifth centuries, but again there is no suggestion of sacramental use, although two of them are said to serve as reliquaries. Towers with doves figure among the bequests, and it has been suggested that the dove would have been the immediate container for the Eucharist, while the tower was an ornamental outer casing, but there is no corroborative evidence from this early period.

St. Paulinus of Nola (d. 431) is said by Mabillon[1] to have had a eucharistic dove in mind when writing to Severus:[2]

> Divinum veneranda tegunt altaria foedus,
> Compositisque sacra cum cruce martyribus.
> Cuncta salutiferi coeunt martyria Christi:
> Crux, corpus, sanguis martyris, ipse Deus.

It is possible, although there is nothing to support the assertion.

Gregory of Tours (d. 594) relates how an officer in the army of King Sigebert (574) endeavoured to remove a golden dove hanging above the tomb of St. Denis in the abbey church of that name, and lost his life in the attempt.[3] The dove in question, however, would probably have been no more than a simple ornament.

The first unambiguous reference to a suspended vessel for reservation in the form of a dove is found in a Life of St. Basil, by pseudo-Amphilochus (*c.* eighth century), in which it is said that the Saint, while celebrating the Liturgy, divided the eucharistic bread into three parts, with the third part to be enclosed in a golden dove suspended over the altar.[4] It was possibly this Life, which was translated

[1] Mabil., *De Lit. Gall.*, lib. I, cap. IX, 24.
[2] *Paulin. Nolen.*, *epist.* XXXII *ad Severum*; *Pat. Lat.*, t. LXI, col. 333.
[3] *Greg. Turon.*, *De Gloria mart.*, cap. LXXII; *Pat. Lat.*, t. LXXI, col. 769.
[4] Freestone, *op. cit.*, pp. 194–95; Köster, *op. cit.*, p. 36.

into Latin in the ninth century and in a short time diffused in the West, which led to the introduction of a eucharistic dove in France and elsewhere from about the beginning of the eleventh century.[1] It may well be, as Righetti suggests, that the dove was in use for the chrism from the fifth century, and was only employed for the Eucharist about the eleventh century.[2] An ancient martyrology of Auxerre said that a canon by the name of Frodo gave a silver and gilt dove for the reserved Sacrament to his cathedral church.[3] An onyx pyx for suspension over the altar was presented to the abbey of St. Vanne in Lorraine by the emperor Henry II (1002–24).[4] The eucharistic dove would have had a cavity in its back for the sacred species, and it was closed with a lid. Few other examples are as early in date. Sometimes a smaller pyx containing the particles would be placed within the ornamental dove, and often the Eucharist was wrapped in linen (*pannus eucharisticus*).

Evidence of a golden dove, containing a small pyx made from the bark of a tree (*in pixide cortica*), which hung continually over the altar (*columba jugiter pendente super altare*) was found in the second half of the eleventh century at Cluny, as we learn from the customary arranged by Udalric[5] (*c.* 1085). Other churches of the Order would have undoubtedly followed the practice of the mother house, as well as abbeys which had adopted Cluniac customs without losing their own individuality, as was the case at Hirsau in Germany and Farfa in Italy. In the eleventh century also a eucharistic dove was introduced at St. Benignus in Dijon.

[1] Köster, *op. cit.*, p. 36. [2] Righetti, *Manuale di Storia Liturgica*, vol. I, p. 438.
[3] Martyrol., *Vet. SS. Coll.* VI, 688; Köster, *op. cit.*, p. 37.
[4] 'The emperor Henry also gave . . . a pyx of onyx, in which is kept the Lord's body, hanging over the altar.' *Chron. Hugonis monachi Virdun. et Divion. abbatis Flavinianensis*, lib. I, n. 8; Maffei, *op. cit.*, pp. 41–42; Van Dijk, *op. cit.*, p. 34, n. 5; Köster, *op. cit.*, p. 37. Köster says that the monastery was that of St. Vitus at Verdun.
[5] *Consuet. Clun.*, lib. II, cap. XXX; *Pat. Lat.*, t. CXLIX, col. 722–23.

The term pyx came to be applied indiscriminately to the dove or outer casket, as well as to the inner receptacle containing the particles.

Capsa or Pyx

The Chronicle of St. Alban's Abbey records that in the time of King Edmund (939–46) the fifth abbot, Eadfrith, although his monastic reputation was far from good (*exemplum pastor ovibus dabat perniciosum*), gave to his church a most beautiful vessel (*cyphum quemdam desiderabilem*) as a receptacle for the Lord's body (*ad corpus Dominicum reponendum*), which was as admirable in workmanship as in material.[1] Unfortunately the chronicle does not tell us either the shape of the vessel or where it was to be placed: whether in the sacristy, as was customary in Anglo-Saxon times, or in the church.

Reservation of the Eucharist *in capsis* was prescribed in *Ordo Romanus* I, *Admonitio Synodalis* and the synod of Verona.

About the middle of the ninth century, there were regulations that pyxes and the like must be made of some solid material.[2] A certain amount of carelessness in keeping the eucharistic vessels clean is evident from the admonition of the archbishop of Bourges, Rudolf, who issued instructions that the sacred species should be kept in *vase mundissimo*.[3] Hincmar, archbishop of Rheims (d. 882), ordered deans and other officials to make inquiries in all churches and chapels as to whether due caution was observed respecting the reservation of the Sacrament, and whether a suitable pyx had been provided.[4]

[1] *Gesta Abbatum Monasterii Sancti Albani*, vol. I (*Rolls Series*), p. 20. London, 1867.
[2] Köster, *op. cit.*, p. 40.
[3] *Rodol. archiep. Biruricen.*, cap. VI; Mansi, *op. cit.*, t. XIV, col. 947.
[4] *Hinc. Remen.*, cap. II, 8; *ibid.*, t. XV, col. 480.

A pyx in every church had been insisted upon by both Regino and Burchard, but there were no definite regulations regarding their material or shape. Normally, however, the pyx would have been circular or polygonal, and the *capsa* and *arca* square.[1] It is recorded of Pope Victor III (1086–87) that he bequeathed to the abbey of Monte Cassino, where he had formerly been abbot, a pyx of gold and enamel and a large silver pyx with black enamel.[2]

Aumbry

There would not appear to have been any regulation respecting an aumbry in this early period, but archaeology shows conclusively that they existed in some churches, either in the sacristy or in the church, where they may occur under the altar, in the wall nearby, or in the apse.[3] An aumbry is represented in a mosaic in the mausoleum of Galla Placidia (*c.* 440) at Ravenna, which Righetti calls 'the first tabernacle.'[4] An altar with a cupboard was erected in the baptistery of Parenzo cathedral (Istria) by Bishop Eufrasius, probably in the second quarter of the sixth century. The purpose of the 'storage space,' say Dijk and Walker, is indicated by the symbols of the doves and the cross in the tympanum of the door opening and the fishes at either side above it. The arrangement of these symbols also indicates that they were not intended for the altar as such.[5] The Eucharist would have been required in the baptistery for the Communion of the infant after Baptism

[1] Köster, *op. cit.*, pp. 40–41.
[2] *Leo Ostien.*, *Chron. Casin.*, lib. III, cap. ult.; *Pat. Lat.*, t. CLXXIII, col. 812.
[3] Van Dijk, *op. cit.*, p. 46. [4] Righetti, *op. cit.*, vol. I, p. 436.
[5] Van Dijk, *op. cit.*, p. 46.

and Confirmation, and an eighth-century Mozarabic distich contains the initiatory trilogy:[1]

Carne, cruore pio limfaque et chrismate sacro
Hic Deus est homines vivificare potens

An inscription found by Rossi in a codex of Paris, probably from an old basilica in Seville, says: '*Ad Babtisma, Confirmationem, Eucharistiam, cum babtisterium cum tribunali cohereret.*'[2] Chrism and Holy Communion on the altar of the baptistery are prescribed in a rubric of the baptismal rite in the Mozarabic *Liber Ordinum* (1052).

[1] German Prado, *Textos Inéditos de la Liturgica Mozárabe* (Madrid, 1926), p. 122.
[2] *Ibid.*
[3] Sedente Chrisma vel Sacra Communione superaltare, *Ibid.*, pp. 110–11.

5: RENEWAL OF THE SACRED SPECIES

THE earliest regulations caution against keeping the Sacrament overlong, but they give no indication as to when a renewal should become necessary. Pseudo-Clement, for example, a text of the seventh century, directs the deacons to see that the fragments of the consecrated bread in the sacristy do not get mouldy.[1] The instruction, which was for long ascribed to Pope Clement (88–97), was said by an eleventh-century codex of St. Martial (Limoges) to be the source of a diocesan regulation directing that the body of the Lord should be renewed twelve times in the year, and the old which is changed should be consumed by the clergy, lest through lapse of time any decay should be discovered in the fragments of the Lord's body.[2]

Penalties for permitting the accidents of the sacred species to deteriorate are found in the Celtic and Anglo-Saxon Churches. The Rule of St. Colomban (*c.* 600) determined: 'Let him who has shown negligence towards the sacrifice so that a worm is found in it, even though it be whole, burn it in fire near the altar and put away the ashes underneath the altar, and himself do penance forty days.'[3] The same rule also inflicted penances on those who kept the Eucharist so long that it changed colour, became partially corrupt or entirely dried up (*siccetur*). The reference probably concerned private reservation on the person. Something similar was directed in the Penitential of Theodore (668–90): 'Every sacrifice which has become corrupt through the foulness of age must be burned in

[1] *Pat. Lat.*, t. LVI, col. 893.
[2] Martène, *Ant. Eccl. Rit.*, t. I, lib. I, cap. V, art. III, 9, p. 252.
[3] *Reg. Colomb.*, cap. X; *Pat. Lat.*, t. LXXX, col. 222.

fire.'[1] Again, in the Penitential of Egbert (735–66): 'Let him who has neglected the sacrifice so that there are worms in it, and it has lost its colour and taste, do penance for twenty, thirty or forty days, and let it be burned in fire, and its ashes put away under the altar.'[2]

About the end of the tenth century, we hear of the practice in England of consecrating hosts on Holy Thursday to serve for the sick for a whole year, in imitation of Eastern usage. The custom was condemned in a canon of Aelfric, abbot of Eynsham (*c.* 1000), and it was enjoined that the Eucharist should be renewed every eight or fifteen days.[3] A very firm decision was arrived at by the council of Bourges in 1031: 'Inasmuch as it has been said that the body of the Lord has been neglected in parish churches by being left too long, the bishops in the same council have decreed that the body of the Lord be not reserved longer than from one Lord's day to another.'[4] Regulations of the kind came into general use in the following century.[5]

Instructions for the renewal of the sacred species are issued by Regino of Prüm and Burchard of Worms, when the particles would have been intincted: the former directed '*de tertio in tertium*' and the latter '*de septimo in septimum*.'[6] Detailed regulations are also found in the Cluny customary, edited by Udalric in about 1085: 'It should be known also that the body of the Lord is changed every Sunday. While the priest proceeds to the *pax*, the newly consecrated (host) is placed by the deacon in a pyx of bark, and what was consecrated the previous Sunday is taken out and divided by the same deacon, and the brethren thence communicated;

[1] Haddan and Stubbs, *op. cit.*, vol. III, p. 187. [2] *Ibid.*, vol. III, p. 427.
[3] Can. Aelfric; Thorpe, *op. cit.*, vol. II, p. 361. [4] Counc. Bourges, 1031, can. 2.
[5] Jungmann, *Missarum Sollemnia*, t. III (Paris, 1954), pp. 343–44.
[6] Köster, *op. cit.*, p. 43.

only the two particles of that host which the priest divided are not changed. And while the *psalmi familiares*[1] are being recited after terce, the deacon takes the aforesaid pyx from the dove which hangs continually over the altar, wiping well the dust from the outside with a small linen cloth, and places it upon the right hand corner of the altar, under a veil, and when Mass is finished puts it back in the same place.'[2]

[1] Psalms recited for benefactors.
[2] *Consuet. Cluniacen.*, lib. II, cap. XXX; *Pat. Lat.*, t. CXLIX, col. 722–23.

6: RECEPTION OF RESERVED HOSTS

THE Mosaic law required that what was left over from the sacrifice should be burned, and the regulation was followed in the East for the sacrifice of the new law, although Evagrius (594) says that the old custom at Constantinople was for boys, who had not yet reached the age of puberty (*pueri impuberes*), to consume what remained of the sacred species after the communion in the Liturgy.[1]

Western custom prior to the sixth century is unknown, but the second council of Mâcon (585), following Constantinople, directed that 'innocent boys' (*pueri innocentes*) should be brought fasting on Wednesdays and Fridays to the sacristy, in order to consume what was left over from the Sacrament.[2] This would seem to have been the general practice in Gaul, at least from the sixth to the beginning of the ninth century, as the ordinance appears again in the acta of the council of Tours, held under the emperor Charlemagne.[3] The more ordinary usage, which finally prevailed everywhere, was for the reserved Eucharist to be consumed by the celebrant alone or, if necessity required it, together with other clerics.

[1] Evag., *Eccles. Hist.*, lib. IV, cap. XXXVI; *Pat. Graec.*, t. LXXXVI, part 2, col. 2770.

[2] Counc. II Mâcon 585, can. 6.

[3] Counc. Tours, 813, can. 19.

7: CONTINUOUS LIGHT

THERE was no regulation in this early period for a light to burn continuously before the reserved Sacrament, but a reference by St. Gregory of Tours may possibly indicate that it was sometimes to be found: . . . *avis corydalus, quam alaudam vocamus* . . .: *in sacrario autem sub velo transiens, cicindelum extinguere voluit, sed ab ostiariis prohibita atque occisa est.*[1]

[1] *Greg. Turon., Hist. Eccles. Franc.*, lib. IV, n. 21; *Pat. Lat.*, t. LXXI, col. 294.

8: WORSHIP OF THE RESERVED SACRAMENT

THE rudiments of a cultus definitely paid to the reserved Eucharist first appear in the latter part of the eleventh century, as a reaction to the diffusion of Berengarian views concerning the Sacrament of the altar. Berengarius (*c.* 999–1088), *scholasticus* of the school of St. Martin at Tours and archdeacon of Angers, had disseminated false doctrine as to the presence of Christ in the Eucharist, despite his condemnation in a number of synods. The difficulty for him would seem to have been the mode rather than the fact of the Real Presence, but there is little doubt that he repudiated transubstantiation, as it was defined later by the fourth Lateran council (1215).

It would in all probability have been to counteract these erroneous views that the Norman abbey of Bec decided to carry the Eucharist in the Palm Sunday procession, and in its progress prescribed acts of adoration to the Sacrament. On the appointment of Lanfranc, a former prior of Bec and abbot of St. Stephen's, Caen, to the see of Canterbury (d. 1089), a number of Norman usages were incorporated in his Constitutions, and among them the Palm Sunday procession with the Blessed Sacrament: two priests in albs carry a portable shrine (*feretrum*) in which the body of the Lord has been placed (*in quo et Corpus Christi esse debet reconditum*) . . . and as they pass between, all shall genuflect, not all at once but two by two on opposite sides as the shrine passes by opposite to them.[1] The Canterbury statutes of Lanfranc were adopted at St. Albans by Abbot Paul, the

[1] Lanfranc, *Decreta pro Ord. S Benedicti*, I, 4; *Pat. Lat.*, t. CL, col. 456; *Opera Lanfranci*, edit. Giles, vol. I, p. 100.

first abbot after the Norman Conquest.[1] The Constitutions also prescribed enhanced ceremonial and acts of adoration for the Eucharist reserved on Holy Thursday for the Presanctified rite.[2]

Rouen in the eleventh century, as at Rome, carried only the gospel-book in the procession, although the carrying of the Host was adopted soon after.

[1] *Gesta Abb. S. Alb.*, Rolls Series, vol. I, pp. 52, 61.
[2] Vide Liturgy of the Presanctified, pp. 12–13.

PART II

RESERVATION FROM THE TWELFTH CENTURY TO THE REFORMATION

THE cultus of the Blessed Sacrament, which followed as a reaction from the heretical teaching of Berengarius, became increasingly accentuated in the succeeding centuries of the middle ages. Respect to the reserved Sacrament was inculcated, and instructions were issued by synods and bishops regarding the safe custody of the Eucharist.

9: PURPOSE OF RESERVATION

(*a*) Communion of the Sick and Viaticum

THE primary purpose of the reserved Sacrament has always been the Communion of the sick and dying, and was indeed its sole purpose for nearly a thousand years. Gratian, who has been described as 'the true founder of the science of canon law,'[1] says in his decretal (*c.* 1140), following Burchard of Worms, that 'the Eucharist ought always to be at the disposition of the sick.'[2]

Directions for taking the Sacrament to the sick were issued by English and other bishops throughout the thirteenth century. Thus in 1220 Richard Marsh, bishop of Durham, said: 'When the Eucharist is taken to the sick, let the priest have a clean and decent pyx, so that one always remains in the church, and in the other he carries the Lord's body to the sick, the Eucharist itself being enclosed in a very clean purse (*bursa*). The pyx will be covered with a clean linen cloth.'[3] Very similar injunctions were issued by Peter Quivil, bishop of Exeter, in 1287: 'The Lord's body must be placed in a very clean purse, and this enclosed under lock and key, in a clean and decent pyx of silver or ivory or other fitting material, which the priest must carry on his breast, a light being carried before him, because he who is the brightness of eternal light is being carried forth.'[4] The thirteenth-century 'Dominicanized' Carmelite ordinal, now in the library of Trinity College, Dublin, directed the Eucharist to be reserved '*ad usum infirmorum*,' to which Sibert

[1] Van Hove, art. *Gratian*, *Catholic Encyclopedia*, vol. VI, p. 730.
[2] Gratian, *Decret.* C 93, D.2 de cons.
[3] Wilkins, *op. cit.*, vol. I, p. 580.
[4] *Ibid.*, vol. II, p. 132.

de Beka in the following century added the words: '*et chori devotionem honorifice reservatur.*'[1]

The great English canonist, William Lyndwood (*c.* 1422), quoting from Gratian and following the directions of pseudo-Clement, said: 'the priest will always have the Eucharist ready for the sick.'[2] The all-sufficing reason for reserving the Sacrament—the use of the sick—was stressed so late as 1416 in the council of Breslau (Wratislav): 'No one of the clergy . . . (the feast of the Body of our Lord Jesus Christ, and the occasion of some special commemoration of the same Sacrament being alone excepted) shall presume to expose, exhibit, and *reserve* this most venerable Sacrament, *otherwise than for the use of the sick*, under such penalties as belong to the rebellious and contumacious, the which all transgressors are hereby warned by our synodal authority that they will incur and fall under *ipso facto*.'[3]

In country districts, the taking of the reserved Sacrament to the sick must sometimes have offered much difficulty, and even peril, to the priest, who, in all weathers, and often alone, was obliged to carry the pyx round his neck, with the lantern and bell about his horse's neck. A constitution of the bishop of Worcester, Walter de Cantilupe (1240), was not unmindful of these difficulties.[4] Some two centuries later, we find William Lyndwood explaining just how a priest could manage the lantern and bell, if he were taking the Sacrament to some remote part of the parish, unaccompanied by an assistant. It would not be reprehensible, he said, to attach both of them to the neck of his horse.[5]

[1] Sibert de Beka, *Ordinal*, rubr. XLIV, edit. Zimmermann, p. 86.
[2] Lyndwood, *Provinciale*, *De Consec.*, dist. II, cap. *Presbyter.*
[3] Hartzheim, *Concilia Germaniae*, t. V, pp. 153–54.
[4] If the place is remote or the weather is bad, the casket containing the pyx may be carried round the neck of the priest. *Constit. W. de Cantil.*; Wilkins, *Concilia Magnae Britanniae et Hiberniae*, vol. I (London, 1737), p. 667.
[5] Lyndwood, *Provinc.*, III, 26, note X.

A curious copper lantern, studded with knobs of rock crystal, and, seemingly, of the end of the twelfth or beginning of the thirteenth century is to be seen in the Ashmolean Museum at Oxford. Dr. Rock suggested that this may very well have been a lantern used for taking the Eucharist to the sick.[1]

It was in the thirteenth century also that instructions were issued for the faithful to venerate the Sacrament as it passed them on the road. Giraldus Cambrensis (*c.* 1205) said that 'the deacon is to go ahead with a light, even in the daytime, and the people are to venerate the Sacrament, covering their eyes with their hands.'[2] Something similar was enjoined in the twenty-fifth decree of the provincial constitutions of St. Edmund of Canterbury (*c.* 1236).[3] The ringing of a bell (*tintinnabulum*) was prescribed by the council of Reading (1279), 'so that the people may be roused to due reverence, who are to be discreetly instructed by the priest that they prostrate themselves, or at least humbly pray, wherever it may happen that the King of Glory is carried under the covering of bread.'[4] A similar reason for the bell was given in the statutes of Archbishop Peckham in the following year (1280): 'that the people might kneel down (*prosternandum*) or at least say a prayer.'[5]

The council of Westminster (1138) directed that the priest or deacon should normally take the Eucharist to the sick, but that in a case of 'urgent necessity' it might, 'with the greatest reverence,' be taken by anyone.[6] It was, however, forbidden to deacons, except for some grave reason, by the constitutions of Odo (Eudes) de Sully, bishop of Paris, in

[1] Rock, *op. cit.*, vol. II, p. 374, n. 36.
[2] Girald. Cambr., *Gemma Eccl.*, I, 6; *Rolls Series*, vol. XXI, 2, p. 20.
[3] Wilkins. *op. cit.*, vol. I, pp. 637–38.
[4] Counc. Reading, 1279, can. 7.
[5] Wilkins, *op. cit.*, vol. II, p. 48.
[6] Counc. Westminster, 1138, can. 2.

1198:[1] an injunction repeated in the synodal statutes of the Church of Meaux[2] (1245).

Gifts of a pyx for taking the Eucharist to the sick were not infrequent. Thus in 1396 at the church of St. Benet's, Cambridge, we hear of 'a cup gilte outside with a gilt cover given by Dame Alice Chaumberlyn for this use that the Corpus Christi may be carried to sick parishioners.'[3] The Edwardian inventory of All Hallows in Grimley parish, Worcestershire, gave the entry: 'a lytell box of sylver to bere the sacrament in when the pryst dothe vyset.'[4]

(*b*) Communion of the Faithful in Church

Communion after Mass had been given in the sacristy in Gaul and, probably, elsewhere, but the first mention of Communion in the church itself is found in a statute of Angilbert, abbot of St. Riquier (*d.* 814), in which it was directed to be given after Mass at Easter and Christmas.[5] The practice, however, would not appear to have been followed by other churches until considerably later. In the twelfth century, it was customary for the archbishop of Milan and his clergy to receive Holy Communion in the sacristy at the end of the Good Friday liturgy.[6]

The churches of the religious orders would seem to have been the first to have given Communion after Mass: a custom followed later by parish churches. Cardinal Bona (d. 1674), citing the Oratorian Jean Morin[7] (d. 1659), says that 'the body of our Lord Jesus Christ was in ancient times

[1] *Odo Epi. Paris.*, *Constit.*, cap. V, no. 5; Mansi, *op. cit.*, t. XXII, col. 677.
[2] Martène, *Thes. Nov. Anecdot.* (Paris, 1717), t. IV, col. 893.
[3] *Cambridge Antiquarian Society*, XVII (1911), p. 12.
[4] *Assoc. Architectural Society*, XI (1871), p. 322.
[5] *Pat. Lat.*, t. XCIX, col. 849.
[6] *Beroldus sive Ecclesiae Ambrosianae Mediolanensis Kalendarium et Ordines*, edit. Magistretti, 1894, p. 108.
[7] Morin, *De Poenit.*, lib. VIII, cap. XIV.

kept in the church for the communion of the sick'; to which he adds: 'the actual practice of reserving several consecrated particles for the communion of the faithful outside the sacrifice, owes its origin to the medicant orders, and that finally it was received everywhere, despite the opposition of the Roman ritual, which, still today, says that the Eucharist is reserved for the sick.'[1]

The claim that communion after Mass encouraged more frequent communion was quite certainly false, and it was only prescribed for great feasts, such as Easter or Christmas, or on special occasions, when a large number of communicants was expected. The reason was rather that with so many communicants the Mass would have been too long drawn out. Communion, however, was seldom, if ever, outside the *nexus* of the sacrifice: some considerable time after the Mass.

In the twelfth century, we find the practice of waiting until the end of the liturgy prescribed in the ritual of the Canons Regular of St. Augustine, the Benedictine convent of Schönau, and in a letter of Abelard (d. 1142) to Heloise. The ordo of the Lateran basilica (twelfth century) directed neophytes to receive Communion every day in the octaves of Easter and Pentecost *post finem missae*.[2] The custom of receiving Communion after Mass was greatly extended in the following century when Communion under one kind had become general in the Western Church. The Dominican ordinal (1256) gave the priest permission, when there was a large congregation, to defer Holy Communion *usque post missam*, except on Holy Thursday.[3] Somewhat similar instructions are found in the Carmelite ordinal (after 1250), *ordo* of Sens (1213), canonical visitation charges of certain

[1] Bona, *Rer. Lit.*, cap. XVII. [2] *Ordo eccl. Lateran.*, edit. Fischer, p. 73.
[3] Guerrini, *Ordin. juxta ritum sacri Ord. Frat. Praedic.*, p. 248.

of the English bishops, and the pastoral directions of Durandus of Mende (d. 1296).

The decision of the fourth Lateran council (1215), making it obligatory for the faithful to receive Holy Communion at least once a year,[1] was not conducive to frequent Communion, and shortly before the Reformation the ritual of Schwerin (1521) actually forbade all who were not priests to communicate outside Paschaltide, allegedly for fear of profanation of the Sacrament.[2] Yet on the rare occasions of Communion, there would have been no need to reserve the hosts, as the parish priest would know the number of intending communicants on each occasion, and consecrate the required number of particles accordingly.

As the middle ages drew to a close, the once exclusive idea of Viaticum gradually fell into the background, and reservation of the Eucharist at the altar grew to be dominantly connected with Communion. So much was this the case, and so naturally did all this come about that in the parish church of Neisse in Silesia, with its forty-five altars, the large host for the weekly procession of the Blessed Sacrament on Thursdays and the hosts for the sick were reserved in the sacrament house apart from the altar, while the hosts *pro communicantibus* were reserved in the tablenacle which was on the high altar.[3]

A note book of Pastor Dreygerwolt, parish priest of St. James', Munster (1521–25), throws light on the practice in that church just prior to the Anabaptist revolt. It tells us that a notice is to be given out on the Sunday before Christmas to 'bid those communicants who do not come

[1] 'Receiving reverently the sacrament of the Eucharist at least at Easter.' Counc. IV Lateran, 1215, cap. XXI. Denzinger-Schönmetzer, *op. cit.*, p. 264.

[2] Schönfelder, *De Custodia eucharistiae, Die Agende der Diözese Schwerin von* 1521 (Paderborn, 1906), p. 6.

[3] Edmund Bishop, *Liturgica Historica*, pp. 36–37.

to confession here (St. James' church) to give notice of their intention to communicate, on account of the (number of) hosts to be consecrated.'[1] Holy Communion was given on Christmas Day after the High Mass, which was at 5.30 in the morning, and the celebrant was directed to remove his chasuble before distributing the Sacrament.[2]

At Stralsund on the Baltic coast, communion was invariably given after the Mass was finished, as we learn from a tract written by Franz Wessels, the burgomaster of the town at the time of the Reformation (*c.* 1550). He tells us also that on Holy Thursday, after the Blessed Sacrament had been taken to the place of repose and the whole office was over, the celebrant took off his chasuble and gave Communion (*et deinde communicant, postquam omnia rite peracta*). *Veni, Sancte Spiritus* was sung immediately before; and, generally, an antiphon of the Blessed Virgin afterwards.[3]

(*c*) Worship of the Reserved Sacrament

The purpose of the reserved Sacrament continued to be that of Communion, especially for the sick, but as the middle ages progressed, signs of devotion to the Eucharist in the pyx became more frequent.

The *Ancren Riwle* or *Regula Inclusarum* for anchoresses, which may well have been written for the nuns of Tarrant in Dorset by Richard Poore, who died there in 1237, after having held the sees of Salisbury and Durham, gave a form of devotion to the reserved Sacrament:[4] 'Sprinkleth you with holy water, that ye shoulen ever have with you, and thinketh o Godes flesh and on his blod, that is over the

[1] *Ibid.*, XXV, p. 446. [2] *Ibid.*, p. 447. [3] *Ibid.*, p. 451.

[4] *Ancren Riwle*, 16 (c. S. 1853); British Museum, Cotton MS., Nero, A. XIV, fol. 4.

high altar (*heie weovede*), and falleth each one theretoward with this greeting:

> Ave, principium nostrae creationis.
> Ave, precium nostrae redemptionis.
> Ave, viaticum nostrae peregrinationis
> Ave, premium nostrae expectationis.
> Tu esto nostrum gaudium, etc.

The cells of the anchoresses had windows into the church. Richard Poore, who was born in Tarrant and had a sister in the convent, was looked upon as the 'Second founder' of the house. The Anglo-Saxon language would seem to make it earlier than the time of Simon of Ghent, a later bishop of Salisbury (1296–1315), who has often been accredited as the author.[1]

As we have seen, the Carmelite Sibert de Beka added the words '*et chori devotionem*' to '*ad usum infirmorum*' in the ordinal of the Order.[2] A 'visit' to the Blessed Sacrament, much as we know it today, also seems to have been encouraged by the Benedictine poet, John Lydgate (d. *c.*1450): 'When thou comest to the holy place, cast holy water in thy face. Then look to the high altar, and pray to him that hangeth there.'[3]

[1] Gasquet, *Acren Riwle or Regula Inclusarum*, *Catholic Encyclopedia*, vol. 1, p. 464.
[2] Sibert de Beka, *Ordinal*, rubr. XLIV, edit. Zimmermann, p. 86.
[3] Lydgate, *Merita Missae*, pp. 37 seq.

10: PLACE OF RESERVATION

(*a*) Reservation outside a Church

THE practice of reserving the Eucharist elsewhere than in a church became increasingly rare, as the cultus of the Blessed Sacrament developed, with a greater insistence on exterior acts of veneration and intensified anxiety for the safety of the sacred species.

St. Louis (*d.* 1270), however, is said to have carried the Sacrament on his person, by permission of the papal legate, at the time of the Crusades.[1] The Eucharist was also reserved on the ship for the Communion of the sick, while the King attended a *missa sicca* each day, with the ministers in vestments according to the colour of the day.[2]

The old Celtic custom of a priest carrying the Sacrament as a safeguard against the perils of the way and for Viaticum is recorded of four priests in the life of the archbishop of Dublin, St. Laurence O'Toole (*c.* 1150).[3]

St. Godric (1110–70), who was not a priest and lived as a hermit at Finchdale near Durham, reserved the Eucharist for more than thirty years over the altar in his oratory, ministered to by the monks of Durham. A life of the Saint related how in 1138 the Scots 'rushed into his oratory and plundered whatever was of value, trampling the Eucharist under their filthy feet, and crushing the offletes (unconsecrated altar breads) into pieces.'[4]

[1] Guillaume de Nangis, *Gesta Sancti Ludovici*; Martène, *De Ant. Eccles. Rit.*, I, 5, art. 4. i; Bouquet, *Receuil des Historiens des Gaules* (1840), t. XX, p. 388.
[2] Bona, *op. cit.*, I, cap. XV, 6.
[3] Köster, *op. cit.*, part 2, cap. II, p. 56.
[4] *Vita S. Goderici*, edit. Stevenson, *Surtees Society* (1847), p. 114.

St. Thomas of Canterbury was accustomed to carry the Sacrament with him when it was necessary to have an audience with the King (Henry II).[1]

The fifteenth-century historian, Charles Veranus, related that Ferdinand of Spain, after being captured by the Moors, left the Eucharist with them as a pledge for his return to captivity, should he fail to find the ransom money.[2]

In the fourteenth century, it was customary for the Pope to carry the Sacrament processionally with him on his journeys.[3] The first known example is that of Gregory XI (1370–78), who even when travelling in the mountains for recreation was preceded by the Eucharist. Muratori said of Benedict XIII (1394–1424) that, whenever he left his residence to go to some church, or went on a journey outside the city, he was preceded by a cross and the Body of Christ.[4] Popes and antipopes throughout the fifteenth and sixteenth centuries followed a similar practice. This apparent revival of an ancient custom was, however, neither to have the Eucharist at hand for Viaticum, nor to serve as a talisman against danger, but rather to enhance the person of the pope as he entered or left the cities of his territory. The central figure of these processions was not the Sacrament, but the pope, and from at least the fifteenth century was a personal privilege which was rarely granted to others. In 1446, Paul II had forbidden the archbishop of Benevento to carry the Eucharist with him on his visitations, although it had been a custom of the diocese. Three years later (1449), however, Nicholas V accorded the privilege to the antipope Felix V after his submission.[5]

[1] Bernard, *Cours de Liturgie Romaine, Le Rituel*, t. I (Paris, 1893), p. 582.
[2] Rocca, *Thes. Pontif.*, vol. I, p. 41; Freestone, *op. cit.*, p. 47.
[3] Köster, *op. cit.*, pp. 56–57.
[4] Muratori, *Rer. Ital. Script.* (Milan, 1723–51), III, II, p. 781. Also pp. 795, 806, 820.
[5] Köster, *op. cit.*, p. 57.

Rijksmuseum, Amsterdam

PLATE I

EUCHARISTIC DOVE
Thirteenth century

Facing page 66

PLATE 2

HIGH ALTAR WITH EUCHARISTIC SUSPENSION
Arras Cathedral, Thirteenth century

(*b*) Reservation inside the Church

Cathedrals and Parish Churches

The Blessed Sacrament, as we have seen, was reserved for the sick, and therefore primarily in those churches to which a cure of souls was attached.

The first official regulation was the decree *Sane* of Innocent III in the fourth Lateran council of 1215. The purpose of the decree was not to legislate how or where the Eucharist was to be reserved, but that it was to be kept with strict care under lock and key. The same vigilance was required for the chrism, 'that no presumptuous hands may be able to lay hold on them for any horrible or evil purpose.'[1] The security measures of Innocent were repeated by his successor, Honorius III (1216–27): 'The Eucharist is always to be kept in a special place (*in loco singulari*), clean and locked (*signato*), with all reverence, devotion and faithfulness.'[2] This all-important provision of 'lock and key' appeared also in the decretals of Gregory IX (1227–41).[3]

The papal requirements, however, had been anticipated and even exceeded by Odo de Sully, bishop of Paris, in 1198, who not only required the eucharistic vessels to be locked, but directed that the Sacrament should be reserved in a pyx of ivory on the fairest (*pulchriore*) part of the altar.[4] In a final series of miscellaneous provisions, the bishop made it plain that his requirements were to be obeyed by the clergy: 'for some are so negligent that, though it is now three years since they received copies of these regulations, they have not yet provided . . . a tabernacle (*tabernaculum*)

[1] Counc. IV Lateran, 1215, cap. XX; Mansi, *op. cit.*, t. XXII, col. 1007.
[2] Honor. III; *ibid.*, t. XXII, col. 1100.
[3] Greg. IX, decr., cap. I, can. 20.
[4] *Odonis Episc. Parisien.*, *Synodicae Constit.*, 1198, cap. V, n. 7; Mansi, *op. cit.*, t. XXII, col. 678.

wherein the body of the Lord may be reserved with honour. . . .'[1]

Throughout the thirteenth century, councils and synods endeavoured to enforce the security measures of the decree *Sane*. Many of the bishops also issued regulations as to the mode and place of reservation, which differed in the various countries and dioceses. With a view to greater security, the Cistercian general chapter in 1262 advised the substitution of a 'suitable vessel' (*vas idoneum*) for the customary chalice (*calix*) to serve as a receptacle for the reserved Sacrament in the churches of the Order.[2] Instructions for the carrying out of the Lateran decree were given in the councils of Oxford (1222), Rouen (1223), Trier (1227, 1238), Fritzlar (1246), Mainz (1261), Cahors (1273) and Padua (1284) to name but a few. In the course of the century, there was hardly a diocese of England in which the security measures of Innocent were not enjoined. The bishop of Lincoln, Robert Grosseteste (*c*. 1238), warned his parochial clergy that 'the Eucharist . . . must be devoutly and faithfully preserved, and be always honourably laid up in a place apart (*in loco singulari*), clean and locked (*signato*).'[3]

Perhaps the most important regulations which figure in William Lyndwood's *Provinciale* affecting the reservation of the Eucharist in medieval England are contained in the Constitutions of John Peckham, archbishop of Canterbury, for the year 1281: 'that in every parish church there shall be made (*fiat*) a tabernacle (*tabernaculum*) with a lock (*clausura*), fitting and decent according to the importance and means of each church, wherein the body of the Lord itself shall be placed in a most fair pyx, wrapped in linen,

[1] *Ibid*., n. 35; *ibid*., col. 683. The word tabernacle had a variety of meanings, and is here used for a pyx.
[2] Cap. Gen. 1262, 8; Canivez, Stat. Capit. Gen. Ord. Cist., t.III, p. 2.
[3] *Roberti Grosseteste*, epist. LII, *Rolls Series* (1861), p. 155.

but under no circumstances in a purse (*loculo*[1]), so as to avoid the danger of breaking; and we charge that this be renewed every Lord's Day.'[2]

The episcopal requirements had been most sedulously expounded and explained, and yet in 1289 it was found necessary for the bishop of Chichester[3] and also the provincial council of York to threaten three months' suspension *ab officio* to any parish priest who failed to keep the Eucharist, baptismal font and holy oils under lock and key. In 1393, one of the questions asked in every church at the visitations of the bishop of Salisbury, John Waltham, was as to the condition of the locks and keys on the pyx, font and chrismatory.[4]

It seems strange that injunctions in respect to security measures regarding the Eucharist should still have been found necessary in the fifteenth and early sixteenth centuries. However, in 1470 the council of Passau was forced to remind the clergy of their obligation to see that the vessels containing the Sacrament and the oils were securely fastened.[5] The council of Seville (1512) felt it incumbent, not only to enjoin locks and keys, but also to direct that the Eucharist should be reserved in all cathedrals and parish churches.[6] Nor were these the only examples of the kind, as we learn from the synod of Warmia[7] (1497), provincial council of Cologne[8] (1536), etc.

Legislation was forthcoming also as to the custody of the keys for eucharistic vessels and receptacles. The council of Eichstätt (1447) was most insistent that the keys should

[1] *Loculus* is here the equivalent of *bursa*, which is found in some manuscripts. It may also mean a cupboard.
[2] Counc. Lambeth, 1281, cap. I; Wilkins, *op. cit.*, vol. II, p. 52.
[3] Wilkins, *op. cit.*, vol. II, p. 171.
[4] Cox and Harvey, *English Church Furniture*, (London, 1907), pp. 43–44.
[5] Harzheim, *op. cit.*, t. V, p. 483.
[6] Köster, *op. cit.*, p. 59.
[7] Harzheim, *op. cit.*, t. V, p. 664.
[8] *Ibid.*, t. VI, p. 282.

never be in the care of seculars,[1] and the provincial council of Seville (1512) was no less emphatic.[2] A similar decree was issued also by the synod of Ratisbon (1512).[3]

Churches of Regulars

The custom of reserving the Eucharist was found in the churches of the Benedictines from the sixth century, and by the twelfth had become universal in conventual churches.[4] In 1238, the general chapter of the Cistercians passed a statute in conformity with the decree *Sane* of Innocent III.[5] There was no attempt to legislate as to the mode of reservation, and the security measures were repeated in the *Institutiones capituli generalis* of 1240 and 1256.[6]

In some of the convents, in which the priest was permitted to enter for Mass and the renewal of the sacred species, the Eucharist was allowed to be reserved in the enclosure of the nuns. Indults for the purpose were sometimes granted by Rome, as, for example, by the antipope Clement VII (1378–94) for convents under the jurisdiction of the Friars Minor.[7] The Sacrament had been reserved in the nuns' choir at Toess near Winterthur (Switzerland) since the beginning of the thirteenth century.[8]

[1] *Ibid.*, t. V, pp. 367, 560.

[2] Tejada y Ramiro Juan, *Coleccion de Canones y de todos los Concilios de la Iglesia de España y de America* (Madrid, 1859–63), t. V, p. 103.

[3] Harzheim, *op. cit.*, t. VI, p. 97.

[4] Köster, *op. cit.*, p. 61.

[5] 'That the Eucharist be reserved under lock and key in all the houses of our Order.' *Cap. Gen.* 1238, I; Canivez, *Stat. Capit. Gen. Ord. Cist.*, t. 2 (Louvain, 1924), p. 185.

[6] '. . . Hosts must be of pure wheat: and the Eucharist reserved under lock and key.' *Instit. Cap. Gen.* 1246, 1256, dist. i. cap. VII; *Nomasticon Cisterciense* (edit. Séjalon, 1894), p. 288.

[7] 'That nuns or religious under the jurisdiction of the Minister General of the Friars Minor may have the Eucharist in some suitable place in the enclosure chapel, as well as in the outside church.' Köster, *op. cit.*, p. 63.

[8] *Ibid.*

Permission, however, was by no means always given, and in some cases it was abrogated.

In Other Churches or Chapels

In the middle ages, the Blessed Sacrament was not normally reserved in churches or chapels other than those of the foregoing categories. The purpose of reserving the Eucharist was for the communion of the sick, and bishops would have regarded indiscriminate permissions as a violation of the *jus parochialis*. The provincial statutes of Upsala in Sweden (1443–48) expressly prohibited reservation in small chapels away from the parish church.[1]

There were, however, exceptions, and royal personages, on occasions, were permitted by the Pope to reserve the Sacrament in their private chapels. The privilege was accorded to Sancia, Queen of Sicily, in 1331,[2] and Eugenius IV issued an indult to Henry VI of England in the twentieth year of his reign, allowing him to keep 'the blessed Sacrament in his oratory wheresoever he may be.'[3]

Sacristy or some similar place

It had become customary by the twelfth century to reserve the Sacrament in the church, but the practice of keeping it in the sacristy lasted longer in Italy, although even here this was by no means universal, and from at least the beginning of the thirteenth century a number of churches reserved on or near the altar.

The choice of several places, the sacristy among them, was sanctioned by the synod of Pavia in 1297, and a similar

[1] Provinc. Stat., Upsala, 1443–48, n. 84; Hefele, *Hist des Conc.*, t. VII (Paris, 1916), part 2, p. 1171.

[2] Köster, *op. cit.*, p. 64.

[3] *Vat. Regesta*, 12 Eugenius IV, vol. CCCLX, p. 240. The original, one of the unpublished letters of Eugenius IV, is at Eton College. 10 Kal. Aug. Florence, f. 186 d.

freedom of choice was permitted by the council of Ravenna in 1311.[1] The Eucharist was still reserved in the sacristy of the Lateran basilica in the time of Gregory XI (1370–78).[2] In the province of Milan, sacristy reservation persisted down to the reforms of St. Charles Borromeo (d. 1584), although aumbries by the side of or behind the altar were used in some churches, while at S. Nazaro (Milan) there was a hanging pyx in the form of a dove (twelfth-century).

There is documentary evidence respecting the usage in the cathedral church of Milan. Beroldus said that in his day (twelfth century) the archbishop and clergy received Communion in the sacristy at the end of the Good Friday liturgy,[3] and that a lamp was kept burning there throughout the night. The function of Beroldus was to tend the candles and lamps of the cathedral church, for which he received the title of '*cicendelarius*.'[4] The lamp still burns in the south sacristy, in an uninterrupted tradition.[5] A document of 1395 referred to an altar in the sacristy, dedicated to St. John the Evangelist, on which Mass was said; while an ordinance, drawn up in 1408, directed a tabernacle of wood to be made for the high altar, to contain the Eucharist on the Fridays of Lent, because no Mass was said on those days in that church.[6] The same annals, for the year 1465, in recording the adornment of the '*capsa tabernaculi*' in which the body of the Lord is placed, stated that the place of reservation in the cathedral church of Milan was the

[1] 'That the Eucharist, viaticum or body of Christ, chrism, holy oil, and oil of the sick, be devoutly, safely and secretly kept and reserved in either churches or sacristies, in a place appointed for the purpose.' Counc. Ravenna, 1311; Mansi, *op. cit.*, t. XXV col. 453–54.

[2] Martène, *Ant. Eccles. Rit.*, t. I (1700), lib. i, cap. V, art. 3, pp. 646–47.

[3] *Beroldus sive Ecclesiae Ambrosianae Mediolanensis Kalendarium et Ordines*, edit. Magistretti (1894), p. 107.

[4] The *cicendelarius* tends the candles, lamps and other vessels used for the purpose of giving light in a church. Du Cange, *op. cit.*, t. II, p. 416.

[5] Tamborini, *Il Corpus Domini a Milano*, chap. II, p. 24.

[6] *Annali Fab. Duomo*, an. 1409 (Milan, 1877–85), vol. II, p. 287.

sacristy.[1] This was continued until at least 1529, as we learn from the Chronicle of that year: 'The tabernacle remained on the altar of the cathedral until the evening. At the end of vespers the *Signori Ordinarii* removed it into the sacristy.'[2] It would seem probable that the Eucharist remained in the cathedral sacristy until the reforms of St. Charles Borromeo (1560–84), although the decree for visitations passed in the provincial synod of 1579 referred exclusively to aumbry reservation: the '*antiquae custodiae*' in the wall were either to be removed or diverted to other uses.[3] The *transitorium*, a chant sung during the Communion in the Ambrosian rite, may well have originated, as Dr. Cattaneo has suggested, as the processional chant, during which the sacred species would have been taken to the sacristy.[4]

Italy was not the only country in which reservation in the sacristy was permitted, and so late as 1745 Dom Chardon, in his *Histoire des Sacrements*, cited certain churches in France: 'Aujourd'hui encore il y a d'anciennes églises où il n'y a point de tabernacle où l'on réserve l'Eucharistie, entr'autres celle de Lyon, de Vienne, de Besançon... A Verdun l'Eucharistie pour les malades se reservoit dans une boëte que l'on reportait dans le sacraire après la messe. C'est qui étoit encore en usage vers le commencement du sixième (sic, but obviously 16th) siècle, comme il paroît par les statuts (fol. 251) que l'on ne garde pas le corps de Jésus-Christ que l'on met en réserve pour les malades audelà de huit jours sous les peines portées par les canons... et

[1] *Ibid.*, p. 243.
[2] Burigozzo, *Cronaca Milanese*, an. 1529; *Archivio storico Italiano*, t. III (Florence, 1842), p. 142.
[3] *Acta Eccl. Mediol.*, edit. Ratti, vol. II, p. 548.
[4] Cattaneo, *I Canti della Frazione e Communione nella Liturgia Ambrosiana, Miscell. Mohlberg*, vol. 2 (Rome, 1949), p. 170.

qu'après la messe on mette dans une boëte les hosties consacrées à cet usage, et qu'on les porte dans le sanctuaire où on a coutume de conserver le corps de notre Seigneur, ayant soin de le faire précéder de lumière dans le trajet: et reportetur ad sanctuarium ubi consuetum est dictum sacratissimum corpus, observari lumine eum praecedente, et que là on l'enferme sous la clef. Les statuts ajoutent que l'endroit dans lequel on garde ce précieux trésor doit être un lieu éminent et honnête, et que si les facultés de l'église le permettant, il doit toujours y avoir devant une lampe allumée.'[1]

Although the *sacrarium* was seldom distinct from the sacristy or treasury, that of Notre-Dame des Victoires au Sablon in Brussels is altogether true to type and solely devoted to eucharistic reservation.[2] Its entrance faces that of the sacristy on the gospel side in the second bay of the heptagonal apse. It served for reservation until recently, when there was a tabernacle in the form of a tower, coming from an old altar (sixteenth century) dismantled in the last century. The *sacrarium* itself has the appearance of a eucharistic tower.[3]

In medieval England, it was customary for two hosts to be taken to the sacristy after the Mass on Holy Thursday: one to serve for the Presanctified rite and the other, enclosed in a pyx, to be placed with the cross in the 'sepulchre' from after the veneration on Good Friday until early on Easter morning.[4]

As the middle ages progressed, the reserved Sacrament came to be given an increasingly honourable and important

[1] Chardon, *Histoire des Sacrements*, t. II (Paris, 1745), chap. X, pp. 253–54; Maffei, *op. cit.*, pp. 19–20.

[2] Maffei, *op. cit.*, p. 20. [3] *Ibid.*

[4] *Processionale . . . Sarum*, edit. W. G. Henderson (Leeds, 1882), pp. 72, 91–92; Rock, *op. cit.*, vol. IV, p. 277.

position in the church. This, however, had not been the case in the cathedral church of Verona. In 966, its bishop Ratherius, a native of Liège, had accepted the *Admonitio Synodalis*, in which reservation on the altar was sanctioned,[1] and yet in 1524, when Matthew Giberti (1524–43) was appointed to the see, the Eucharist was still reserved in 'some odd corner' (*in quodam angulo*).[2]

On the Altar

The directions of the *Admonitio Synodalis* were followed by a number of synods and episcopal regulations, but, as we have seen, the use of the word '*super*' makes it uncertain whether 'on' or 'over' the altar was intended. Honorius, one time praelector of Christ Church, Canterbury, and later living the life of a hermit at Ratisbon (twelfth century), referred, as of current usage, to the *propitiatorium* or 'mercy seat,' which is on (*super*) the altar: '*Propitiatorium*, which is located on the altar, is the divinity of Christ, who is the mediator for the human race.'[3] Durandus of Mende[4] (d. 1296) said that the '*propitiatorium*,' which is found in some churches (*in quibusdam ecclesiis*), recalled the temple of Solomon.[5] The thirteenth-century wooden tabernacle, with its roof in the form of a pyramid, now in the Bargello at Florence, is an example of this kind of eucharistic vessel.

A synodal constitution of Odo, bishop of Paris (1198), to which reference has already been made, clearly envisages the Eucharist to be reserved on the altar.[6] The term

[1] Syn. Verona, 966, 6; *Pat. Lat.*, t. CXXXVI, col. 559.
[2] Bishop, *op. cit.*, p. 34.
[3] Honor., *Gemma animae*, lib. i, cap. CXXXVI; *Pat. Lat.*, t. CLXXII, col. 587.
[4] Durand, *Rat. div. offic.*, lib. 4, cap. I, no. 15.
[5] *Ibid.*, lib. i, cap. II, no. 16.
[6] 'The most holy body of the Lord should be reserved in a locked vessel on the fairest (*pulchriore*) part of the altar.' *Odo. Episc. Paris.*, *Synod Constit.*, cap. V, n. 7; Mansi, *op. cit.*, t. XXII, col. 678.

'*tabernaculum*' is used here, possibly for the first time, and, although it would not suggest the ornament which we know by that name today, anticipated the general ruling of the Church in the second half of the sixteenth century.

Medieval inventories of cathedral and monastic churches often list small boxes or caskets of some precious material, and although there is no evidence as to their use, it may well be that they were sometimes used to contain the Eucharist, and were placed on the altar. The inventory of Clairvaux, for example, included: 'Une petite boete ronde avec son couvercle d'yvoire, en façon de cassolette, haulte de plus de deux poulces.'[1]

The use of a burse for the reserved Sacrament may have implied that it was on the altar. The visitation of the church of Hill Deverel in the diocese of Salisbury in 1220 revealed that there was no pyx, and that the Eucharist was kept in a silk burse: *Non est ibi pixis continens Eucharistiam, sed deponitur in quadam bursa serica.*[2] So late as the beginning of the fifteenth century, a visitation report from the diocese of Grenoble said that the Sacrament was reserved *in quadam modica bursa in panno piloso.*[3] If these 'burses' were indeed left lying on the altar there would have been a great danger of profanation. Whether burse, covered chalice, or veiled pyx, it was an easy prey to the sacrilegious.

The thirteenth-century wooden tabernacle from the Cistercian abbey of Senanque would almost certainly have stood on the altar. It is octagonal in shape, painted within and without, in two storeys with twin lights (thirty-two in all), furnished with greenish glass, mounted on a base, and crowned with an octagonal spire. The inscription has

[1] Lalore, *Le Trésor de Clairvaux du XIIe au XVIIIe siècle.* Troyes, 1875; Rohault de Fleury, *La Messe: Etudes archéologiques sur ses Monuments*, vol. V (Paris, 1887), p. 70.

[2] *Regist. S. Osmundi Epi.*, *Rolls series*, vol. I (1883), p. 312.

[3] Chevalier, *Visites Pastorales des évêques de Grenoble*, p. 195.

been repianted, but it is considered by Viollet de Duc to be the original text: *Qui*: *Manducat*: *Hunc*: *Panem*: *Vivet*: *In*: *Aeternum*.[1] It is possible that one of the storeys was used for the holy oil.

Reservation on the altar was enjoined by a number of decrees and instructions in the thirteenth century. St. Francis had legislated in his Rule (1223) that the Order should follow the liturgy of the papal court in the Lateran, which seemingly reserved the Eucharist on or above the altar. St. Francis himself said that he had on a number of occasions seen the body of the Lord reserved unworthily, but without specifying in what manner. He wished to send his brethren 'comely and spotless chalices' (*cum pulchris et puris calicibus*), in order that they might rectify the dishonour shown to the Eucharist, by substituting more fitting vessels.[2]

The Augustinian friars had also taken the papal liturgy as their model, and the *Ordinationes* of the two Orders in describing the censing of the altar during vespers and lauds on solemn days stated clearly that '. . . the priest should kneel upon the highest step before the altar. Then, going up to the altar, he begins (to cense) . . . towards the body of Christ or the crucifix.'[3] The Augustinian ceremonial gave full directions for the reserved Sacrament: 'We wish that in all our houses the body of Christ be reserved upon the high altar in *ciboria* with pyxes of ivory or other precious material, both secured with locks, in small or moderate quantity, and wrapped in a clean cloth.'[4] The church of the Austin Friars at Southampton, at the time of the dissolution

[1] Viollet le Duc, *Dictionnaire raisonné du mobilier français*, t. I, p. 246; Corblet, *Essai historique et liturgique sur lés Ciboires et la Réserve de l'Eucharistie* (Paris, 1858), p. 52.

[2] Thomas of Celano, *Vita secunda S. Francisci Assisiensis*, cap. CCI, edit. *Collegii S. Bonaventurae* (Ad Claras Aquas, 1927), pp. 196–97; Köster, *op. cit.*, p. 82.

[3] Van Dijk, *op. cit.*, p. 50.

[4] Van Dijk, *op. cit.*, pp. 50–51.

of the monasteries by Henry VIII, would have retained this method: 'in the myddes of the auter a proper frame gylt for the sacrament.'[1]

A synod of the diocese of Valence (1255) seemed to prefer reservation on the altar, while admitting the possibility of other methods.[2] The altar was prescribed as the correct place for the reserved Sacrament in the council of Münster (1279), and also in the diocesan synod of Cologne (1281), which was in the same ecclesiastical province.[3] It is in Cologne that the oldest 'tabernacle' in Germany is found, dating from the first half of the fourteenth century. Formerly in the church of St. Clara, it is now in the cathedral. The synods of Liège (1287) and Cambrai (1300) have very similar directions respecting the reserved Sacrament, except that Liège enjoined *sub altare* (or in an *armarium*[4]) and Cambrai *super altare*.[5] The prescription *sub altare* was certainly very unusual, although it may have been no more than a scribal error: *sub* instead of *super*. Errors of the kind were not infrequent, and a statute of the synod of Exeter (1287) may possibly be a further example of the kind. The bishop, Peter de Quivil, ordered every parish to be provided with a *sacramentarium lapideum et immobile*.[6] This may well be, as Fr. van Dijk suggests, a faulty transcription for *baptizarium* or font. It is the more probable, says the Franciscan scholar, in view of the ordinance of David, bishop of St. Andrews, some twenty years earlier.[7] The synod of Exeter also prescribed a *celatura super majus altare*:[8]

[1] Micklethwaite, *Ornaments of the Rubric*, *Alcuin Club* (London, 1897), p. 29.

[2] '. . . and in the centre of the altar with the greatest care, and locked, if it can be conveniently done.' Syn. Valence, 1255; Mansi, *op. cit.*, t. XXIII, col. 890.

[3] 'We direct that the Eucharist reserved for the sick . . . be kept on the altar in a suitable place.' Harzheim, *op. cit.*, t. III, pp. 648, 663.

[4] *Ibid.*, t. III, p. 692; Moreau, *Hist. de l'Eglise en Belgique*, t. IV, liv. 6, chap. II, p. 372.

[5] *Ibid.*, t. IV, p. 72.

[6] Wilkins, *op. cit.*, vol. II, p. 139.

[7] Van Dijk and Walker, *op. cit.*, p. 45.

[8] Syn. Exon., 1287, can. 12; Mansi, *op. cit.*, t. XXIV, col. 801.

'a carved canopy' of which Du Cange says: *Forte id, quod tabernaculum vulgo dicunt: incertum tamen.*[1] A confirmation of the accuracy of *sub altare* is thought by Fr. Maffei to be forthcoming from the discovery in 1860 of a thirteenth-century pyx under the *tombe* of the high altar in the church of St. Leonard at Léau.[2]

In this last connection, there is also the evidence of Notre Dame in Paris, where, at the extremity of the choir on the site of the new altar of Louis XIV and behind the old one, was the altar of the Trinity, commonly called also '*des Ardens*,' raised up so that it could be seen over the high altar from the stalls of the choir. Underneath it was a place called the '*conditoire*,' kept locked, in the cupboard of which all the vestments, etc., for high Mass were kept; in former times the Blessed Sacrament had also been reserved there. It would seem from a paper sent to Lebrun that a somewhat similar arrangement existed in Troyes cathedral. His informant was writing about 1714–16.[3]

The council of Oxford (1222), which had enjoined compliance with the decree *Sane* (1215), directed that the greatest reverence and honour should be shown to the sacred altars, and especially to the one on which the most holy body of the Lord was reserved and Mass was celebrated.[4] The statutes of the council were confirmed in the provincial constitutions of Walter Raynald, archbishop of Canterbury.[5]

A tabernacle (*tavernielken*) *on* the high altar of the collegiate church of Anderlecht (Belgium), which was in a bad state of repair and had served for a number of years, was renovated in 1495.[6]

[1] Du Cange, *op. cit.*, t. II (Halle, 1773), col. 20.
[2] Maffei, *op. cit.*, p. 44.
[3] Bishop, *op. cit.*, p. 33.
[4] Wilkins, *op. cit.*, vol. I, p. 594.
[5] *Ibid.*, vol. II, pp. 512–13.
[6] *Betaelt Janne Cloot op de Coelmert* (*coal market*) *van den tavernielken te repareren dat staet opten autaer op den hoogen choer autaer, dwelc zere erstucken was, 18 st.* Lavalleye, *Archives des Arts*; *Bulletin Soc. Roy. Arch. Brux.* (1932), p. 107, Maffei, *op. cit.*, p. 70, n. i.

Scotland, shortly before the Reformation, provides examples of a fixed tabernacle on the altar or in immediate connection with it. The inventory of King's College Chapel, Aberdeen, drawn up by the rector at the visitation in 1542 says: 'the altar of the venerable Sacrament built by the rector of Kinkell. On this altar is a place (*locus*) for the Sacrament of pyramidal form, given by the same rector.'[1] Yet in the church at Kinkell the Eucharist was reserved in an aumbry.[2] About the same time, an arrangement of altar and tabernacle, similar to modern usage, appears to have existed at Holyrood (Edinburgh).[3]

In altari was one of the modes of reservation permitted by the synod of Pavia (1297), which was endorsed in 1303 by the synod of Gubbio: 'in some place within the church, either behind the altar or upon it, or in some other seemly place especially made or intended for the purpose.'[4]

A thirteenth-century Dominican missal under the rubric *De sacra communione* enjoined that the Eucharist should be reserved *in altari*,[5] and this is made clear in the ordinal of Humbert de Romans, when describing the censing of the high altar: ' . . . (the priest) having taken the thurible from the thurifer, first genuflects on the altar step and then goes up to the altar, censing first the body of Christ; then he censes to the right, afterwards to the left and (again) the body of Christ a second time.'[6] The statute of Odo of Paris regarding reservation was repeated in the synod of Soissons (1403), but with the proviso: *si fieri potest*.[7] *Ordo Romanus XV*, a work of the fourteenth century,

[1] Kennedy, *Annals of Aberdeen*, vol. 2, p. 444, Bridgett, *op. cit.*, vol. II, p. 90.
[2] *Collections for a History of Aberdeen and Banff*, *Spalding Club*, p. 571; *ibid.*, p. 90.
[3] Eeles, *King's College Chapel*, *Aberdeen* (Edinburgh, 1956), p. 59.
[4] Hardouin, *Concil.*, t. VII (Paris, 1715), p. 861.
[5] Wickham Legg, *Tracts on the Mass* (*Henry Bradshaw Society*, 1904), p. 85.
[6] Guerrini, *Ordinarium . . . Ordinis Fratrum Praedicatorum* (Rome, 1921), 12 f., no. 290; Van Dijk, *op. cit.*, p. 54.
[7] Köster, *op. cit.*, p. 68.

speaks of the officiant as censing not only the altar, but also the *cophinus*, 'in which the body of Christ is reserved,'[1] making it evident that the eucharistic vessel was on or near the altar.

In this same century, we find an attempt to associate the 'tabernacle' with the altar, by inserting it at the centre of the gradine, which stood at the base of the reredos (*dossale*). A fourteenth-century example is found at Venice, in the reredos of S. Tarasio in the church of S. Zaccaria.[2] Something of the kind existed in Belgium from the first half of the sixteenth century. The church of St. Martin at Hal has a masterpiece of the Renaissance in a three-storeyed alabaster retable, surmounted by a perforated tabernacle with a pelican at the top (1533). Formerly in the sanctuary, it has now been relegated to a side chapel.[3] Spain, in the fifteenth century, reserved the Sacrament for the sick 'in a kind of room behind the *retablo* of the high altar.'[4] The hanging pyx was well-nigh universal in medieval England, but there were exceptions, at least in London. An inventory taken at the church of St. Stephen, Coleman Street, in 1466 recorded under the heading 'cheste and Almoryes': 'One coffyn for to kepe the Sacrament on the by auter.'[5] In the following century, the churchwarden's accounts for 1531 showed the theft of a pyx from the church of St. Margaret's, Westminster: 'for mette for the theff that stalle the pyx, 4d.'[6] The same accounts for 1547, possibly making

[1] O.R. XV, LI, *De Collectis Rubrica*; *Pat. Lat.*, t. LXXVIII, col. 1298–99. A similar prescription is found in the *Constitutiones Lateranenses*.
[2] Righetti, *op. cit.*, vol. I, p. 439; *Enciclopedia Cattolica* (1950), t. V, col. 777.
[3] Maffei, *op. cit.*, pp. 124–25.
[4] Braun, *Altar*, vol. II, pp. 590, 635.
[5] Micklethwaite, *Ornaments Rubric*, *Archaeologia*, vol. L, p. 44; Comper, *The Reasonableness of the Ornaments Rubric . . .*, *St. Paul's Ecclesiological Society*, vol. IV, (1900), p. 80, n. i.
[6] Comper, *Practical Considerations on the Gothic or English Altar . . .*; *St. Paul's Eccles. Society*, vol. III (1895), p. 202.

good the loss, gave the entry: 'Also paid for making of a little pyx upon the hie altar, for to set in the Sacrament, with other necessaries, 1s. 4d.'[1]

Over the Altar

The hooks which are still visible in the interior of the altar canopy or ciborium in some of the Roman basilicas may point to a suspension of the Eucharist,[2] but there is no evidence to confirm this, and they may well have served for a corona of lights.[3] Mabillon stated categorically that the reserved Sacrament was never suspended at Rome, nor even in all Italy, and such eucharistic doves as there might be, he dismissed, as 'French importations'.[4] The copper or brass dove[5] at Bobbio, for example, the Maurist thinks that it might have been introduced by the founder of the monastery, St. Colomban. Lebrun and other writers have said much the same.[6] French influence at Bobbio is certainly possible, but the donor of the dove could not have been St. Colomban, who died in 615. It may, however, well have been the emperor Henry II who, on the occasion of his coronation in 1014, obtained from the pope the elevation of Bobbio as an episcopal see. He had already, as we have seen, given an onyx pyx for suspension over the altar to St. Vanne in Lorraine.

There is no doubt that a hanging pyx was a rarity in Italy, but it may be noted that the Congregation of Rites,

[1] *Ibid.*; Cox and Harvey, *op. cit.*, pp. 42–43.
[2] Martigny, *Dictionnaire des antiquités chrétiennes* (Paris, 1865), p. 164.
[3] Hooks of the kind are found at S. Clemente, S. Agnese fuori le Mure, S. Lorenzo fuori le Mure, S. Cecilia and S. Maria in Trastavere, and also in S. Elias at Nepi.
[4] Mabillon, *Museum Italicum*, t. II (Paris, 1687), col. 140; *Pat. Lat.*, t. LXXVIII, col. 932. [5] *Aurichalcum*.
[6] Lebrun, *Explication de la Messe*, t. III (Liège, 1777), p. 270; Chardon, *Histoire des Sacrements*, t. II (Paris, 1745), pp. 242, 245, 246; Martène, *De Antiq. Eccles. Rit.*, lib. i, cap. V, art. 3, no. 4.

PLATE 3

STANDING PYX

Silver-gilt with medallions champlevé enamel and niello.
Italian, Fourteenth century

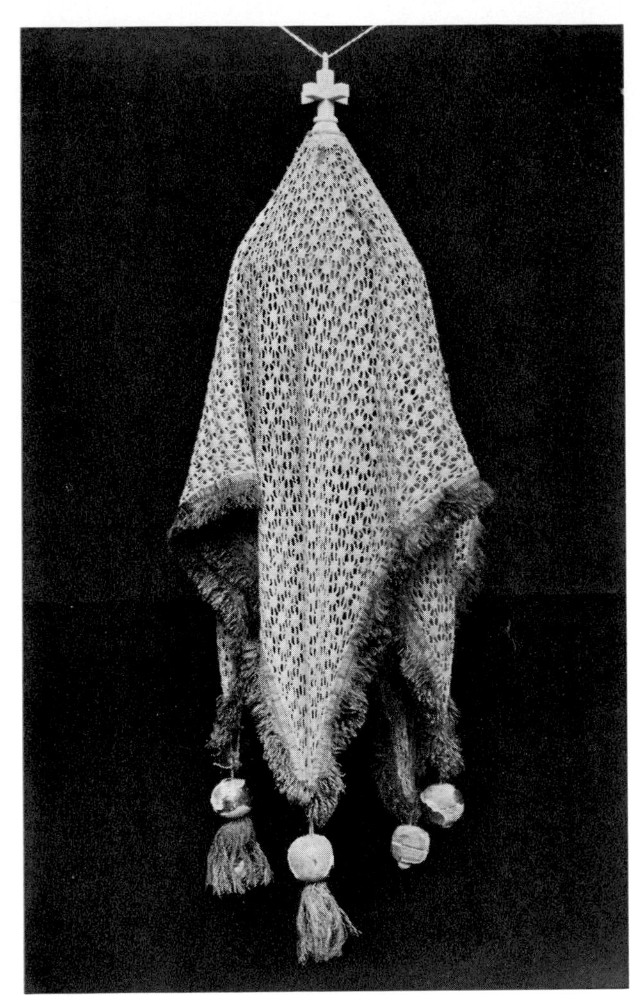

British Museum

PLATE 4

MEDIEVAL PYX-CLOTH

The only extant example of the pre-Reformation cloth or canopy in England, belonging to Hessett Church, Suffolk. It is square in form, measuring on each side two feet five and a half inches

on November 22nd, 1659, in a decree to the chapter of the Church of Bologna, said expressly that it admitted the legitimacy of reserving the Eucharist in a vessel suspended over the altar.[1]

Somewhat fancifully, this method of reservation is said to have been suggested by St. John's vision of the holy city let down from heaven: *ecce tabernaculum Dei cum hominibus*.[2]

The hanging pyx was very general throughout England and France in the middle ages, and also in Scotland before the introduction of the aumbry in the fifteenth century. The usual method of fixing the pyx was for a crane or pulley to be so arranged over the altar as to permit of the ready raising or lowering of the pyx, which was suspended by a cord or chain attached to a ring on its top. Above the pyx was hung the canopy, a circular tent-like construction, formed of some costly fabric, which was generally attached to a ring and ornamental crown of metal.[3] The pyx itself was veiled in a pyx cloth, which often had the form of a square napkin, with a hole in the middle, through which the suspending cord passed, and weighted tassels at the four corners which kept it down close by the pyx.[4] A drawing in the Islip Roll of Westminster Abbey (1532) shows a flat tester projecting over the high altar with the pyx hanging from the front, surmounted with a triple crown.[5] At Wells cathedral there is an oak, lantern-like canopy of the thirteenth century, which is believed to have been a pyx container. Cylindrical in form, it is divided into three stages of pierced tracery surmounted by trefoiled cresting, and was originally coloured and gilded. The

[1] Köster, *op. cit.*, p. 126, n. 41. [2] *Apoc.*, XXI, 2, 3.
[3] Cox and Harvey, *op. cit.*, p. 40.
[4] Micklethwaite, *Ornaments of the Rubric*, p. 28.
[5] Cook, *English Cathedrals through the Centuries*, p. 121.

container was suspended from the high vault or from a tester by iron rods.[1] Its purpose, however, has been contested, and Micklethwaite considers that it was a lantern for a light rather than a container for a pyx.[2] In the chancel roof above the altar at West Grinstead in Sussex there is still to be seen a wooden lever hung on its middle, but thicker and therefore heavier at one end than the other. The pyx was suspended by a cord from the lighter end and lifted by the weight of the other.[3] A fifteenth-century hanging 'tabernacle' or pyx container is found at Milton Abbas in Dorset, attached to the west wall of the south transept. It is made of wood in the form of a steeple: richly carved and painted on three of its sides.[4] A tall, slender canopy, made of one piece of wood and dating from about the year 1500, is suspended above the altar at Dennington in Suffolk,[5] and at Tewkesbury, on the north wall of the chancel, a further example of a pyx canopy has been preserved. Durham at the time of the Reformation must have had something of the kind: 'over the high altar did hang a rich and most sumptuous canapie for the blessed Sacrament to hang within it, which had two irons fastened in the French Peere (altar screen of French stone), very finely gilt, which held the canapie over the midst of the high altar that the pyx did hang in it that it could not move nor stir,' when, as is mentioned further on, the pyx was drawn 'upp and downw.' The description was written down from memory in 1593.[6] There are traces of the irons at Milton Abbas, and they may have been for the same

[1] *Ibid.*

[2] Comper, *The Reasonableness of the Ornaments Rubric illustrated by a comparison of the German and English altars. Transactions of the St. Paul's Ecclesiological Society*, vol. 4 (1900), p. 85.

[3] Micklethwaite, *op. cit.*, p. 28, n.i.

[4] Comper, *op. cit.*, pp. 80–82.

[5] Pevsner, *Buildings of England: Suffolk*, p. 170.

[6] *Rites of Durham, Surtees Society*, vol. XV (1842), pp. 6–7.

purpose as at Durham.[1] By their aid the 'tabernacle' would hang square and not swing round, so as to show its plain side, but the opening would always face the east, and the priest, turning from the altar, could without difficulty remove the pyx, when the tabernacle was lowered. In this way also the tabernacle would be sufficiently in advance of the altar screen, so as not to black out its imagery, and the steadying irons would be concealed by the canopy above.[2] The great stone crown projecting from the top of the reredos of the high altar of Winchester cathedral was to canopy the pyx, and bears the marks of the cords by which it was raised and lowered. A like arrangement existed at Christchurch in Hampshire and St. Alban's Abbey, but it has been mutilated in each.[3]

The earliest evidence for a eucharistic suspension in England is found in the chroniclers, Matthew Paris[4] and Roger de Hoveden,[5] who both record an accident that befel the hanging pyx in the cathedral church of Lincoln. The date is given in Matthew Paris as 1140 and in Roger de Hoveden as 1141. It was the feast of the Purification (February 2nd) and, in the presence of King Stephen (1135–54) and the bishop of Lincoln, the chain broke and the pyx containing the body of the Lord fell on the altar. The mishap, together with the breaking of the king's candle, was interpreted by the bystanders as foretelling disaster to the royal cause.

Lightning caused a similar accident in the church of St. Laurence at Liège in 1182: 'The lightning entered by the door and leaping over the Lenten curtain which hung

[1] Comper, *op. cit.*, p. 84. [2] *Ibid.*, pp. 84–85.
[3] Micklethwaite, *op. cit.*, p. 28, n.i.
[4] Matt. Paris, *Chronica Major*, edit. Rolls Series (1874), vol. II, p. 172.
[5] *Chronica Magistri Rogeri de Houedene*, edit. Rolls Series (1868), vol. I, p. 201.

over the great crucifix and before the chancel, it darted to and fro about the high altar, dividing without burning the altar cloth, and so out of the door again.' One of the monks (Raineri) ran to the altar: 'I found the silver pyx, in which the Lord's body was kept, fallen on the altar, for the great heat had consumed the iron chains by which it used to hang, as if it were straw, so that we could scarcely find a few links. Full of fear I took it in my hand, and I found it firmly locked (*serratam*), though blackened like ink, and having only a little opening made by I know not what workman. I rubbed off the black smoke with my hands and opened it, and found three particles within perfectly entire, though a little discoloured, and I showed them to those that stood near me.'[1]

The eighteenth abbot of St. Albans, Robert (d. 1166), had the Eucharist placed in a precious vessel under a silver crown;[2] while his successor, Simon (1166–83), had made by Brother Baldwin the goldsmith a most magnificent vessel of pure red gold (*ex auro obryzo et fulvo*) with gems of inestimable value set about it, which was to be hung over the high altar. When King Henry II heard of this, he sent a most noble and precious cup to the abbey, in which the shrine (*theca*) immediately containing the body of Christ should be placed.[3] The abbot, in addition to the hanging pyx, gave also a costly vessel, made after the manner of a shrine (*per modum scrinii*), in which the Blessed Sacrament was to be carried on Palm Sunday.[4] The gift to St. Albans was not the only eucharistic vessel to be presented to a church by Henry II, and we read that his eldest son, when warring against his father, broke into a monastery in France, and

[1] *Pat. Lat.*, t. CCIV, col. 141; Bridgett, *op. cit.*, vol. II, p. 89.
[2] *Gesta Abbatum Monasterii Sancti Albani, Rolls Series*, vol. I (1867), p. 179.
[3] *Ibid.*, p. 190. [4] *Ibid.*, pp. 191–92.

stole the very golden dove that the king had given to the church.[1]

The second of the regulations of King Henry V to his soldiers before their embarkation to France in 1419, entitled 'For Holy Church,' warned them against profaning the Eucharist: 'That no man may be so hardy, of less than he be priest to touch the Sacrament of God's body, upon pain to be drawn and hanged therefor; nor that no manner man be so hardy to touch the box or vessel, in which the precious Sacrament is in, upon the pain aforesaid.'[2] Shakespeare would have been alluding to this decree in his *Henry V*, act III, scene vi:

> Fortune is Bardolph's foe, and frowns on him;
> For he hath stol'n a pyx, and hanged must a'be.

Gervase, a monk of Canterbury, in describing the fire and subsequent restoration of the cathedral church (1180) said that he 'received from a certain monk the pyx with the Eucharist, which was accustomed to hang over the high altar.'[3]

An elaborate eucharistic vessel for suspension, reminiscent of those found in the French Cistercian churches of the baroque centuries, was provided for Canterbury by Prior Chillendon in the fourteenth century: 'An image of the blessed Virgin with four angels of silver-gilt, and in the hand of the Virgin a cup of pure gold with gems, for placing the Corpus Christi in, able to be pulled up or let down at will.'[4] Something similar existed at Ludlow, where the

[1] 'In the meanwhile the boy king violently snatched the treasure of the monastery of Grandmont, and, horror to relate, he did not spare the golden dove in which the Lord's body was enclosed, which his father had previously given.' *AA.SS.* June, t. V, p. 571; Rock, *Church of our Fathers*, vol. IV, p. 235.

[2] Bentley, *Excerpta Historica* (London, 1831), p. 30.

[3] Gervase, *Chronicle of the Reigns of Stephen, Henry II and Richard I*, Rolls Series (1879), vol. I, part 1, p. 23.

[4] Oman, *English Church Plate*, p. 81.

hanging pyx was described as an 'Image of our Lady of Pity, for the Sacrament.'[1] And, again, in St. Stephen's chapel, Westminster, with the inclusion of a representation of the Trinity: 'A Trinity of silver and gilt, four angels of silver and gilt, and an image of our Lady and the Holy Ghost bearing the Sacrament of silver and gilt, hanging over the high altar, weighing 316 oz.'[2] Gifts of costly eucharistic vessels were frequent throughout the middle ages, as, for example, Godfrey of Croyland, abbot of Peterborough (1299–1321), who presented his church with 'a silver-gilt cup with three chains and a silver circlet and within it a silver-gilt case (*capsula*) for the Corpus Christi.'[3]

At the cathedral church of St. Paul in London, the Eucharist was reserved in three places, though in distinct buildings. The inventory taken at the visitation in 1295 says that for the high altar there was a cup of silver all gilt with engraved work of lions and other beasts, hung by a silver chain to contain the Eucharist, to be hung before the altar on feasts, the gift of King Henry (probably Henry III). Also another gilt silver pyx, 'with scalloped work' and silver chain. In the church of St. Faith in the crypt there was a gilt cup of copper, with an ivory pyx, without lock, closed within (*sine serura*, *interius clausa*), in which the Eucharist is placed. Lastly, the charnel house in the cemetery had 'a ciborium of crystal above the altar, to hold the Eucharist.'[4] It may be noted that the first of these eucharistic vessels was used only *in festis*, following the practice described by Durandus, that 'on great feasts the treasures

[1] *Transactions of the London and Middlesex Archaeological Institute*, vol. 4, p. 373.

[2] Waterton, *Pietas Mariana Britannica*, part 2, pp. 99, 229; *London and Middlesex Archaeological Society Transactions*, vol. 4 (1873), p. 373; Oman, *op. cit.*, p. 81.

[3] Rock, *Church of our Fathers*, vol. 4, p. 236, n. 6.

[4] Dugdale, *Monast. Ang.*, t. 3, i, p. 310.

of the church are exposed for the people to view.'[1] Something similar is found in the fourteenth-century inventory of Amiens cathedral (1347) in which the silver-gilt 'tabernacle' was said to have been hung over the high altar *in magnis sollempnitatibus*.[2]

Country churches, no less than cathedral and collegiate churches, were accustomed to reserve the Eucharist in a hanging pyx. Canonical visitations refer to the practice as one which ought to be followed everywhere. Thus in 1220 at St. Nicholas chapel, Hurst: 'Item, a pyx hanging over the altar with the Eucharist of Limoges work' (*de opere Lemovicense*),[3] and again four years later at Horningham in the same diocese: 'a wooden pyx in a silk "tabernacle," hanging over the altar, containing the Eucharist.'[4]

A eucharistic dove, frequently met with in France, was seldom used in this country, and no more than two examples are known: Battle Abbey[5] and Salisbury cathedral.[6] The inventory, taken at Salisbury in 1222, had the following entry: Item, a silver *corona* with three silver chains, with a silver dove for the Eucharist.[7] The canonist William Lyndwood (d. 1446) testified to the universality of the hanging pyx in England, although he was severely critical of its use, because, as he said, it was against the intention of the aforesaid cap. *Sane*, which prescribed that the Eucharist should be reserved, not in an open place, but in one set apart (*non in loco patenti sed singulari*). 'For although the

[1] Durandus, *Ration. divin. offic.*, lib. i, cap. III, no. 42.
[2] Garnier, *Inventaires du trésor de la cathédrale d'Amiens*; *Mémoires de la Société des Antiquaires de Picardie*, vol. X (1850), p. 259.
[3] *Vetus Registrum Sarisberiense alias dictum Registrum S. Osmundi Episcopi* Rolls Series, vol. I (1883), p. 281.
[4] *Ibid.*, p. 313.
[5] *Chronicon Monasterii de Bello* (1846), p. 138.
[6] *Vetus Registrum*, *op. cit.*, vol. II, p. 129; Wordsworth, *Salisbury Ceremonial*, p. 171.
[7] *Ibid.*

English custom was praiseworthy in this, that the Sacrament was more readily brought before our eyes that we might worship it, still it was not praiseworthy in this, that it was kept in a public place where presumptuous hands might easily be put forth to seize it. . . . Therefore in my opinion the custom of other places, which I have seen, was more to be commended, e.g. in Holland or Portugal, where a separate and becoming place was appointed close to the altar, where the blessed Eucharist was placed to be kept under lock and key, either in the wall itself (aumbry) or in some secure receptacle (sacrament house), so that no one could reach the sacred species but the priest of the parish, who kept the key.'[1]

In 1549, one of the demands of the Devonshire rebels, as they were called, was that the hanging pyx should be restored to their churches: 'We will have the Sacrament hung over the high altar, and there to be worshipped, as it was wont to be; and they will not thereto consent, we will have them die like heretics against the holy Catholic faith.'[2] Thomas Becon, the author of *The Displaying of the Popishe Mass*, written abroad in the time of Queen Mary, gave no less than twelve references to the reserved Sacrament, all of which spoke of the hanging pyx. No other method of reservation would seem to have been contemplated in pre-Reformation England, as Thomas Harding (d. 1572) showed in his controversy with Jewel: though divers customs in divers countries, yet 'the hanging up of it on high hath been the manner in England.'

Yet for all that, the hanging pyx entailed difficulties, and the apparatus for raising and lowering it could easily get

[1] Lyndwood, *Provinc.*, III, 25, p. 248, Oxford, 1679.
[2] Art. 4, Cranmer, *Miscellaneous Writings and Letters*, *Parker Society*, Vol. II, pp. 172–73.

out of order. The churchwardens' accounts for St. Mary at Hill, London, contain several references to the repairs of the pyx pulley, pyx rope and pyx plumb. The last of these was the plumb of lead which acted as a counterpoise to the weight of the suspended pyx.[1]

Scotland, as we have seen, very largely abandoned the hanging pyx in favour of the aumbry in the fifteenth century, but a visitation of his cathedral church by the bishop of Aberdeen (Elphinstone) in 1496 revealed a 'silver-gilt cup (*cowp*) hanging before the great altar.'[2] This was seemingly not suffered to remain, as a description of the ornaments of the high altar in the time of his successor, Gavin Dunbar (*c.* 1530), speaks of a *domus sacramenti*.[3] The pyx was probably retained at St. Nicholas, Aberdeen, and Trinity College, Edinburgh. Melrose, also, is said to have had a hanging pyx at the time of its suppression, although the ruins show a large fifteenth-century aumbry by the side of the altar: set, high up into one of the pillars, so that it could be reached only from wooden steps.[4]

The eucharistic dove was very general in France, as may be gauged from the old popular saying: 'On voit bien qu'il n'a pas couché dans l'église, il n'a pas volé le Saint Esprit.'[5] Bossuet, the 'Eagle of Meaux' (d. 1704), in his treatise, *Défense de la tradition sur la communion sous une espèce*, remarks: 'L'Eucharistie, que le Saint Esprit, figuré par la colombe, consacre, d'où le Saint Esprit se répand pour vivifier les âmes et les corps.'[6]

There were, however, other forms of suspension in use, especially in the later middle ages. Sometimes the Eucharist

[1] Cox and Harvey, *op. cit.*, pp. 40–41.
[2] *Regist. Episc. Aberdon.*, vol. II, p. 167.
[3] Comper, *Practical Considerations on the Gothic or English Altar . . .*; *St. Paul's Eccles. Society*, vol. III (1895), p. 203.
[4] Van Dijk, *op. cit.*, p. 44. [5] Maffei, *op. cit.*, p. 30.
[6] Bossuet, *Défense de la tradition sur la communion sous une espèce*, part 2, chap. XIX.

was suspended from the beak of the bird, as at Saint-Thibaut in Burgundy, where it survived until 1846.[1]

Extant eucharistic doves are for the most part of the twelfth and thirteenth centuries: Saint Yrieux, Leguenne (Corrèze), Musée de Cluny (Paris) and Amiens (Museum). A modern example, used for the reserved Sacrament, is found in the Cistercian abbey of Hauterive in Switzerland.

A dove had been introduced in the eleventh century at Dijon[2] (St. Benignus) and Cluny,[3] from whence it was adopted at Hirsau, whose second abbot, William (1071–91), had initiated a number of Cluniac usages.[4] In the twelfth century, it was enjoined in the *Ordinarium* of Laon,[5] appearing also at Angers[6] (*c.* 1150) and, possibly, in the Ordinal of the Priory of Val des Choux (*c.* 1200).[7] The Cistercian church of Le Pin near Poitiers reserved the Eucharist in a dove in the first quarter of the twelfth century.[8] The mode of reservation in the Benedictine priory of Bohon (Manche) was criticized in a visitation report of the archbishop of Rouen, Odo Rigaud, in 1266. The prior was ordered to remove the Eucharist from the *fenestra*, as those who said office in choir turned their backs to it. A pyx was to be provided, and the Sacrament kept either 'over' (*supra*) the altar or close to it (*vel juxta*).[9]

Eucharistic vessels in the middle ages had a variety of names, as we see in an inventory of the Sainte Chapelle

[1] Maffei, p. 35.

[2] *Divionenses St. Benigni consuetudines*, cap. XXI.

[3] *Pat. Lat.*, t. CXLIX, col. 653, 722.

[4] *St. Wilhelmus, Constitutiones Hirsaugienses seu Gegenbacenses*, lib. 2, cap. LXII; *Pat. Lat.*, t. CL, col. 1133.

[5] Chevalier, *Ordinaire de l'Eglise cathédrale de Laon* (Paris, 1897), p. 44.

[6] Rohault de Fleury, *La Messe: Etudes archéologiques sur ses Monuments*, t. II (1883), chap. V, p. 72.

[7] 'After the *pax*, the body of the Lord is taken from the vessel over the altar, and is placed on the paten to be consumed at that time.' Köster, *op. cit.*, p. 69, n. 31.

[8] Lavialle, *Vie du bienheureux Giraud de Sales*, p. 81.

[9] Guitrancourt, *L'Archévêque Eudes Rigaud et la vie de l'Eglise au XIIIe siècle . . .* Paris, 1938), p. 332; Freestone, *op. cit.*, p. 65.

in Paris in 1376: 'Item, a certain receptacle (*repositorium*), known in French as "*cyboire*," which is hung over the high altar, in which there is a kind of golden cup, where the Sacrament is reserved.' Cups without lids were sometimes suspended over the altar, and Maffei thinks that it was a cup of this kind which was listed in an inventory of the collegiate church of Saint-Ame at Douai (1377): '*Une coupe d'argent pendant deseure l'autel pour le chiborre*.'[1]

In 1470, an inventory at the same church showed the pyx suspended by chains or cords from a crozier fixed above the altar: 'Item, le cibole d'argent doré pendant à la croche devant le grant autel ouquel repose le corps de N.S.'[2] This form of suspension, frequently to be found in Cistercian churches in the baroque centuries, existed in the Sainte Chapelle (Paris) in 1298,[3] and it is found again in the cathedral church of Cambrai in 1462: 'A maistre Jehan Lachet, fondeur de métail, pour avoir faict à la croche, dessus le grant autel, par lequel on monte et descent Corpus Domini, sur le led grant autel, 17 feuillez.'[4]

A hanging pyx in the form of a tower was not unknown in France, although no example has survived. Martène (d. 1739) witnessed to a silver tower suspended over the altar at Marmoutier, and said that something of the kind had been recently given up in the church of St. Laurent, Rouen.[5] In other countries, suspensions were the exception, and almost all those known in Germany and Italy show Limoges work.[6] Eucharistic doves of the twelfth century are to be found at Göttweig (Austria) and Florence (Bargello), with

[1] Maffei, *op. cit.*, p. 50. [2] *Ibid.*, p. 53. [3] *Liturgia* (Paris, 1930), p. 283.
[4] Maffei, *op. cit.*, p. 53. It has, however, been suggested that *à la croche* means no more than 'on a hook.'
[5] Martène, *De Antiq. Eccl. Rit.*, lib. i, cap. V, art. 3, no. 6.
[6] Köster, *op. cit.*, p. 70.

later examples at Bari (S. Sepolcro), Milan (S. Nazaro), Salzburg (cathedral) and Silos (Spain). The dove in the treasury of the Benedictine abbey of Silos has a moveable head, which was turned sideways when it was not in use. The cathedral church of Prague had a hanging pyx in the chapel of St. Wenceslas from 1354 to 1420, when, owing to the Hussite troubles, it was removed.[1] Reservation at a side altar was unusual, and the synod of Brixen in South Tyrol (1318) specifically enjoined that the Sacrament should hang over the high altar in a clean pyx, and be covered by some fitting ornament.[2]

In Italy, Bernard of Besse, secretary of St. Bonaventure (*c.* 1278), referred to the hanging pyx as an 'undesirable novelty': 'Now they suspend over the altar,' he says. 'Hence, in the presence of the people, they are, at times, unable to have it, because the cord on which it is hung either gets entangled or snaps and breaks; and thus, with much scandal and danger, it falls to the ground.'[3] It is possible, however, that the friar, who had been *custos* of the Franciscan house at Cahors, may have been condemning the very prevalent French practice, rather than alluding to its existence in Italy.[4] The Benedictine abbeys of Frassinoro, near Modena and Farfa certainly reserved the Eucharist in a dove, but the former had been under the jurisdiction of Chaise-Dieu (Haute-Loire) since 1107; while the latter had early adopted Cluniac customs, without, however, abandoning its independence.

A hanging pyx, while by no means general in Spain, is depicted in the miniature in the palace constitutions of James II, king of Majorca, and further examples are found

[1] Braun, *Altar*, vol. 2, pp. 603–04. [2] Van Dijk and Walker, *op. cit.*, p. 52.
[3] *Ibid.*, pp. 51–52; Braun, *op. cit.*, t. 2, p. 603. [4] Köster, *op. cit.*, p. 70.

in Braun.[1] French influence would certainly have accounted for the eucharistic dove at Silos.

The English canonist, William Lyndwood, had said that an aumbry was the customary mode of reservation in Portugal,[2] but a letter from the Benedictine abbot of Paço de Sousa to his community, dated December 24th, 1467, directed the Eucharist to be reserved on the 'Thursday of the Washing of the Feet' and the 'Friday of Suffering,' above the altar, covered by a veil, and that it was to be replaced there after it had been removed from the sepulchre on the morning of Easter.[3] There is, however, no indication as to whether such reservation was peculiar to the house.

The 'common practice' of reservation in Norway during the Romanesque period was to suspend a pyx from the middle of the roof of the ciborium over the altar, as we find at Kinservik.[4] An exceptionally fine and richly ornamented ciborium of the transitional period is found at Hopperstad, but the pyx has long since disappeared.[5] The sacrament house would seem to have become very general in the later middle ages, although it has been suggested that some of the small models of Gothic churches which have survived in Norway were in fact receptacles for the Eucharist. Bendixen, however, is of the opinion that they were reliquaries.[6]

Aumbry

Reservation in the sacristy would undoubtedly have entailed in many of the churches some recess or cupboard

[1] Braun, *op. cit.*, pp. 610, 612, 602. [2] Lyndwood, *Provinc.*, III, 25, p. 248.

[3] *Memorias do Mosteiro de Paço de Sousa e Index dos Documentos de Arquivo. Academia Portuguesa de História, Publicacoēs Comemerativas do Duplo Centenario da Fundacão e Restauracão de Portugal*, doc. 2, 9, pp. 126–27. Lisbon, 1942. The notes on the fifteenth century liturgical reform at Paço de Sousa were kindly supplied to the author by the master of ceremonies of the primatial church of Braga, Mgr. de Azevedo.

[4] Fett, Harry, *Norges Kirker i Middelalderen* (Kristiania, 1909), p. 42.

[5] *Ibid.*, pp. 42–43. [6] *Ibid.*, p. 101.

in the wall. The first known document attesting to the use of an aumbry (*armarium*) for the reserved Sacrament within the church itself is that of Rupert, abbot of Tuy (Deutz), in a description of the fire of 1128 in the parish church of St. Urban. The recess or cupboard in the wall near the altar (*in fenestra sive abside*), with its locked door, had been gutted by the fire, and the wooden pyx containing the Eucharist remained safe and intact, although the other vessels that were with it had been destroyed.[1] The occurrence was looked upon as a miracle, and the pyx placed on the altar, as was customary with relics. The first known decree authorizing an aumbry was issued by Giovanni Parente, the first Franciscan minister general after the death of St. Francis, in the general chapter of the Order in 1230.[2] Nothing in heaven or earth was more worthy of veneration than the body of the Lord, which was to be kept in a securely locked '*casella*.'[3] This *casella*, says Köster, must surely indicate a wall tabernacle or sacramental tower.[4]

An interesting point, which seems to have been very generally overlooked, has been made by van Dijk and Walker: the distinction between 'open aumbry reservation,' that is a locked casket or pyx, displayed openly in a recess of the altar or in the church wall, and 'closed aumbry reservation' in a cupboard set in a niche or recess closed by a locked door.[5] Evidence of the 'open aumbry' is found in the legend of St. Clare of Assisi, for, when the Saracen troops of Frederick II attacked the convent of S. Damiano, the saint took 'the silver casket (pyx) enclosed in ivory, in

[1] *Ruperti Abbatis Tuitiensis, De Incendio Oppidi Tuitii*, cap. V *Liber Aureus*; *Pat. Lat.*, t. CLXX, col. 337–38; Mabillon, *Annal. Bened.*, cap. XLIX.

[2] Braun, *op. cit.*, vol. II, p. 603; Köster, *op. cit.*, p. 72.

[3] *Ibid.*; *ibid.* [4] Köster, *op. cit.*, pp. 72–73. [5] Van Dijk, *op. cit.*, p. 41.

which the body of the Holy of Holies was most devoutly kept,' and, carrying it to the door, saved the house. The casket was kept in a small window at the left hand side near the altar.[1] 'Closed aumbry reservation' became increasingly customary after the decree *Sane* of Innocent III (1215), as it ensured safety under lock and key, although the council had said nothing as to the manner of reserving the Eucharist. The synod of Liège (1287) suggested a 'small locked cupboard' as one of the more seemly ways of reserving the Eucharist,[2] and much the same thing was approved by the synods of Pavia (1297), Cambrai (1300) and Gubbio (1303).

Aumbry reservation was by no means usual in medieval England, but it was found at Pattishall in Northamptonshire (*c.* 1317–39),[3] and the accounts of the church of Thame in Oxfordshire mentioned 'an aumbrye for the Lorde's Boddye.'[4] Despite the desire of Cardinal Pole to introduce a tabernacle, we find a definite statement in Waterman's translation of the 'Fardle of Facions' (1555) recommending wall aumbries for the reserved Sacrament: 'Upon the right hande (north side) of the highe aulter, there should be an almorie either cut in the wall or framed upon it, in the whiche thei would have the sacrament of the Lorde's Bodye; the Holy Oyle for the sicke, and chrismatories, alwai to be locked.'[5] Many of the aumbries to be met with in parish churches and cathedrals would have served as Easter sepulchres, reliquaries or receptacles for books and sacred vessels.

Is it possible that 'cista' was ever used to denote an aumbry? Some writers have suggested that two late

[1] *Ibid.*, pp. 52–53. [2] Mansi, *op. cit.*, t. XXIV, col. 899.
[3] Cox and Harvey, *op. cit.*, p. 316.
[4] Bond, *The Chancel of English Churches* (Oxford, 1916), p. 214.
[5] *Ibid.*

fourteenth-century references bear this connotation. The accounts of the keepers of the fabric of Ripon Minster (1399–1400) show the sum of 3d. that was given to the man who mended the lock of the *cista* 'in which the body of Christ is placed.'[1] Again, in the inventory of St. George's Chapel, Windsor, in the time of Richard II, we read of an 'iron cista,' with many keys, a pyx of beryl for enclosing the body of Christ, somewhat broken.[2]

Scotland, on the other hand, largely abandoned the hanging pyx in favour of the aumbry in the fifteenth and sixteenth centuries. The term 'sacrament house' was in general use, but it bore little or no resemblance to those in Germany and the Low Countries, and was in fact a recess in the wall, often enriched with sculpture. The earliest known example, probably not before 1460, is in the College of St. Salvator in St. Andrews. Twenty of these 'sacrament houses' or aumbries are to be found in Scotland today, not including those of a plain locker type.[3] The aumbry at Kintore, which is five feet high, has sculptures of a monstrance, crucifix and angels vested in albs and crossed stoles, with the legend: '*Jesu, Maria.*'[4] That of Kinkell in the diocese of Aberdeen is a recess in the north wall of the chancel, with an inscription over it in green stone: '*Hic est servatum corpus de Virgine natum*' and underneath: '*obiit M.A.G.* 1528.' The initials are those of Magister Alexander Galloway, a prebendary of Aberdeen, who probably erected the aumbry and a crucifix in the wall near

[1] *Memorials of Ripon*, edit. Fowler, *Surtees Society*, vol. III, p. 129; Micklethwaite, *Ornaments of the Rubric*, p. 29.

[2] Dugdale, *Monasticon Anglicanum* (1846), vol. VI, p. 1365.

[3] St. Salvator's College (St. Andrews), Fowlis, Easter, Aberdeen (cathedral), Kinkell, Dyce, Kintore, Auchindoir, Deskford, Cullen, Turiff, Fintray, Pluscarden, Airlie, Benholm, Cortachy, Tealing, Lundie, Kilmahew, Elgin (Franciscan church) and Kirkwall (St. Ola).

[4] Mackensie, E. C. Walcott, *Scoti-Monasticon*: *The Ancient Church of Scotland* (London, 1874), p. 34.

H. A. Wahltuch

PLATE 5

AUMBRY

Pluscarden Priory, Scotland, Fifteenth century.
Note carving of monstrance

Facing page 98

PLATE 6

Grille of Sacrament House
South Germany, Fifteenth century

it.[1] A number of references to the 'sacrament house' are found in the episcopal registers of Aberdeen at the time of the Reformation. We read that in 1559 the bishop, distributing the treasures of the cathedral for safety, gave 'the covering of the sacrament-house' to one of the canons. The inventory for 1562 had the entry: an 'antipend for the sacrament-house with a dornick towle to the same,'[2] and in the list of things stolen by robbers: 'Four knops of gold and silk with their great cords of green silk that hang at the sacrament-house, price 3s.'[3]

There is evidence of aumbry reservation in France during the middle ages, although the hanging pyx was the more general method. Dom Martène expressed astonishment at the aumbry in the Cistercian church at Auberive: '*une chose assez singulière*,' as he expressed it. In his description he said: 'Le Saint Sacrement n'y est point conservé au grand autel, mais dans un tabernacle ou armoire quï est dans le fond de l'église du côte de l'épître, et qui n'est fermé que d'une grille de fer; en sorte que tout le monde peut voir le S.ciboire.'[4] The literary journey was made at the beginning of the eighteenth century, but it is unlikely that this method of reservation was initiated in baroque times. It may be noted that the aumbry in question was on the epistle side of the church, and the visiblity of the eucharistic vessel through the grille was reminiscent of the sacrament houses in Germany and the Low Countries. The twelfth-century chevet is all that remains of the church today, but in it are two niches in exactly the same position as the aumbry described by

[1] *Collections for a History of Aberdeen and Banff*, *Spalding Club*, p. 571; Bridgett, *op. cit.*, vol. II, p. 90. Mackensie, *op. cit.*, p. 34.
[2] *Regist. Episc.* I, *Spalding Club*, p. lxxxvi; *ibid.*, p. 91.
[3] *Regist. Aberd.*, vol. II, p. 192; *ibid.*, p. 91.
[4] Martène, *Voy. Lit.* (Paris, 1717), part I, p. 113.

Martène. One of these had certainly been furnished with a grille or door, but it has a drain, as if for ablutions.

The narrow bay in the east wall of the south transept in the Cistercian church of La Bussière (Côte d'Or), one and a half metres above the ground and slightly splayed towards the exterior, is believed by Marcel Aubert to have been at one time a eucharistic aumbry sheltering a lamp.[1] A '*petite armoire grillée au fond du choeur*' would seem to have been the customary method of reservation in the district of Bresse, north of Lyons.[2] As we have seen, a hanging pyx was given to St. Benignus, Dijon, in the latter part of the eleventh century, but Martène says that the Sacrament was formerly reserved in '*un vase de pierre comme de l'albastre*,' which in his day served as a reliquary.[3] At the beginning of the eighteenth century, the Eucharist was reserved in the collegiate churches of Angers in two places simultaneously, and there is no reason to suppose that it had been otherwise in the middle ages. Thus in the church of St. Julien there was an aumbry, called the '*sacraire*' or '*sacrarium*' in the wall on the gospel side, which served for the administration of Viaticum in the parish; while there was also a suspension of the Eucharist over the high altar for the religious of the collegiate church: '*le saint ciboire est suspendu en haut au-dessus de l'autel sans pavillon : il y a une colombe au-dessus.*'[4] Something similar was reported from the church of St. Pierre: '*Il y a la suspension du saint ciboire au haut de l'autel, sans pavillon, mais il y a un dais au-dessus . . . Dans la muraille ex parte Evangelii on garde encore le St ciboire dans une armoire ou sacraire pour la paroisse.*'[5]

[1] Aubert, *Architecture Cistercienne en France*, vol. I, chap. IV, p. 323, n. 1.
[2] Bishop, *Liturgica Historica*, p. 36. [3] Martène, *Voy. Lit.*, part I, p. 22.
[4] De Moléon (Lebrun-Desmarettes), *Voyages liturgiques de France* (Paris, 1718), p. 103. [5] *Ibid.*, p. 105.

A sacrament house became very general in the Low Countries towards the end of the middle ages, although the 'wall tabernacle' was by no means abandoned, especially in the smaller churches. In the earlier centuries, the aumbry would probably have been the normal method of reservation. A thirteenth-century example was brought to light in the last restoration of the church of Lennick-Saint-Martin in the north wall of the choir: it had suffered from mutilation at the hands of the iconoclasts.[1] The gospel side of the sanctuary was the normal position for the 'wall tabernacle,' as in the church of St. Nicholas, Droogenbosch (fourteenth century), but at Duisbourg it is found in the wall of the chevet (*c.* 1400). Examples of the fifteenth century are met with at Hal, Buvrines and in the little church of the Augustinian canonesses at Ter Cluysen (L'Ermite). The finest specimen of an aumbry in the Low Countries is in the church of St. Martin at Hal, dating from 1409: in a buttress separating two of the chapels of the choir, and ornamented with magnificent bas-reliefs. A miraculous Host was at one time reserved in an aumbry at the end of the choir in St. Gudule, Brussels, but its further use was made impossible by the erection of a new high altar in 1560.[2]

Germany in the later middle ages favoured the sacrament house, but the Cistercian abbey church of Eberbach in the diocese of Mainz has an aumbry with fourteenth-century sculpture on the north side of the presbytery. The church of St. Nicholas at Enns in Austria provides an aumbry in the wall on the north side of the choir apse, dating from 1480, where the door is an iron open-work grille, permitting the Eucharist to be seen. The use of an aumbry as a method of reservation was advocated, probably as more conducive to safety than the hanging pyx, in the synods of Schwerin

[1] Maffei, *op. cit.*, pp. 75–76. [2] Maffei, *op. cit.*, pp. 77–81.

(1492), Warmia (1497), Basle (1503) and Cologne (1536), although the specification was sometimes no more detailed than 'in a fitting and securely locked place.'[1] Schwerin, while deploring reservation 'in little caskets (*capsulis*) or in public places where they could be opened at the will of the parishioners,' enjoined the use of *ciboria*.[2] Earlier in the century, the synod of Breslau (1416), as the Eucharist had been burnt in a fire shortly before, prescribed the construction of 'stone *sacraria*' (*sacraria ex lapide naturali*).[3] The former Franciscan church in Basle has retained the aumbry that may well have been introduced in obedience to the synod of 1503.

An aumbry was the traditional mode of reservation in pre-Reformation Sweden, either in the north wall of the sanctuary or in the east wall to the right of the altar (north). A thirteenth-century example is found at Gothard, and in the island of Gotland the majority of its ninety-two churches, all built before 1360, have preserved their aumbries. An exceptionally fine Gothic specimen is to be seen in one of the pillars of the sanctuary in the cathedral church of Linköping.[4] After 1152, there was a eucharistic aumbry in the wall of the choir of Hamar cathedral in Norway.[5]

Wall tabernacles were in very general use in Italy throughout the middle ages, which Gothic and Renaissance art enriched with sculpture, especially on the wall above and on either side. A number of these, conspicuous for their grace and beauty, are to be found in the country. The subjects of the sculptures are varied, but favourite themes

[1] Köster, *op. cit.*, p. 73. [2] Hartzheim, *op. cit.*, t. V, p. 646.
[3] *Ibid.*, t. V, p. 154.
[4] Letter from Dr. Eric Segelberg of Uppsala University to the author, May 2nd, 1963.
[5] Dietrichson, L., *Den Kirkelige Kunstarkaeologi med saerligt hensyn paa den norske kirke* (Kristiania, 1909), p. 112.

include adoring angels and Christ divested of His garments, from whose wounds flows the blood which is collected in the chalice.[1] Two fine examples may be seen in the churches of S. Lorenzo and SS. Apostoli in Florence. The former has an angel on either side holding a candlestick with a pricket for a candle (fifteenth century); while the latter, in the east wall of the north aisle, is an early work of Giovanni della Robbia (1469–*c.* 1529). The churches of Florence, Prato, Pistoia, Lucca and Pisa are for the most part furnished with wall tabernacles of the fifteenth and early sixteenth centuries, but many of them are little more than featureless cupboards. In accordance with post-Tridentine regulations, the purpose of these aumbries was changed, when reservation in a tabernacle on the altar became more or less obligatory, and they were made to serve for the holy oils. '*Oleum Infirmorum*' or '*Oleum Sanctum*' has been inscribed on a number of them, as, for example, at S. Egidio and S. Maria Novella in Florence, S. Domenico in Prato, S. Paolo, S. Francesco al Prato and S. Bartolomeo in Pantano, in Pistoia and S. Frediano in Lucca. At Rome, however, in the Sessorian basilica of S. Croce, the Sacrament was reserved in the wall behind the high altar until 1839. The aumbry, which had been given by Cardinal Quignonez, the titular of the church, was protected by a wooden door and iron grille, which were covered by a curtain of silk.[2] The sacred species was enclosed in a crystal vessel.[3] Several of these wall tabernacles have survived in Rome, although no longer used for the Eucharist: S. Clemente, S. Maria in Cosmedin, S. Maria in Trastevere. The tabernacle at S. Clemente dates from

[1] Righetti, *op. cit.*, vol. I, p. 438.
[2] *Bulletin de la Société des Antiquaires de l'Ouest* (1839), p. 30; Corblet, *op. cit.*, p. 35.
[3] Corblet, *op. cit.*, p. 49; Rohault de Fleury, *op. cit.*, t. V, p. 84.

1299, and at S. Maria in Cosmedin, the work of Deodato Cosmati, from about the same period; while the elegant aumbry in S. Maria in Trastevere was designed by Mino da Fiesole (d. 1484).

As we have seen, the Milanese Church very generally reserved in the sacristy until the second half of the sixteenth century, but the cathedral church of St. Thecla had erected an aumbry and altar of the Blessed Sacrament in the apse behind the high altar in the previous century. When the Winter church was demolished, the altar was transferred to the Summer church and placed in the chapel of S. Galdino, later known as St. Catherine, where a wall tabernacle is still to be seen. There is evidence that this aumbry was in use for the communion of the faithful until 1737, despite the very clear directions of St. Charles Borromeo.[1] Exceptions to sacristy reservation were found also in other churches of the province: behind the high altar at S. Eustorgio (Milan), and by the side of it at Castiglione Olona and Trezzo d'Adda. The former monastic churches of S. Paolo presso S. Eufemia and S. Maurizio (Monastero Maggiore) still retain their wall tabernacles.

A remarkable canopied altar, with a wall tabernacle, surmounted by a bas-relief of the Pietà by Bernardino da Bissone (1498), is found to the right of the apse in the patriarchal basilica of Aquileia.[2]

Sacrament House

The elaborate stone structure in which the Eucharist is reserved in many of the churches of Germany and the Low Countries, isolated from the altar and normally on the gospel side of the chancel or sanctuary, is known as a sacrament

[1] Ratti, *Acta Eccles. Mediol.* (Milan, 1890), vol. II, p. 1186.
[2] Brusin, *Aquileia e Grado*, pp. 36–37.

house. They were often sculptured in the form of a monumental tower, approached by several steps, and with a railing round, on which candles were placed. Sometimes, also, there were two or more storeys and a space above for a light.

These sacrament houses appeared first in Germany in the fourteenth century (*c.* 1380), and became increasingly popular both there and in the Low Countries in the two subsequent centuries. It is thought that they originated as a compromise, enabling the faithful to see the Blessed Sacrament or at least the eucharistic vessel without contravening the synodical decrees, which sought to discourage frequent expositions and processions, as they tended to superstition. The council of Cologne (1452), presided over by the papal legate, Cardinal Nicholas of Cusa, forbade either the one or the other, except in the octave of Corpus Christi and on one other day in the year, which must be for a serious reason and with the permission of the bishop: *nullatenus visibiliter in quibuscumque monstantiis ponatur aut deferatur, nisi....* The decision was made 'for the greater honour of the Blessed Sacrament': *ad majorem honorem sanctissimi sacramenti.*[1] Similar decrees were passed in the synods of Mainz.[2] (1451), Passau[3] (1470) and Schwerin (1492).[4] This eagerness to gaze at the Sacrament was particularly marked along the Baltic coast and in Westphalia.

The compromise of the sacrament house was effected by a door of metal lattice work, with a light to make the Eucharist more visible, and sometimes with candles burning on prickets affixed to the outside railings. The railings thus formed an 'enclosed garden,' conformable to the Flemish

[1] Hartzheim, *op. cit.*, t. V, p. 416; Mansi, *op. cit.*, t. XXXII, col. 149.
[2] *Ibid.*, p. 408. [3] *Ibid.*, p. 486. [4] *Ibid.*, p. 646.

'*thuynkens*.'[1] Contemporary archives speak of the tabernacle in the church of St. Ursula at Delft, as surrounded with a '*thuynken*' (1494): as also in St. Sulpice, Diest, in 1527.[2] At Vadstena in Sweden, the mother house of the Brigittines, there is the record of the erection of a sacrament house in 1454. It is styled '*ciborum sive columna*,' and a monstrance with a lamp was directed to be placed in it.[3]

The desire to gaze on the Sacrament was the purport of a will made in Munich in 1395, which provided funds for an erection of stone behind the high altar, wherein the Eucharist was to be kept in a monstrance perpetually exposed to view. Whether the beryl mentioned in the document was to be set in the stone-work of the sacrament house or was intended to form the face of the monstrance is not clear.[4] Superstition respecting the Sacrament would seem to have been rife in Germany in the centuries preceding the Reformation. A fifteenth-century writer (Henry Gorychum) recounts how it was the custom in some places for the priest, after an infant had been baptized, to fetch the pyx containing the Eucharist, to lift up one of the particles, show it to the godparents, replace it, and then, purifying his fingers, to offer the water to the infant to drink.[5] The Reformation would seem to have failed to warn German Catholics of the danger of suchlike superstition, and a book printed at Cologne in 1560 complained bitterly of the 'unusual, continuous and almost daily exposition, as they call it, of the Blessed Sacrament in transparent monstrances.'[6] An altogether different reason for the erection of sacrament

[1] Maffei, *op. cit.*, p. 97. [2] *Ibid.*, pp. 99–100.

[3] Thurston, *Exposition of the Blessed Sacrament*, *Catholic Encyclopedia*, vol. V, p. 713.

[4] Thurston, *Benediction of the Blessed Sacrament*, *The Month* (September, 1901), p. 266.

[5] Gorychum, *De Superstitionibus*, prop. 8; *ibid.* (June, 1901), p. 594.

[6] Gropper, *De Veritate Corporis et Sanguinis Christi in Eucharistia* (Cologne, 1560), pp. 515–16.

houses, separated, as they were, from the altar, was alleged by a fifteenth-century writer, who maintained that they were established by way of protest against a heretical opinion, widespread in Germany, which affirmed that the Real Presence was inseparable from the Sacrifice of the Mass.[1]

Germany had a variety of names for these sacrament houses: *sakramenthäusen*, *herrgottschäuschen*, *gotteshüttchen*, *fronwalme*, *sanktuarien*. They were often the gift of corporations, confraternities or even of a single donor, and were found in many of the religious houses. Stone, marble, metal or wood were used in their construction, but those in wood have disappeared, with the exception of the '*Monstranhuus*' of Gilminge (1500), in the museum of Copenhagen,[2] and some few in Sweden. Our Lady's church in Lubeck had a sacrament house in bronze (1479).

A number of examples have survived in Germany, for the most part of the fifteenth century: e.g. Münster, Kiedrich, Wilderstadt, Frankfurt (cathedral), Nuremburg (St. Laurence), Constance (St. Stephen), and in the Cistercian churches of Doberan, Altenberg, Salem and Heilsbronn. The Eucharist is reserved today in the sacrament houses of Altenberg and Salem, although they are now parish churches. An open-work grille, to view the Sacrament, exists in the Heilsbronn exemplar, which was constructed by Adam Krafft in 1515. Drosendorf in Austria, has a sacrament house of the early sixteenth century.

Wall tabernacles and sacrament houses were well-nigh universal in the Low Countries before the devastations of the Gueux, but a large number are still to be found. Their popularity may be gauged from a sixteenth-century writer, John Molanus (1533–85), who mentioned, as '*vetustiora*

[1] Maffei, *op. cit.*, pp. 92–93, n. 4. [2] *Ibid.*, pp. 93–94.

templa,' the '*turriculae*' in the dioceses of Belgium, which are to be found by the side of the high altar, generally of brass.[1] The fate of the sacrament house in the abbey of the Dunes has been given in a report of the state commissioners in 1567.[2] The *repositorium sanctae Eucharistiae*, says the chronicle of the house, had been erected in the time of Abbot Robert de Clercy (1519–57), with the lower part serving as a reliquary. On August 15th, 1566, a band of Gueux burst into the abbey church and well-nigh destroyed the high altar and the sacrament house. An attempt to repair the fragment of the latter was to no purpose, as twelve years later (1578) the iconoclasts returned and totally demolished what was left.

The oldest extant sacrament house in Belgium, St. Pierre, Louvain (1450), was erected by the *Confrérie du Saint-Sacrement* under an arch of the choir on the gospel side of the church. Three years later the confraternity charged a locksmith to erect a surrounding enclosure or *tuine*, which was to be surmounted by candles.[3]

Mention of the 'finest' and the 'most extraordinary' of the sacrament houses must suffice, as the Low Countries have preserved too many to make a description of them possible. The 'finest' is considered to be that of St. Jacques, Louvain (1539), a hexagonal structure, dominated by a pelican, and resting on a pedestal with small columns. The panels of the 'tabernacle' have sculptures from scenes in the life of our Lord. Ancient mural decoration has been preserved on the wall behind. The Renaissance railing with caryatids and statuettes was added in 1568.[4] The church of

[1] Molanus, *De Historia SS. Imaginum et Picturarum* (Louvain, 1771), p. 493, note P.
[2] Archives of Bruges, no. 1722: 15.
[3] Maffei, *op. cit.*, pp. 101–02. [4] *Ibid.*, pp. 108–09.

St. Leonard at Léau, is said to possess the 'most extraordinary' sacrament house, eighteen metres high, which has retained its Gothic form, with sumptuous Renaissance ornament (1552). It was the gift of Martin de Wilre, lord of Oplinter, and cost six hundred *florins Carolus*. Reached by a staircase in the wall, it is used today as the 'altar of repose' in the night of Holy Thursday to Good Friday.[1] Some of the churches disposed of their sacrament houses to other churches, in order to obtain new and, possibly, larger structures. Such was the case at Diest, which sold its 'tabernacle' to Gheel, and Léau, where it was disposed of to Hal.[2]

The late medieval tradition in Holland would have been similar to that of Belgium, but the Calvinists, unlike the Lutherans, wantonly destroyed the ornaments of the churches. Dutch Limburg, however, which remained predominantly Catholic, has a small stone sacrament house, dating from about 1500, at Holset,[3] and in the Chapel of St. Roch at De Kamp, there is a further late Gothic example, taken from the neighbouring Well church.[4]

The use of an aumbry was the more usual form of reservation in Sweden, but a number of sacrament houses still exist, for the most part of wood, some with their paintings intact.[5]

Sacrament houses are found also in France, although they are comparatively rare. In 1404, a visitation report from the cathedral church of Grenoble referred to a suspension for the Eucharist, as if it was something exceptional: 'The body of the Lord is reserved over the altar in a small

[1] *Ibid.*, pp. 109–111. [2] *Ibid.*, p. 100.
[3] *Kunstreisboek Voor Nederland, Voor de Monumentenbeschrijving*, p. 573, Amsterdam, 1960. [4] *Ibid.*, p. 576.
[5] Letter from Dr. Eric Segelberg of Uppsala University, to the author (May 2nd, 1963).

"laton"[1] pyx (*bustia*) within a little tabernacle, hanging by a cord, without a key': a manifestly unsatisfactory arrangement.[2] Later in the century, we find the bishop, Siboud Allemand, in his visitation charges (1457–58) counselling reservation in an aumbry near the altar.[3] A stone sacrament house, more than forty-five feet high, was erected at this time (1455–57) in the cathedral church. There is a sacrament house in the cathedral of St. Jean de Maurienne, in which the Eucharist was reserved until 1757. We find them also in the former Cistercian churches of Le Bénissons-Dieu (Loire) and Silvacane (Bouches-du-Rhône), but in the latter no more than the base and sculptured canopy have survived. A wooden sacrament house in the form of a tower was noted by Dom Martène on his visit to the cathedral church of Digne: 'dans l'ancienne cathédrale il eroit a côteé de l'autel, dans un tour de bois, qu'on voit encore aujourd'hui.'[4]

A severely damaged sacrament house supported on two pillars is found on the north side of the presbytery in the former Cistercian church of Arbona, near Chieti, in Italy. This type of tabernacle, looking rather like a clock on a short column and pedestal, was sculptured for Volterra cathedral by Mino da Fiesole in 1471.

[1] Laton (*orichalcum*) was a mixture of brass and the dross of a furnace (*cadmia*). Du Cange, *op. cit.*, t. IV, p. 345.

[2] Chevalier, *Visites Pastorales* . . . p. 59.

[3] Köster, *op. cit.*, p. 76.

[4] Martène, *Voy. Lit.*, part I, p. 27.

11: RESERVATION OF EUCHARIST AND HOLY OILS

THE 'tabernacle' in the middle ages was often used for the holy oils at the same time as the Sacrament. Innocent III had said no more in the decree *Sane* (1215) than that the chrism and the Eucharist should be kept faithfully under lock and key.[1] Following the prescriptions of the council, Walter de Cantilupe, bishop of Worcester, had enjoined in 1240 that the Eucharist should be reserved *sub competenti clausura*, at the same time as the oil and the chrism.[2] There was no suggestion that they ought to be kept in separate receptacles, and the synods of Trier[3] (1238) and Gubbio[4] (1303) make it clear that they would be reserved together. The sick required holy oil as well as the Eucharist, and it was a matter of convenience that they should be found together. Sometimes they were in the same vessel: the lower part for the Sacrament and the upper part for the oil.

There were, however, instructions in the middle ages for the two to be kept in separate receptacles, as the synods of Liège (1287) and Cambrai (1300) directed.[5]

[1] Can. 20; Mansi, *op. cit.*, t. XXII, col. 1007.
[2] Wilkins, *op. cit.*, vol. I, p. 667. [3] Hartzheim, *op. cit.*, vol. III, p. 560.
[4] *Archivio per la storia ecclesiastica dell'Umbria*, vol. I (1913), p. 320.
[5] Hartzheim, *op. cit.*, t. III, p. 629, t. IV, p. 72.

12: FORM AND MATERIAL OF THE PYX

THE Eucharist was normally reserved within two vessels: the pyx proper containing the hosts, and a larger and more elaborate receptacle: from country to country, church to church, and century to century.[1] The eucharistic vessels depended for their size and material on what a church could afford.

The term pyx has been generally accepted from at least the ninth century, when regulations for reserving on the altar became traditional,[2] although a number of other names were in use. The oft-quoted statute of Archbishop Peckham (1280) confined itself to enjoining reverence, decency and security, with a condemnation of the use of a burse, presumably on the altar. No more was said than that the pyx was to be the finest obtainable (*pulcherrima*), lined with linen and surmounted by a silken covering.[3]

The original form of a pyx was a small cylindrical box with a flat lid, such as was found in the sarcophagus of S. Nazaro in Milan, but at an early stage there were a number of other forms: square, polygonal or oval,[4] with, later, a cover frequently in the form of a cone to which a hinge was attached.[5] Sometimes the pyx was mounted on feet, in the form of a little tower, as we find at St. Omer (twelfth century), Argelès-sur-Mer (end of the thirteenth century) and Lesmont (fifteenth century).[6] Covered cups (*ciboria*) came to be established gradually from the thirteenth century, and the term 'ciborium' was current in the fourteenth. The word is found in a pastoral letter of Mahaut d'Artois in

[1] Van Dijk, *op. cit.*, p. 39.
[2] *Ibid.*, p. 33.
[3] Wilkins, *op. cit.*, vol. II, p. 48.
[4] Van Dijk, *op. cit.*, pp. 33–35, 44.
[5] Maffei, *op. cit.*, p. 42.
[6] *Liturgia*, pp. 286, 188.

1325: 'Pour un chyboire . . .' and 'Pour la painture dudit chyboire.'[1] In 1399, the accounts of the cathedral church of Cambrai speak of: '14 toises de corde pour prendre le chyboire dessus le grand autel.'[2] The term 'cup' or 'ciborium' would have been synonymous with 'pyx.' The more usual English shape was of a circular cup-like form, with a dome-cover, surmounted by a cross and ring. A latten (brass) pyx of this type, probably of the last half of the fifteenth century, was found at Exning in Suffolk, buried in the earth: a covered cup with a conical spire and crowned with a crucifix.[3]

This cup-like form is frequently met with in inventories, as, for example, those of Amiens (1247), St. Paul's, London (1297) and the Sainte Chapelle in Paris (1376).[4] The inventory of Saint Sepulchre, Paris (1379), gives the entry: 'Une coupe d'argent dont le pié et la jambe et le couvescle sont d'argent esmailliez et le buvent (la coupe) est de cristal brodé d'argent doré et dessus le couvescle a un crucefix. Et dedens la coupe a une boiste d'argent dorée et sacrée ou repose le corps de Nostre-Seigneur; et est tout ensemble dedenz le thabernacle, pendant sus le grant autel.'[5] Again at Dol in 1440: 'Une coupe d'argent couverte, pendue sur le grand aulter où est corpus Domini.'[6] Cups for the reserved Sacrament were listed also in the inventories of Laon in 1523 and Notre Dame, Paris, in 1577.[7] The fourteenth-century accounts of the Constable of Dover Castle mention (1344): 'One cup of silver-gilt with its cover (of silver) to receive the body of Christ, and a cover of silk knotted to hang

[1] *Ibid.*, p. 289. [2] *Ibid.* [3] Cox and Harvey, *op. cit.*, p. 42.

[4] 'A gold cup, wherein the holy sacrament is hidden, with a silver-gilt tabernacle suspended by three silver chains. Another "*vernaculum*": *La coupe d'or et le tabernacle d'argent doré a iii chaesnes d'argent.*' Van Dijk, *op. cit.*, p. 36.

[5] *Ibid.*, Maffei, *op. cit.*, p. 29; Gay, *op. cit.*, vol. I, p. 377.

[6] Maffei, *op. cit.*, p. 45; Gay, *op. cit.*, vol. I, p. 377. [7] *Ibid.*, p. 47.

over the said cup.'[1] For the year 1361, the accounts have an entry in old French: 'A cup of copper-gilt and a cover of silk to put over it, and a box of ivory to be placed inside the said cup and to contain the body of our Lord.'[2] 'A cup of berill, garnished with gold, pearls, and precious stones, to put the holy Sacrament in,' was left to the church of St. Catherine, near the Tower of London, by John, Duke of Exeter, in 1447.[3]

The form of eucharistic vessel varied greatly in the middle ages, and several of the inventories refer to a 'coffer.' In the inventory of Charles V of France (1364–80), we find: 'Ung reliquaire d'or en facon d'une nef, à porter le corps de Nostre Seigneur, que deux angelotz soustiennent; et poise neuf marcs sept onces d'or.'[4] Less costly was the coffer in the inventory of the church of St. Paul, Orleans (1462): 'un escrain de bois garni de fer et de laton ou cuivre doré, à mettre Corpus Domini.'[5] It may have been a coffer to which an inventory of the cathedral church of Aberdeen referred in 1436: *Unum jocale eucharistie de argento deauratum ad modum castri cum laberello*, given by the bishop, Henry de Lychton: *in cujus summitate ponitur jocale aureum cum ymagine pietatis*, the gift of another donor.[6] The eucharistic vessel in the form of a dove has been described elsewhere.

Ivory may well have been one of the less costly materials, and consequently suitable for small country churches, as is recorded of Histon, near Cambridge, in the thirteenth century.[7] The synodical constitutions of Eudes de Sully, bishop of Paris (1198), enjoin the use of ivory, without citing

[1] *Archaeological Journal*, vol. XI, p. 382; Bridgett, *op. cit.*, vol. II.
[2] *Ibid.*, p. 384; *ibid.*
[3] Bridgett, *op. cit.*, vol. II, p. 94.
[4] Freestone, *op. cit.*, p. 65.
[5] Gay, *op. cit.*, vol. I, p. 377.
[6] *Regist. Episc. Aberdon*, vol. II, p. 144. For *jocale* see Du Cange, *op. cit.*, t. 4, p. 253, where *theca* is given as a possible meaning.
[7] 'An ivory pyx with lock.' *Churches of Cambridgeshire, Camden Society*, p. 60.

PLATE 7

WALL TABERNACLE

St. Clemente, Rome, late Thirteenth century

PLATE 8

Wall Tabernacle
Lucca, late Fifteenth century

any other material,[1] as also did the synods of Autun (*c.* end of the thirteenth century) and Soissons (1403). A choice of silver or ivory was given by the council of Oxford[2] in 1222 and endorsed by the synod of Exeter[3] (1287) and the Carmelite ordinal (*c.* 1312).[4]

A third alternative was sometimes permitted, as in the injunctions of the bishop of Worcester (1229, 1240), with Limoges enamel (*de opere lemonitico*[5]) and the synod of Liège (1287) with burnished copper (*cuprea bene elimata*).[6] An enamel pyx was mentioned in an inventory of the chapel of Hurst in Berkshire in 1220.[7]

In later centuries there was a tendency in some quarters to despise ivory as a material for the pyx, and Mabillon recorded how a general of the Canons Regular had described the use of ivory as 'unworthy of so great a mystery,' ordering all such to be replaced by pyxes of silver-gilt.[8] This is the more curious, as it was possible to combine the most costly magnificence with the 'humble' material. St. George's Chapel, Windsor, for example, in 1385 possessed 'a noble ivory pyx, garnished with silver plates, gilt, with a foot covered with leopards and precious stones, having a cover of silver-gilt with a border of sapphires, and on the top of the cover a figure of the crucifix with Mary and John, garnished with pearls, with three chains meeting in a disk of silver-gilt, with a long silver chain by which it hangs.'[9] The same inventory mentioned also: *Item una pyxis de eburneo gemellato argenteo, cujus coopertorium frangitur.*[10] Salisbury cathedral (1536) had 'a pyx of ivory, bound above and beneath with

[1] *Odon. Epi. Paris, Synod. Constit.*, cap. V, n. 5; Mansi, *op. cit.*, t. XXII, col. 677.
[2] Wilkins, *op. cit.*, vol. I, p. 594. [3] *Ibid.*, vol. II, p. 139.
[4] *Ordin. Carm.*, edit. Zimmermann, rubr. XLIV, p. 86.
[5] Wilkins, *op. cit.*, vol. I, pp. 623, 666. [6] Mansi, *cp. cit.*, t. XXIV, col. 897.
[7] Cox and Harvey, *op. cit.*, p. 42.
[8] Mabillon, *Mus. Ital.* (Paris, 1687), t. I, p. 198.
[9] Dugdale, *Monast. Anglic.*, t. VI, p. 1365. [10] *Ibid.*

silver and gilt, having a squared steeple on the top, with a ring and a rose, and an escutcheon in the bottom, having within a case of cloth of gold with I.H.S. on every side set with pearls.'[1] An ivory pyx with plates of silver at the four corners was listed in an inventory of Aberdeen cathedral in 1549.[2]

Silver was the most usual material for the pyx, as may be gauged from constitutions and inventories. Frequently also inferior vessels were replaced by those of silver or silver-gilt. It had been the intention of King Henry VII (d. 1509) to effect this in 'every house of the four Orders of friars, and in likewise every parish church within this our realm,' as seen in his last will. The king had been shocked to see so many 'ful simple and inhonest pixies, specially pixies of copre and tymbre,' and gave instructions to the 'treasurer of the chamber and master of the jewel house' to see that the required number of pyxes were provided, each of which was to be of the value of four pounds, 'garnished with our armes, and rede roses and poortcolis crowned.'[3] The wish of the king would not seem to have been fully carried out, and on the eve of the Reformation, Thomas Doddington, priest of All Saints, Northampton, left, in 1530, ten pounds in money or plate to make a pyx for the Sacrament, requesting that his brother should 'make the said pix after such a goodly manner as he can devyse.'[4] Four years earlier, Henry Godwin of Irchester bequeathed forty shillings 'towards the bying and purchasing of a pyxe of sylver and gylte to ley the blessed Sacrament or body of our Lord Jhesu Cryste, there to remain for ever.'[5]

[1] Nightingale, *The Church Plate of the County of Wilts* (Salisbury, 1891), p. 237.
[2] *Regist. Episc. Aberdon.*, vol. II, p. 182.
[3] Astle, *The Will of King Henry VII* (London, 1775); Cox and Harvey, *op. cit.*, p. 44.
[4] Cox and Harvey, *op. cit.*, p. 44 [5] *Ibid.*

Expense necessarily limited the number of gold pyxes, but they were prescribed in the synods of Münster (1279) and Cologne (1281).[1] They were, however, found in a number of the more important churches. One such was given by Eustace, bishop of Ely (1187–93) to his church,[2] and among the 'cups for the Lord's body' at Canterbury was one of gold, a present of Louis, king of France.[3] The *Rites of Durham* said that 'the pyx, wherein the blessed Sacrament hung, was of most pure gold, curiously wrought of goldsmith's work.'[4] Winchester cathedral, also, had a gold pyx, which was among the treasures stolen by Henry VIII.[5] 'A silver (portable) tabernacle with a gold pyx for the reservation of the body of Christ' were among the sacred vessels given by Nicholas III (d. 1280) to St. Peter's, Rome, and listed in a contemporary inventory.[6]

No fixed regulations as to the material of the pyx existed in the middle ages, and prescriptions were very varied. Pyxes of crystal were not unknown, and the inventory of Winchester cathedral, taken at the time of the dissolution of the priory, recorded no less than 'nine pixies of christal, partly garnished with silver and gilt.'[7] The inventory of the Celestines of Esclimont in the diocese of Chartres (1546) mentioned: 'deux ciboires: ung de cristal, garny d'argent doré de perles et roses de vermeilles, et l'autre de fonte (metal) bien doré.'[8] Cups of beryl were frequently noted. William of Wykeham (d. 1404) left to his church of Winchester: 'one vessel of berill ordained for the body of Christ,'[9] and, as we have seen, it was 'a cup of berill . . . to put the holy Sacrament in' that John, Duke of Exeter,

[1] Hartzheim, *op. cit.*, vol. III, pp. 647, 663.
[2] Bridgett, *op. cit.*, vol. II, p. 94. [3] *Ibid.*
[4] *Rites of Durham, Surtees Society*, vol. CVII (1903), p. 7.
[5] Bridgett, *op. cit.*, vol. II, p. 94; Dugdale, *op. cit.*, vol. I, p. 204.
[6] Van Dijk, *op. cit.*, p. 37. [7] Oman, *op. cit.*, p. 80.
[8] Maffei, *op. cit.*, p. 41. [9] Bridgett, *op. cit.*, vol. II, p. 94.

bequeathed to the church of St. Catherine near the Tower in 1447.[1] Copper was expressly permitted by the synods of Münster (1279), Cologne (1281), Liège (1287) and Cambrai (1300),[2] and was by no means uncommon. An inventory of St. George's Chapel, Windsor, in the time of Richard II (1377–99) had the entry: 'A pyx of copper for placing the body of Christ in, with a chain of the same metal, with two canopies, large and small.'[3] The church of Heybridge, near Malden in Essex, had two pyxes: one of silver and one of copper.[4] In the last centuries of the middle ages, the material was often unspecified: '*aliam idoneam*,' '*aliam convenientem*,' etc.; while no more was required of the pyx than that the Eucharist should be reserved 'in a clean vessel, proof against mould or damp.'[5]

Tin was but rarely used and only in poor churches, for which it was expressly permitted by the synod of Amiens in 1454.[6] It is found, however, in a number of country churches in England at the time of the Reformation. In Worcestershire, Salwarpe St. Michael had 'one pyxe of tynne,'[7] and St. John Baptist, White Lady Ashton: 'a pix of tyn and pewter.'[8] The *Inventory of Superstitious Monuments*, recounting the church furnishings that were destroyed in Lincolnshire in 1566, had a number of examples. At Markby: 'a pix, sold the said tynne to William Swane, who hath made a paire of balance of the same.'[9] Market Rasen: 'a pix—the foresaid South pursevant had the sayd tynne and pmised to break it and to redeliver the barres

[1] *Ibid.*
[2] Köster, *op. cit.*, pp. 83–84.
[3] Dugdale, *op. cit.*, t. VI, p. 1365.
[4] Bridgett, *op. cit.*, vol. II, p. 93.
[5] Köster, *op. cit.*, p. 84.
[6] *Ibid.*
[7] Walcott, *Inventory of Church Goods, Worcester Architectural Society*, p. 30.
[8] *Ibid.*, p. 34.
[9] *English Church Furniture, Ornaments and Decorations at the Period of the Reformation, as exhibited in a list of the goods destroyed in certain Lincolnshire Churches, A.D.* 1566; edit., Edward Peacock (London, 1866), p. 117.

of silver whe'wth it was bound who hath not accordingly restored the said silver barres and whether the pix be defacid wee ar not certaine.'[1] At Greatford the pyx had disappeared: 'a pixe of pewter wt an old white clothe goune in the tyme of two former churchwardens,'[2] but at Swayfield the 'pyx was broken and defaced and sold to a pewterer,'[3] and at Stickford: 'broken in peces and sold to a tinker, 1562.'[4]

Latten or brass was also not excluded. 'A lytle cuppe of silver within the brasen pyxe' was found in the chantry of St. Michael Elmley Lovett[5] and at Norton St. James juxta Kemsey there was a 'pixe of brasse with a little boxe of silver within the same pixe.'[6] The two vessels appear again at St. Martin's, Worcester: 'a pix of laten and a little box thearin of silver.'[7] At Harby in Leicestershire there was 'a pixe of latyn with canope'[8] and at Hose in the same county: 'one pyxt of latine a canopye.'[9] A brass pyx was reported as 'broken in peces' by the churchwardens at Alkborough in Lincolnshire in 1565.[10]

The 'thirteenth-century' bronze 'goblet' receptacle for the Sacrament, made by Vecchietta (1467–72) for Siena cathedral, is said by Dix to have 'features derived from the hanging pyx, sacrament house and tabernacle in combination.' That may be so, but it is not of the thirteenth century.[11] A visitation report from the diocese of Grenoble (1399–1414) mentioned lead as a material for the pyx, but it was rarely found.[12] Wooden pyxes were cited in the same

[1] *Ibid.*, p. 124. [2] *Ibid.*, p. 90.
[3] *Ibid.*, p. 147. [4] *Ibid.*, p. 147.
[5] Walcott, *Invent. Worcester Architect. Society*, p. 18.
[6] *Ibid.*, p. 26. [7] *Ibid.*, p. 38.
[8] Walcott, *Inventories of Framland Deanery, Leicestershire, Leicestershire Architectural Society*, p. 4. [9] *Ibid.*, p. 5.
[10] *English Church Furniture* . . . , edit. Peacock, p. 35.
[11] Dix, *op. cit.*, pp. 42–43. [12] Köster, *op. cit.*, p. 84.

report, concerning which the bishop said: '*hae pyxides per alias metalleas supplerentur*.'[1] It was a pyx of wood that was spared in the fire at Tuy (1128), and they were found in 1220 at St. Peter Swallowcliffe and Horningham at the visitation of the churches in the deanery of Mere.[2]

[1] *Ibid.*, pp. 84–85.
[2] *Regist. St. Osmundi*, *Rolls series*, vol. I (1883), pp. 291, 311, 313.

13: CANOPIES AND COVERINGS

A CANOPY was normally hung above the pyx: a silken hood thrown upon the chains of the corona or hoop, so as to form the tabernacle of which Peckham speaks: sometimes changed according to the season or feast. Over the cup itself was cast the Sacrament cloth or piece of thin cloud-like muslin—*pannus nebulatus*.[1]

'The white cloth' at Durham 'that hung over the pix was of very fine lawne, all embroydered and wrought about with gold and redd silke, and four great and round knopes of gold, marvelous and cunningly wrought, and with great tassels of gold and redd silke hanging at them, and at the four corners of the white lawne clothe; and the crooke that hung within the cloth that the pix did hang on, was of gold; and the cords that did draw it upp and downe was made of fine white strong silke.'[2] The great canopy above was surmounted by 'a pelican, all of silver . . ., very finely gilded, giving her blood to her young ones in token that Christ did give his blood for the sins of the world.'[3] In 1470, St. Margaret Pattens in the City of London had 'a canape with iii crownys of laton to hang ov'e the Sacrament.'[4]

Sometimes the canopy was covered with leather, as in the collegiate church of All Saints', Derby: 'a redde leddr case to doe abowte the canappe.'[5] The churchwarden's

[1] Rock, *Church of our Fathers*, vol. I, pp. 238–39.
[2] *Rites of Durham*, *Surtees Society*, vol. CVII (1903), p. 7. [3] *Ibid.*
[4] *Archaeological Journal*, 1885, p. 315.
[5] Cox and St. John Hope, *Chron. of the Colleg. Church of All Saints, Derby* (London, 1881), pp. 163, 171.

accounts at St. Mary at Hill, London, for 1485 mentioned: 'a pyx-cloth for the high altar of *sipers* (Cyprus silk) fringed with gold, with knopps of gold and silk of Spanish making, of the gift of Mr. Doctor Hatcliff, parson'; 'Item, a pyx-cloth of *sipers* fringed with green silk and red with the knopps silver and gilt with corners going, of Master Suckling's gift'; 'Item, a canopy for the pyx of white baudekin.'[1] Later accounts (1529–30) of the same church record a payment of 2d. for the 'wasshyng and starchyng of the pix clothe.'[2] A unique survival of an English pyx cloth from Hessett in Suffolk is on loan in the British Museum. It is of a square shape with a round hole in the centre, and a silk fringe of rose and yellow. At one corner a gilt wooden ball is still suspended by a tassel of silk, of the same colour as the fringe.[3] The following entries are found in an inventory of St. Stephen's, Westminster, taken at the time of the Reformation: 'A Sacrament clothe (over the pyx) of ffyne white sarcynet ffrynged with gold with this scripture: "*Xpo gloriam canamus*," with knoppys of sylver and gylte'; 'Another Sacrament clothe of red sarcenet for every day, of Xpofer Goodhappys gyfte'; 'A canopy of clothe of gold garnysshed with sylver and gylt, of ye gyfte of or reverent father J. Islyppe.'[4]

Legacies were sometimes left for the renewal or beautifying of the pyx canopy, as at Walberswick, Suffolk, in 1500: to provide 'a canope over the hygh awter welle done with our Lady and IIII aungelys and the Holy Ghost (i.e., the dove) goyng upp and down with a cheyne.'[5] There is also a group of Northamptonshire bequests for a similar purpose: 'To mendynge the canopye of the blessed Sacrament of the

[1] Bridgett, *op. cit.*, vol. II, p. 95. [2] Cox and Harvey, *op. cit.*, p. 41. [3] *Ibid.*
[4] Walcott, *Inventories of Westminster Abbey* (n.d.), p. 15.
[5] Cox and Harvey, *op. cit.*, p. 40; Micklethwaite, *op. cit.*, p. 28, n. 2.

aulter, XIId' (Holcot); 'Towards the maintenaunce of a canopye over the hie aulter, IIIId' (Daventry); 'To the Sacrament of the aulter to by a canopye, Xs' (Great Billing); 'A canope to hang over the holy and blessyd Sacrament' (Brafield).[1]

An inventory taken at Faversham in 1512 mentioned: 'a canapy for the Sacrament of crymson sarsenett with knoppis of golde and tacellys of sylke.'[2] A 'canape of tissue for the Sacrament and a lawne with iiii botons wrought with gold, and tassels of gold for the pix' was listed in an inventory at St. Lawrence, Reading, in 1517.[3]

The Islip Roll of Westminster Abbey (*c.* 1532) shows a triple crown hanging immediately above the altar, and beneath it the fold of the cloth concealing the pyx. The triple crown, which probably had no intended connection with the papal tiara, is met with again in Lydgate's fifteenth-century *Life of St. Edmund*, where the pyx in the miniature is visible through a transparent veil which surrounds it like a bag.[4]

In Scotland, the inventory of the ornaments, given by the bishop of Aberdeen, Gavin Dunbar (1518–31), to his cathedral church, included: 'a most magnificent veil of very fine linen (*bisso villosa*) of a light blue colour, with most handsome representations worked in gold, together with wooden supports and rods beautifully painted, with good iron keys to guide these supports to the sacrament house, with balls decorated with gold; together with a table for carrying the venerable Sacrament, with antipendia decorated with letters of gold and scriptures embroidered as befits

[1] *Ibid.*
[2] *Archaeologia Cantiana*, vol. XVIII, p. 109; Micklethwaite, *op. cit.*, p. 28, n. 2.
[3] Kerry, *History of the Municipal Church of St. Lawrence, Reading* (Reading, 1883), p. 108.
[4] Brit. Mus., *Harl.* MSS. 2, 278, fol. 53.

the house of God.'[1] The *epistolare* of the bishop mentions also: 'a canopy to carry over the venerable Sacrament *ex bisso villosa hyacinthina*, with images, designs and sculpture of gold work with poles.'[2]

Number of Hosts Reserved

The Cistercian *Liber Usuum*[3] (twelfth century) and the Dominican *Missale Conventuale*[4] (1256) approved a single host, but normally there were at least two in the pyx. The Cluniac customary[5] directed four, and the synod of Exeter (1287) seven.[6]

[1] *Regist. Aberdon.*, vol. II, p. 251; Bridgett, *op. cit.*, vol. II, p. 91.
[2] *Ibid*; *ibid.*
[3] Martène, *op. cit.*, t. IV, pp. 64-65.
[4] Wickham Legg, *Tracts on the Mass, Henry Bradshaw Society* (1904), p. 85.
[5] Udalric, *Consuet. Clun.*, lib. I, cap. XXX; *Pat. Lat.*, t. CXLIX, col. 722.
[6] Wilkins, *op. cit.*, vol. II, p. 132.

14: TIME FOR THE RENEWAL OF THE SACRAMENT

It had been forbidden for many centuries to reserve hosts for the communion of the faithful until the following day, but, already from the eleventh century, there had been exceptions, especially in monastic churches, where there were relatively more communions. This would seem to have been the case at Cluny[1] and also at St. Benignus, Dijon, which had adopted Cluniac usages.[2] Something similar was practised by the Cistercians in the twelfth century,[3] and we find it in the Dominican missal of 1256.[4] The usage, however, was not confined to religious houses, and it appears in a number of liturgical books, including the Ordo of John Burchard (1502).[5]

Regulations for the renewal of the sacred species varied from place to place. In England and Scotland it was normally enjoined that the Eucharist should be renewed every seven days. The reason for this was given in the constitutions of the bishop of Lincoln, Robert Grosseteste[6] (*c.* 1238), and something very similar was said by the bishop of Worcester, Walter de Cantilupe (1237–66).[7] The weekly renewal was enjoined by the council of York[8] (1195), and

[1] *Consuet. Clun.*, lib. II, cap. XIII; *Pat. Lat.*, t. CXLIX, col. 662.

[2] 'At the will of the celebrant, they were either reserved in the pyx or consumed by the subdeacon.' Martène, *op. cit.*, t. IV, pp. 140, 64.

[3] *Ibid.*, pp. 64–65.

[4] 'If there were but few hosts remaining after communion, they were put into the eucharistic vessel with those already reserved for viaticum.' Wickham Legg, *op. cit.*, pp. 85–86.

[5] *Ibid.*, p. 163.

[6] 'Lest the holy Eucharist through error or keeping it from day to day might get mouldy or damp, so that it either changes its appearance or becomes unpleasant to the taste.' *Roberti Grosseteste Episcopi quondam Lincolniensis Epistolae, Rolls Series* (1861), epist. LII, pp. 155–56.

[7] Wilkins, *op. cit.*, vol. I, p. 667.

[8] *Ibid.*, vol. I, p. 501

again by the councils of Westminster[1] (1138, 1200), and Oxford[2] (1222), and the synod of Exeter[3] (1287). 'Those that remain after seven days,' says the synod of Exeter, 'are to be consumed on the Sunday, before the ablution of the chalice, by the celebrant or another priest, worthily and devoutly, when others are to be consecrated in greater or smaller numbers, according to the extent of the parish.'[4] Exceptions to this weekly renewal were rare. The council of Reading[5] (1279) and the statutes of Peckham (1280) prescribed fifteen days as the maximum, but the archbishop corrected this in the following year. A similar period was enjoined also in the Carmelite ordinal, with a warning that hosts must never be kept longer than a month.[6] This fortnightly renewal was mentioned in the *Isagogicon* (1523), written by the Carmelite Nicholas Audet. Innocent IV (1243–54), in his condemnation of the Byzantine practice of 'toasting' the Sacrament and keeping it for a year, with a renewal on Holy Thursday, said in a letter (*Sub Catholicae*, 1254) to the bishop of Tusculum, who was the Apostolic legate to the Greeks, that the Eucharist must never be kept longer than fifteen days.[7]

On the Continent, there was a greater variation as to the time of renewal, although seven days was very general. Twice in the month was prescribed by the provincial synod of Trier (1238), and the synods of Münster (1279), and Cologne (1281)[8]; while twelve times in the year were enjoined for the diocese of Limoges.[9] 'Each Communion day' was prescribed in the thirteenth-century *liber ordinarius*

[1] *Ibid.*, p. 505. [2] *Ibid.*, p. 594. [3] *Ibid.*, vol. II, p. 132. [4] *Ibid.*
[5] Counc. Reading, 1279, cap. VII.
[6] *Carm. Ordin.*, edit. Zimmermann, rubr. XLIII, p. 86.
[7] Denzinger-Schönmetzer, *Enchir. Symb.* (1963), n. 834, p. 271.
[8] Hartzheim, *op. cit.*, vol. V, pp. 560, 648, 663.
[9] Martène, *op. cit.*, t. I, p. 252.

of Liège, which would imply about every month.[1] Several of the German councils and synods had ordered a monthly renewal of the sacred species: Freising (1440, 1480), Salzburg (1490), and Ratisbon (1512).[2] Even every second month was permissible in certain circumstances according to decrees of the councils of Eichstätt (1447) and Constance (1463, 1483), but warning was given against the danger of putrescence.[3] The season of the year was considered by the synod of Cambrai (1300) to affect the time for the renewal of the Sacrament: 'in winter and summer according to what was fitting.'[4]

[1] Jungmann, *Missarum Sollemnia* (Paris, 1954), vol. III, p. 344, n.ii.
[2] Hartzheim, *op. cit.*, vol. V, pp. 276, 520, 582; vol. IV, p. 95.
[3] *Ibid.*, vol. V, pp. 367, 464, 560.
[4] *Ibid.*, vol. IV, p. 72.

15: RECEPTION OF RESERVED HOSTS

THE hosts taken from the pyx at the renewal were consumed either at the altar or in the sacristy, and normally by the priest himself. An alternative was permitted by the bishop of Durham in 1220: 'some innocent person of good life.'[1] Something similar was contemplated by the synods of Exeter[2] (1287) and Aberdeen (thirteenth century).[3] The custom of '*pueri innocentes*' receiving the reserved Sacrament was known also on the Continent, especially in France, but the practice was forbidden by a number of synods, including Paris (1198), Bordeaux (1255), Clermont (1268), Bayonne (1300), and Würzburg (1298).[4]

[1] Wilkins, *op. cit.*, vol. I, p. 84.
[2] *Ibid.*, vol. II, p. 132.
[3] Robertson, *Concilia Scotiae* (Edinburgh, 1866), p. 33.
[4] Köster, *op. cit.*, p. 91.

16: CONTINUOUS LIGHT

THE early centuries knew nothing of any light before the reserved Sacrament. The first known reference is found in the Nestorian synod of Seleucia (904), but this would not have affected the Western Church. A light to burn continuously before the Eucharist from Holy Thursday to Good Friday was prescribed in the eleventh-century Cluniac customary, as well as in those of St. Vitus, Verdun, and St. Augustine's, Canterbury, but the regulations only concerned the ceremonial of the *Triduum Sacrum*, and it was not before the end of the twelfth and the beginning of the thirteenth century that instructions appeared in respect to the normal reservation in church: St. Martin, Auxerre (1189), Harlebeke (1190), Ninove (1210), Paris (*c.* 1220), Vernon (*c.* 1265), etc.[1] In 1240, the bishop of Worcester, Walter de Cantilupe, enjoined that 'a lamp must burn day and night before the Eucharist, in churches which can afford it,'[2] and something similar was prescribed at Passau in 1284.[3] Synods and episcopal constitutions in the three following centuries were increasingly concerned with the maintenance of a continuous light to burn before the reserved Sacrament, but the obligation would not seem to have been universally accepted before the sixteenth century. Ludovicus Ciconiolanus said in the *Directorium Divinorum Officiorum* (1503): 'I often see the Body of Christ without a light, which, according to law, ought to burn before it,'[4] and a number of councils and synods endeavoured

[1] Köster, *op. cit.*, pp. 93–94.
[2] Wilkins, *op. cit.*, vol. I, p. 667.
[3] Hartzheim, *op. cit.*, vol. III, p. 673.
[4] Wickham Legg, *op. cit.*, p. 215.

to enforce the regulation: Basle (1503), Narbonne (1509), Seville (1512), Ratisbon (1512) and Augsburg (1548).[1]

The 'light before the Sacrament of the Altar and the light above the Sepulchre' were permitted by Thomas Cromwell in 1536 to be continued,[2] and five years later (1541) Henry VIII in a letter to Cranmer said: 'no offering, or setting of lights by candles, should be suffered in any church, but only to the Blessed Sacrament of the Altar.'[3] There seems little doubt as to the meaning of these injunctions, but the Royal Injunction of 1547, permitting the retention of 'two lights upon the holy altar before the Sacrament,' is not so clear. Micklethwaite says that, when compared with the earlier injunction of Thomas Cromwell, the reference would be to lights before the reserved Eucharist, rather than to the altar candles.[4] This, says the author of a recent book, *The Use of Lights in Christian Worship*, is 'linguistically possible, but the interpretation appears unlikely.'[5] It is in the highest degree improbable that Edward in 1547 intended an increase of ceremonial. The only reasonable interpretation, especially bearing in mind subsequent legislation, is that the Injunctions marked a further reduction, by forbidding the lights allowed by Cromwell. This view is confirmed by the fact that Cranmer's visitation articles of the same year for his own diocese say merely 'whether they suffer any torches, candles, or tapers, or any other lights to be in your churches, but only two lights upon the high altar.'[6] It would certainly appear that Micklethwaite was mistaken, and that the lights in question were altar candles.

[1] Köster, *op. cit.*, p. 95.

[2] Wilkins, *op. cit.*, vol. III, p. 816; Dendy, *The Use of Lights in Christian Worship* (London, 1959), chap. X, p. 151.

[3] Strype, *Cranmer*, I, i, XXIII, edit. 1812 Oxon, p. 132; Dendy, *op. cit.*, p. 152.

[4] Micklethwaite, *Ornaments of the Rubric*, pp. 29–30.

[5] Dendy, *op. cit.*, p. 152. [6] *Ibid.*, pp. 152–53.

Alinari

PLATE 9

WALL TABERNACLE, 1469–1529
Church of SS. Apostoli, Florence

Facing page 130

Alinari

PLATE 10

WALL TABERNACLE

St. Egidio, Florence, Fifteenth century.
Used later for Oil of the Sick

Either wax or oil would have been used in lamps of the kind. A hanging basin was perhaps the commonest form of lamp, but brackets projecting from the wall were also used, and sometimes a lamp-stead in the wall in the form of a niche, generally with a sort of hood above to catch the smoke, and less often with a small flue to carry it away.[1] Buscot, near Lechlade, has a lamp-stead without a flue in the east jamb of the window, the sill of which forms a thirteenth-century sedilia. A further example, with a flue in the north wall of the chancel, is found at Meppershall in Bedfordshire. Two curious examples, both near Peterborough, are met with at Tollington in Lincolnshire and Castor in Northamptonshire. That of Tollington is of the twelfth century on the south side of the chancel; while at Castor it is on the north side and of the fourteenth century. Each has a flue above, and a pierced basin in the bottom of the niche, as if to drain away the spilled oil. The flues are generally very small.[2]

Benefactions were sometimes made for the maintenance of the light, and in 1306 a sum of money was left to the Cistercian house of Doberan in Mecklenberg for a candle to burn before the reserved Sacrament '*diu noctuque sine intermissione*.' Similar donations were made in the same century to the Danish abbeys of Sorö (1327) and Esrom (1338).[3] In England, also, we hear of William Sedman, who 'settled a wax taper to burn continually day and night for ever before the Body of our Lord in the chancel of the church of St. Peter of Mancroft, Norwich.'[4]

[1] *Ibid.* [2] *Ibid.*, p. 30, n.i. [3] Köster, *op. cit.*, pp. 95–96, n. 214.
[4] Blomfield, *Norfolk*, vol. IV, p. 206.

17: TABERNACLE

THE term 'tabernacle' has been employed to signify a number of altogether disparate objects. In the first place, the name was given to a kind of small 'tent' which covered the pyx suspended over the altar. Thus a visitation report of Horningham, near Salisbury, in 1220 spoke of a 'wooden pyx in a silk tabernacle, hanging over the altar and containing the Eucharist.'[1] Its use as a covering or canopy was referred to in a French document of 1675: 'Un tabernacle de drap d'or avec figures, doublé en satin de soie cramoisie, rouge. . . .'[2] 'Tabernacle' came also to signify the eucharistic vessel itself, irrespective of the mode of reservation, and only received its present connotation, the receptacle in the middle of the altar, about the end of the sixteenth century.

English documents after the thirteenth century rarely spoke of a pyx as a tabernacle,[3] but an exception is found in an inventory of church goods in St. Botolph, Billingsgate, in the city of London in the reign of Edward VI. Here there is an entry: 'It'm a tabernacle that dyd hange over the altar, 5s.'[4] The term, however, was employed for a niche to receive a statute or triptych: Henry VI gave to Winchester College a 'tabernacle of gold adorned with precious stones and with the images of the Holy Trinity and of the blessed Virgin of christal.'[5] Again, in an inventory of the cathedral church of Lincoln: 'a tabernacle of

[1] *Regist. St. Osmundi epi.*, *Rolls Series* (1883), vol. I, p. 313.
[2] *Les Tabernacles de la Renaissance à Rome*, *Revue de l'Art Chrétien* (1789), p. 258; Bridgett, *op. cit.*, vol. II, p. 87.
[3] Bridgett, *op. cit.*, vol. II, p. 88.
[4] Walters, H. B., *London Churches at the Reformation* (London, 1939), p. 215.
[5] Bridgett, *op. cit.*, p. 87; *Lowth*, *Life of William of Wykeham*, p. 81.

ivory standing upon four feet with two leaves, with one image of our Lady in the middle, and the salutation in one leaf and the nativity in the other.'[1] A late fourteenth-century (1391) Parisian statute for craftsmen used the term 'tabernacle' as a receptacle for images, as well as for the Eucharist: 'Nul tailleur d'images ne fasse aucun tabernacle à mettre corpus Domini ne autre pour images, qu'ils ne soient taillez de bon bois et sec, et par especial ceux à mettre le corpus Domini doivent estre dorez de fin or et d'argent bruny, dorez de teinte, et à leur ordonnance ancienne et accoustumée, doivent estre le verre assis et ouvré et enclavé bien et suffisament.'[2]

'*Tabernacolo*' is also the name given to certain of the street shrines in Florence, as well as to shrines of venerated Madonnas in the churches of Or San Michele and SSma Annunziata. The *Caeremoniale Episcoporum* (1600) regards the tabernacle as synonymus with a monstrance: '*Sequitur episcopus portans manibus suis SS. Sacramentum in tabernaculo sive ostensorio inclusum.*'[3]

'*Tabernaculum*' was the term used in inventories and accounts in the latter part of the middle ages for a type of altar-piece in many of the churches in Scotland: an altar retable incorporating a centre-piece with carved work and hinged doors or wings. Clearly it had no connection with eucharistic reservation. A charter of the prior of Pluscarden, dated October 13th, 1508, mentioned: 'twa tabirnaclez in ye said abbey: that is to say, ane to ye hie alter and ane oyer to our lady alter to ye making in flandris.'[4] The altar-piece brought from the Continent by the abbot of Paisley, Thomas Tervas, is referred to in the Auchinlech Chronicle

[1] *Ibid.*; Dugdale, *op. cit.*, t. VIII, p. 1204.
[2] Gay, *op. cit.*, vol. II, p. 365; Freestone, *op. cit.*, pp. 68–69.
[3] *Caerem. Episc.*, lib. II, cap. XXXIII, n.8.
[4] Macphail, *The Religious House of Pluscardyn* (Edinburgh, 1881), p. 236.

as 'the statliest tabernakle that was in all Scotland and the mast costlie.'[1]

The term 'tabernacle,' to denote the receptacle fixed to the altar in which the Eucharist is reserved, was largely the outcome of the reforming measures of the bishop of Verona, Matthew Giberti (*c.* 1525), who, finding the Sacrament in 'some odd corner' (*in quodam angulo*) of his cathedral, hung it in a tabernacle of marble and crystal borne by four angels of brass suspended over the high altar, 'that he might thus excite the devout minds of priests and people to godly piety.'[2] The example of the bishop influenced the Tridentine reformers, with the result that a tabernacle fixed to the altar came in due course to be the normal manner of reservation throughout the Western Church.

[1] R.C.A.M., *Inventory of the City of Edinburgh* (1951), pp. 38–39.
[2] Dix, *op. cit.*, p. 51.

18: CIBORIUM

THE term 'ciborium' may be derived either from the Latin *cibus*, 'food' or from the Greek χιβώριον, 'pod of a large Egyptian bean,' which had a cup-like form. The Romans called a cup used at feasts a 'ciborium':

> *Oblivioso levio Massico*
> *Ciboria exple.*[1]

In Christian times, 'ciborium' came to be applied to the canopy which was supported by four columns over the altar. Then, in the sixteenth century, to a little 'temple on the altar,' rectangular, octagonal or circular, in which the Eucharist was reserved. 'Temples' of the kind are met with in many of the Italian cities.[2]

The silver chalice-like vessel with a cover, which in England is called a ciborium, developed from a pyx placed upon a stem. Pyxes of this type first appeared in the twelfth century, but they did not at first cease to be suspended, as at Alpais[3] (end of twelfth century) and Sens (thirteenth century).[4] The treasury at Alsemberg in Belgium has a somewhat similar pyx, surmounted by the crucifixion group, with a receptacle for the holy oil in the base.[5]

[1] Horace, *Odes*, II, 7. [2] E.g. Florence, Rome, etc. [3] Now in the Louvre.
[4] Maffei, *op. cit.*, pp. 45–46. [5] *Ibid.*, p. 88.

19: MONSTRANCE

A MONSTRANCE, designed for the purpose of showing the Sacrament to the people, became an important eucharistic vessel in the closing years of the middle ages. Something of the kind, however, was depicted in a miniature of a Franciscan psalter, transcribed in northern France in the third quarter of the thirteenth century.[1] The pyx carried by St. Clare (d. 1253) in the well-known illustration of her repelling the Saracens was obviously designed for the purpose of exposition.[2] The most ancient monstrance extant is preserved in the church of St. Quentin, Hasselt (Limburg), a gift of the prioress Edwige to her convent (Cistercian) of Herkenrode in 1286. It is a hexagonal tower-shaped vessel, surmounted by a crucifix and small statues, with an inscription recording the gift.[3]

The earliest evidence for a monstrance designed for the express purpose of showing the Sacrament to the people comes from Danzig in east Germany in the first half of the fourteenth century, and appears in a life of Blessed Dorothea of Prussia (d. 1394). The *Beata* was accustomed to contemplate the Host after having assisted at several Masses, going to a little church outside the city dedicated to the Body of Christ, where she gazed on the Sacrament exposed to view in a monstrance.[4]

The introduction of a procession of the Blessed Sacrament at Corpus Christi made the use of a monstrance inevitable. Religious sentiment, which should have been the very

[1] Paris, *Bibl. Nat.*, ms. lat. 1076, fol. 130r.
[2] Van Dijk, *op. cit.*, pp. 36–37.
[3] Reussens, *Archéologie Chrétienne*, vol. 2, p. 334; Thurston, *op. cit.*, *The Month*, July 1901, p. 65.
[4] Righetti, *op. cit.*, vol. 3, p. 498.

inner life of liturgy, had come to demand that the Eucharist should be visible, in order that devotion might be stirred by gazing on it. This type of devotionalism, which became prevalent in Germany and the Low Countries, was excessive in the northern regions of Germany in the century, or almost the decades, immediately preceding the outbreak of the Protestant Reformation.[1] Expositions and Masses *coram Sanctissimo*, for the purpose of indulging the pious curiosity of the faithful, grew increasingly frequent. The parish priest of St. James', Münster, Pastor Dreygerwolt, has left us a note book in which instructions were given for the exposition of the Host on the feast of Dedication. It was written shortly before the Anabaptist revolt (1521–25). 'I consecrate this Host the day before,' says the pastor, 'as perhaps the priest who comes for the occasion to say the first Mass may not have much experience in the way of placing it' (*quia forte primissarius non peritus in imponendo*).[2] The text was quite explicit: the Host consecrated the day before was exposed (*teneatur*) on the altar during the Masses of the feast, and reserved until the next day at least. The same on Corpus Christi: a host is consecrated the day before, so that on the feast *Ecce panis angelorum* may be sung, and that it may be exposed (*apponatur*).[3] A tract, written by the burgomaster of Stralsund on the Baltic, Franz Wessels (*c.* 1550), says that before the high Mass on the First Sunday in Advent the Blessed Sacrament was placed in a monstrance held in the hand of a silver statue of the blessed Virgin, which was placed over the high altar.[4] The inventory, taken in the parish church of Greifenberg in Pomerania in 1540, contains a description of just such

[1] Bishop, *op. cit.*, chap. II, p. 26.
[2] *Ibid.*, chap. XXV, p. 449.
[3] *Ibid.*, p. 450.
[4] *Ibid.*

another statue.[1] The Mass at Stralsund would seem to have been somewhat eclipsed by the Exposition: 'Of Advent—First, in Advent, before Christmas, a Mass was sung every morning at the stroke of half-past six at the altar in the middle of the choir; a silver Mary image was brought there, about three feet high, with a monstrance in her hand, and therein was a host. The chaplain who said the Mass brought it to the altar from the ciborium (the receptacle from which the host had been taken to be placed in the monstrance). Two "*monstranten*" (deacon and subdeacon) went before, each with a burning torch in his hand, and meanwhile the bells were rung. . . . Before them went twenty or thirty boys, each with a burning wax candle in his hand, and these lights were placed before the altar, which was decked out (*besettet*) with two or three hundred lights and (there were lights) also all about in the church. . . . This Advent Mass was celebrated up to Christmas Eve; that was the last.'[2]

A monstrance combined with an image of our Lord or one of the saints was by no means uncommon. Ste. Menehou in Champagne in 1486 had a silver figure of St. John Baptist, pointing with a finger of his right hand to a lamb that he was holding under his left arm, and on which was a '*soleil*,' in which the Sacrament was exposed.[3] An image of our Lord with the Eucharist enclosed in the breast was not uncommonly used for the Easter sepulchre in some of the largest churches in England. The rites of Durham speak of 'a marvelous beautifull image of our Saviour, representing the resurrection, with a crosse in his hand, in the breast whereof was enclosed in bright christall the holy Sacrament of the altar, through the which christall the

[1] *Ibid.* [2] *Ibid.*, pp. 450–51, n.i.
[3] Thiers, *op. cit.*, lib. 2, cap. II, p. 229; Maffei, *op. cit.*, pp. 131–32.

blessed host was conspicuous to the beholders.'[1] An image of a somewhat similar kind was bequeathed to the cathedral church of Wells by Cardinal Beaufort in the episcopate of John Stafford (1425–52).[2] Lincoln had a special monstrance for Easter and another for the Rogation Days: 'An image of our Saviour silver and gilt, standing upon six lions, void in the breast, for the Sacrament for Easter-day, having a beral before and a diadem behind, with a cross in hand.'[3] And again, 'Item, a round pyx of chrystal, having a foot of silver and gilt, with one image of our Lady in the top, having a place for the Sacrament for Rogation days.'[4] Louis XI, when Dauphin of France, gave a magnificent monstrance to Hal in Belgium in about the year 1460.[5]

The finest example is probably the Belem monstrance, now in the Museum of Ancient Art in Lisbon. Vasco da Gama gave the first gold from the Indies to the king, who commissioned Gil Vicente (1506). Kneeling figures of the apostles in colour surround the lunette.

A monstrance in the later middle ages had a variety of forms, dimensions and ornamentation, and the council of Cologne (1452) spoke of '*in quibuscumque monstrantiis*.'[6] Its name also varied, and the monstrance was frequently referred to as a 'tabernacle,' while at Lincoln it had been spoken of as a 'pyx having a foot.' The constitutions of the Ipswich guild merchants, drawn up for the Corpus Christi procession in 1325, mention 'our tabernacle specially assigned for this procession, in which the body and blood

[1] *Rites of Durham, Surtees Society*, p. 10; Rock, *Church of our Fathers*, Vol. VI, p. 289.

[2] 'A silver-gilt image of the Lord's resurrection standing in an enameled (*amilasatum*) green meadow (*terragium*), having a beryl in the breast for placing the Lord's body in.' Dugdale, *op. cit.*, t. II, p. 280.

[3] *Ibid.*, t. VI, p. 1279. [4] *Ibid.*, Oman, *op. cit.*, p. 80. [5] Maffei, *op. cit.*, p. 129.

[6] Counc. Cologne, 1452; Mansi, *op. cit.*, t. XXXII, col. 149.

of Christ will be contained.'[1] It was listed again as a 'tabernacle' in an inventory of Anjou (1360): 'Un tabernacle de cristal, fait par manière d'une tour . . . et dedenz ledit tabernacle de cristal a un cressant d'argent pour mettre nostre Seigneur. . . .'[2]

Gothic monstrances were frequently in the form of a tower, and sometimes large architectural compositions, as at St. Alban's Abbey, where the abbot, Thomas de la Mare (1349–96), equipped his church with 'a silver-gilt tower . . . in which the *Corpus Christi* is carried about, and can clearly be seen by the people. It has in the lower part of the same tower, in silver-gilt, a Resurrection of Christ, with two angels and four soldiers guarding the sepulchre.'[1] Four bearers were required to carry it.[3]

An early fifteenth-century (1409) inventory of the cathedral church of Hildesheim, lists a 'large silver monstrance after the manner of a pyx with a silver foot, with eight "windows" by way of ornamentation and surmounted by a silver cross.'[4] The monstrance itself may be in the form of a cross, as we find in an inventory of the treasury of Notre Dame, Paris (1438): 'Item, une croix d'argent doré que soutiennent deux angels (sic) pesant en tout douze marcs, en laquelle on porte le Corps de Notre Seigneur au jour du Saint Sacrement, que donna M. Gerard de Montagu, chanoine, et depuis évêque de Paris.'[5]

Monstrances were uncommon in England, yet in 1466 the church of St. Stephen, Coleman Street, London, had no less than three: 'A risen Christ'; 'a monstrance of sylvr for the sacrament wt the hande of our lady'; and 'i mone of

[1] Thurston, *op. cit.*, *The Month*, July 1901, pp. 67–68, n.i.
[2] Gay. *op. cit.*, t. II, p. 365; Maffei, *op. cit.*, p. 130.
[3] *Gesta Abb. S. Alb.*, *Rolls Series* (1870), vol. II, p. 334.
[4] Gay, *op. cit.*, t. II, p. 139; Maffei, *op. cit.*, p. 131.
[5] Chardon, *op. cit.*, i. II, p. 297; Thiers, *Traité de l'exposition du Saint Sacrement*, liv. 2, cap. II, p. 228; Maffei, *op. cit.*, p. 131.

sylv to ber the sact.'[1] There were, however, other churches in London which had a monstrance. Westminster Abbey could boast of two: 'a nooster[2] for the Sacrament of curios work of sylver and gylt haveyng a berall in it of CXLIIII unces,'[3] and 'i stondyng pyx of silver and gylt to bere the Sacrament in, sett with stone and perle besides the cristall.'[4]

An inventory of St. Stephen's, Westminster, mentions a monstrance as part of the loot received by the king: 'Delivered unto his majestie a fair mounstrance gilt parcell of the stuff that came from Westminster weinge iiixx jx oz.'[5] St. Helen's, Bishopsgate, had 'a ring of silver with ii glasses for Corpus Christi'; while 'a ston of chrestall brodered about with silver and gilt' was listed in the Reformation inventory of All Saints, Worcester.[6]

'Eucharist' was a very general term for a monstrance in fifteenth- and sixteenth-century Scotland, and among the ornaments of Holyrood abbey, Edinburgh, in 1493 was 'a great eucharist of silver gilt, weighing 160 oz, and a great silver cup for the Blessed Sacrament.'[7] A monstrance was among the munificent gifts of the Cistercian abbot of Kinloss, Thomas Crystall (1505–35), to his church. The life of the abbot, written by a Piedmontese of the name of Ferserius, recalled that he had 'brought to Kinloss a silver shrine (*theca*) commonly called a eucharist, half a cubit high and exquisitely made.'[8]

[1] Oman, *op. cit.*, pp. 83–84. [2] Ostensorium or monstrance.
[3] Walcott, *Inventories of Westminster Abbey at the Dissolution* (n.d.), p. 5.
[4] *Ibid.* [5] *Ibid.*, note c.
[6] Walcott, *Inventory of Church Goods, Worcester Architectural Society*, p. 35.
[7] Walcott, *Scoti-Monasticon* (1874), p. 306.
[8] John Stuart, *Records of the Monastery of Kinloss* (1872), pp. ii. 32.

20: RITUAL RESERVATION

Palm Sunday: Procession

THE Palm Sunday procession, with the Eucharist carried in a portable shrine (*feretrum*), which had been prescribed in the constitutions of Lanfranc (d. 1089), became very general in England in the succeeding centuries. The Sarum customary (*c.* 1225) said: 'Whilst the blest branches are being distributed, a shrine shall be prepared with relics, from which the body of the Lord shall be suspended in a pyx.'[1] The Hereford missal (1505) referred to an altar of repose to which the body of Christ, with the relics of the saints, had been carried in the morning.[2] A more detailed reference was given in the York missal (1517), directing that the body of the Lord, during the Palm ceremony, was to be carried to its appointed place by a priest in a silver cope. The officiant genuflected three times on the arrival of the procession, as also did the choir. The Sacrament was then taken back to the church by another route. If fine, the Eucharist was placed under a tent (*tentorium*) outside the church, but, if it was wet, the Sacrament was to be taken to the altar of the blessed Virgin, and there honoured.[3] An account of the Palm Sunday procession was given by Clement Maydeston, a Brigittine of Syon convent, Isleworth (d. 1456), in commenting on the use of the Sarum rite in parish churches.[4] At Chichester, a cleric in a white chasuble, supported by two others in copes, carried the eucharistic shrine to a tent prepared in

[1] *Regist. S. Osmundi*, *Rolls Series*, vol. I, p. 120.
[2] *Heref. Missal*, edit. Henderson (1874), vol. II, p. 80.
[3] *York Missal*, *Surtees Society* (1874), Vol. I, p. 86.
[4] Rock, *op. cit.*, vol. III, part 2, pp. 227–28; Bridgett, *op. cit.*, vol. II, pp. 241–42.

the cemetery, and from thence to the chapter house, and so back into the church.[1] The shrine at Durham was timed to appear in the sight of the people just as the words '*Benedictus qui venit*' were being sung at the close of the gospel, and on reaching the station the Sacrament was censed and adored.[2] The Eucharist was never exposed in a monstrance in these ceremonies.

It was not only in England that we find a Palm Sunday procession of the kind, and indeed it originated in north France, and was continued at Aix en Provence until the seventeenth century.[3]

Holy Thursday: *Locus Aptus*

The rite of the Presanctified on Good Friday, whether it entailed a communion of the people or not, necessitated a reservation of the Sacrament after the Mass on Holy Thursday. It was not, however, a 'ceremonial' reservation in the middle ages, and would in all probability have been in the sacristy. The term 'sepulchre' only came to be given to the 'altar of repose' on Holy Thursday after the old idea of the Easter Sepulchre had been abandoned.

The mid-twelfth-century customary of the Benedictines of Polirone (Mantua) directed the Eucharist to be reserved from Holy Thursday onwards between two patens, placed between two *scutella*, all of silver and wrapped in a white cloth.[4]

The thirteenth-century *ordinarius* of the Premonstratensians directed that the Sacrament should be reserved in a suitable and fitting place (*in pulcro et honesto scrinio*) from

[1] Feasey, *Ancient English Holy Week Ceremonial*, p. 72.
[2] *Ibid.*, pp. 72–73.
[3] Marbot, *La Liturgie Aixoise* (Aix, 1899), pp. 300–01. See also: Bishop, *Liturgica Historica* (London, 1918), pp. 279–300.
[4] Padua, *Bibl. Univer.*, fol. 35 v. seq.; Van Dijk, *op. cit.*, p. 38, n. I. *Scutella*: *patena in modum cavitatis scuti*. Du Cange, *op. cit.*, t. 6, p. 147.

Holy Thursday until the following day, with a light continuously burning before it.[1] A later customary of the White Canons (fourteenth and fifteenth centuries) said that after the postcommunion on Holy Thursday the Sacrament was to be taken *in thesaurariam*, accompanied by cross, incense and lights, while the choir sang the antiphon '*Hoc corpus meum*.'[2] Van Dijk and Walker mention a thirteenth-century interpolation in the ordinal of the papal court, which said that after the Pope's communion on Holy Thursday, the presanctified host should be carried with honour by the junior cardinal bishop from the Lateran basilica in a 'tabernacle' to the sacristy of the canons.[3] The sacristy designed for the purpose was probably the church of the canons, known as St. Pancras *de secretario*.[4] *Ordo Romanus XIV*, a work of Cardinal James Gaetani (d. 1343), used the terms *armariolum* and *cophinus* as synonyms for the tabernacle of the altar of repose on Holy Thursday and Good Friday.[5]

The ordinary of Cîteaux (1516) enjoined the celebrant on Holy Thursday to reserve a large host for the office of the following day, and two or three small hosts for the communion of the sick, if there should be a need for them, without specifying where they should be reserved.[6]

Good Friday to Easter: Easter Sepulchre

The *Triduum Sacrum*: 'still days,' when the Church commemorates the resting of our Lord in the sepulchre awaiting the resurrection.

[1] Lefèvre, *L'Ordinaire de Prémontré d'après des manuscrits du XIIe et du XIIIe siècle* Louvain, 1941), cap. XXXIV, p. 59.
[2] Lefèvre, *Coutumiers liturgiques de Prémontré du XIIIe et du XIVe siècle* (Louvain, 1953), usus II, cap. XXIII, p. 52.
[3] Paris, *Bibl. Nat.*, 4162a, fol. 30 rb; Van Dijk, *op. cit.*, p. 37.
[4] Van Dijk, *ibid.*
[5] *Ord. Rom.* XIV, XCIII; *Pat. Lat.*, t. LXXVIII, col. 1216–17.
[6] *Ordin. Cist.* (1516), cap. XXXI.

Every eucharistic vessel is in a sense a 'tomb,' an idea which we find expressed in the *Missale Francorum* (eighth century):

> Almighty God in three Persons, impart the might of thy blessing to our hands, that, through the blessing, this vessel may be sanctified, and a new sepulchre of the body of Christ raised up by the grace of the Holy Spirit.[1]

The term 'sepulchre,' however, could be more precisely applied to the receptacle containing the Eucharist during the *Triduum Sacrum*, when there were symbolical ceremonies of burial (*depositio*) and resurrection (*elevatio*).

The earliest known evidence for reservation of this kind is found in the *Life of St. Ulric* (d. 973), written within twenty years of his death. It was customary, after the rite of the Presanctified in the cathedral church of Augsburg, to place the Eucharist in a kind of sepulchre, closed by a stone (*lapis*), in the church of St. Ambrose. It would appear that the *Corpus Domini* remained in the 'tomb' till Easter morning, but there was no mention of any ceremonial connected with the rite.[2] The setting up of a sepulchre, with a ceremonial 'burial' and 'resurrection,' at first concerned only the cross, as we find in the *Regularis Concordia*. It is uncertain when the Eucharist was first 'buried' with the cross, but an eleventh-century breviary of St. Gall refers to the 'raising' of the *Corpus Domini* at the conclusion of matins on Easter day, with the Sacrament taken to the choir. The sepulchre in which both the cross and the Eucharist were 'buried' would seem to have existed in the Church of Milan from about the eleventh century.[3]

[1] Appendix *ad opera S. Greg. Turon.*, t. LXXI, col. 1185.
[2] *Vita S. Ulrici AA.SS.*, July, t. II (1867), p. 103: Martène, *op. cit.*, t. III (1737), lib. 4, chap. XXV., 7, col. 482–83.
[3] *Ufficio della Settimana Santa secondo il* Rito *Ambrosiano*, p. 347, n. 2. Milan, 1935.

A comparison between the Sarum customary of 1222 and two earlier manuscripts helps to date the placing of the Sacrament in the sepulchre at Salisbury. One of these manuscripts, a codex of the thirteenth century, is among the muniments in the registry of the bishops of Salisbury; while the other, representing a text prior to 1228, is a copy made for the use of Henry de Loundres, bishop of Dublin (1213–28). This second document makes no mention of removing the Sacrament from the sepulchre, as the following text shows, in which the words absent from the Dublin manuscript are in brackets: 'On Easter day before matins two highly placed (*excellentiores*) priests in surplices (after reverently censing the sepulchre, lay the Lord's body on the altar; then) take the cross from the sepulchre.'[1] There is no reference to a '*depositio*' on Good Friday, although earlier in the treatise the treasurer of the cathedral church, 'after the body of the Lord had been laid in the sepulchre,' is directed to provide 'two candles of half pound weight at least from the treasury to burn all day long before the sepulchre, while one such candle is to be kept lighted before the sepulchre all night and during the next day until the Easter procession.'[2] Similar regulations were adopted somewhat later at Wells,[3] but the customary of Norwich cathedral priory (1258–65) made no mention of a burial of the host.[4]

The late thirteenth-century customary of Bayeux showed a certain similarity with Sarum usage,[5] but in an early fourteenth-century ordinal of the Norman church, the clergy and people were directed to be blessed with the

[1] *Regist. S. Osmundi*, *Rolls Series*, vol. I, p. 134. [2] *Ibid.*, vol. I, p. 10.
[3] Reynolds, *Cathedral Church of Wells* (? 1880), p. 32.
[4] *Henry Bradshaw Society*, vol. LXXXII, 1948, pp. 89, 93.
[5] Chevalier, *Ordinaire et Coutumier . . . de Bayeux*, p. 139. Cf. Proctor and Wordsworth, *Breviarum . . . Ecclesiae Sarum*, fasc. i (1882), col. 807.

PLATE 11

EASTER SEPULCHRE
Lincoln Cathedral, Thirteenth century

PLATE 12

Easter Sepulchre

Heckington, Lincolnshire, Fourteenth century

Sacrament in the form of a cross: '*et cum ea clero et populo in modum crucis benedicit more consueto.*'

It was not until the fifteenth century that Hereford accepted Sarum practice, and an ordinal of the fourteenth century continued to follow what had been derived from Rouen, with the cross, but not the Eucharist, in the sepulchre. The rubric in the printed missal of 1502 was no more than a copy of the Sarum. Three hosts were consecrated on Holy Thursday: one for the actual Mass, one for the Presanctified rite, and the third to be put in the sepulchre with the cross, when incense was offered, a candle lighted and the door closed. The scanty rubrics of the York missal say that those who wish may receive Holy Communion with the priest on Good Friday, but there is no mention of reserving a host in the sepulchre, although it is specified that the cross was 'buried.' The Scottish Arbuthnott missal (1491), on the other hand, directs a priest in a surplice, without shoes, to carry the Sacrament and deposit it with the cross in the sepulchre.

In some churches, the host was not reserved with the cross in the sepulchre, although it was brought from the *locus aptus* to be carried in the *elevatio* procession on Easter morning, This was the custom in the Benedictine abbey of Barking at the close of the fourteenth century (1394–1404), with the Eucharist exposed in a monstrance: '*inclusum cristallo.*'[1] At Poitiers, the host was wrapped in a folded corporal between two patens, with a gold cross above it, placed in clean linen, and enclosed, with a ceremonial use of holy water and incense, in a locked receptacle, but not seemingly with the cross in the sepulchre.[2]

[1] *Ordin. and Custom., Barking Abbey*; *Henry Bradshaw Society*, vol. LXV (1927), pp. 100–01, 108.

[2] Feasey, *op. cit.*, p. 164.

The practice of 'burying' the Eucharist in the sepulchre was condemned out of hand in an *ordinarium* of Zurich in 1260. It was 'contrary to reason . . . altogether improper and absurd' that the 'Eucharist, which is the true and living body of Christ, should represent the dead body of Christ.'[1] The prohibition, however, would seem to have been local, and the practice, throughout the middle ages, was very general.

It was not always a host consecrated for the purpose that was placed in the sepulchre, and sometimes we find the hosts left over from the Communion on Good Friday employed in this way. This was prescribed in the *ordinarium* of Prüfening (fifteenth-sixteenth century),[2] and the missal of Eichstätt (1517).[3]

A simple interpretation of the *depositio* and *elevatio* ceremonies appears in a fourteenth-century manuscript from the monastery of St. Blaise in the Black Forest. On Good Friday, when all have received Holy Communion, the *tabulae* are sounded. Then, before vespers, the priest takes the Viaticum and goes to the sepulchre with lights and incense, singing a responsory. The Sacrament is placed in the sepulchre, censed and enclosed, while the responsary *Sepulto Domino* is sung. Then a light is placed before the sepulchre, and vespers follow. The ceremony of the *elevatio* before matins on Easter morning is correspondingly simple. A procession goes to the sepulchre, the inside and outside of which are censed. The Sacrament is taken to the altar and elevated, while the bells are rung.[4]

[1] *Ordin. Turicensense*, 1260, fol. 52r; Zurich, *Zentralbibl.*, ms. c. 8b.
[2] *Ordin. Pruveningense*, fol. 64v, 65v, 66v–67v, 73v–74v; Munich, *Staatsbibl.*, ms. lat. 12018.
[3] *Missale secundum Chorum et Ritum Eiistetensis Ecclesiae*, Nuremberg, 1517, fol. 85r.
[4] Gerbert, *Monum. Vet. Liturg. Aleman* (St. Blaise, 1777), part 2, pp. 335–36.

A considerably more elaborate ceremony took place at Durham: 'After the adoration of the cross on Good Friday, the cross was carried to the sepulchre, which was set up on that morning on the north side of the choir, near unto the high altar, and there laid with great devotion, with another image of our Saviour, in whose breast they enclosed with great reverence the most holy and blessed Sacrament of the altar, censing it and praying to it on their knees a great space, and setting two tapers lighted before it, which burned till Easter day in the morning.' Then—'On Easter day, between three and four in the morning, two of the oldest monks came to the sepulchre, set up on Good Friday after the Passion, all covered with red velvet and embroidered with gold, and then censed it on their knees. Then rising, they took from the sepulchre an extremely beautiful image of our Saviour, representing the Resurrection, with a cross in his hand, in the breast whereof was enclosed, in the brightest crystal, the holy Sacrament of the altar, through which crystal the blessed Host was conspicuous to the beholders. When the anthem *Christus resurgens* was sung, they carried this, upon a velvet cushion all embroidered, to the high altar, knelt, and censed it. When the anthem was sung, they took up again the cushion and statue, and proceeded to the south choir door, where there were four ancient gentlemen belonging to the prior, appointed to attend their coming, holding up a very rich canopy of purple velvet, tasseled round about with red silk and gold fringe; and they bore this canopy over the blessed Sacrament carried by the monks about the church, the whole choir waiting on it with torches and a great number of lights, all singing, rejoicing and praying to God most devoutly, till they returned to the high altar, whereupon they placed the said image, there to remain till the Ascension.'[1]

A dramatic ceremony, recalling certain affinities with the actual use of Braga, is found in the *Liber Sacerdotalis* of Alberto Castellani, which was printed in Venice in 1523. The *depositio* could take place either after the Good Friday liturgy or after dinner. A *solennis sed lugubris processio* was provided by a bier (*feretrum*), carried by four clerics, surmounted by a canopy (*baldachinum*). The host was taken from the altar, as the responsory *Plange quasi virgo* was sung, after which two priests began the *Improperia* (*Populе meus*), and the choir responded with the Trisagion (*Sanctus Deus*). The procession to the sepulchre, with the Host in a bier, was made with four stations, at the last of which the host was taken out, and held aloft. Then, having blessed the people, the Eucharist was placed in the sepulchre, which was closed and sealed, as *Sepulto Domino* was sung.

The Easter sepulchre was a universal feature in England before the Reformation.

The actual receptacle for the Sacrament was normally of wood, enriched with costly hangings, placed for the occasion within a permanent structural recess on the north side of the choir or sanctuary. The sole surviving wooden sepulchre, a box of oak, richly painted and gilded, with a door on iron hinges, is preserved at Warkleigh in Devon.[2] The temporary character of the sepulchre is evident from a number of churchwarden's accounts, as at St. Nicholas, Yarmouth, for the year 1465: 'Paid for setting up of the sepulchre; drying the sepulchre's cloth; bearing the whip; for two pullies over the sepulchre, in the chancel roof; for taking down the sepulchre; for mending the sepulchre; for

[1] *Ancient Monuments, Rites, etc. of Durham*; *Surtees Society*, 1903, pp. 10–11.
[2] Cox and Harvey, *op. cit.*, p. 43.

mending an angel standing at the sepulchre—for a new house in the vestry to put the sepulchre—for dressing and watching the sepulchre; for fetching the sepulchre; for tending the sepulchre's light.'[1] An ornate sepulchre was provided for St. Mary Redcliffe in Bristol in 1470: 'Master Canynge delivered this day, fourth of July 1470, a new sepulchre well gilt with gold . . . and an image of God Almighty rising out of the same sepulchre . . . four knights armed keeping the sepulchre with weapons in their hands.'[2] Various embellishments appear in the records of St. Stephen, Coleman Street, London: 'Item, one sepulchre over gilded with a frame to be set on with four posts and crests thereto; Item, four great angels to be set on the sepulchre with divers small angels; Item, two stained cloths with the apostles and prophets beaten with gold with the Creed; Item, eight bears beaten with gold to be set about the sepulchre with divers small penons.'[3]

The accounts of another London church, St. Andrew Hubbard, East Cheap, for 1480–82 said: 'Item, paid to a man for taking oute of a stone, and setting in of the face of the Resurrection, that the tabernacle stondeth upon, 4d. Item, paid to a carver for making bace, and for lyne for tabernacle cloth, 22d.'[4] Ten ewes were bequeathed for the making of a sepulchre, by Thomas Hunt of Cransley, Northants, in 1516: 'and that the increase of them may be to the supportacion of the same.'[5]

The rood loft served for the sepulchre at St. Lawrence's, Reading: 'Ye loft over the chancell crosses, where the sepulchre lighte dyd stand' (1498).[6] Fifteen years later

[1] Swinden, *History and Antiquities of the Ancient Burgh of Great Yarmouth* (Norwich, 1772), sect. XXII, p. 811.
[2] Cook, *The English Mediaeval Parish Church* (1955), p. 171.
[3] *Ibid.*
[4] Feasey, *op. cit.*, p. 132.
[5] *Ibid.*; *Archaeological Journal*, 1913.
[6] *Ibid.*, p. 131.

(1513), the churchwardens 'payd for settying upp the frame aboute the sepulchre,' and in the following year '5d was paid for ale to the carpenters at the removal of the sepulchre.'[1] 'For the setting up of God's house and taking it down again' was an expenditure at St. Margaret's, Westminster in 1520.[2]

The hangings and draperies of the sepulchre were of the finest and most costly materials. The records of the time make frequent mention of them. In 1498, the churchwardens of St. Lawrence's, Reading, mention: 'a sepulchre cloth of right crymson satten imbrowded wt image wt a frontaill of pays conteyng in length iiii yards wt ii cloths of lawnde for the sepulchre.'[3] A number of draperies for the sepulchre are recorded in the inventories of London churches at the time of the Reformation. Westminster Abbey: 'a greate cover of bedde called a sepulcher clothe of nedle worke'; St. Stephen's, Westminster: 'A sepulchre cloth of clothe of gold, with red fygury and blewe tynsyn'; St. Dunstan's in the East: 'a shete to laye in the sepulture'; St. Mary Woolnoth: 'a sharyne for the sepulture, covered with cloth of tyssue.'[4] So late as 1550, the fourth year of King Edward VI, we read of 'a pece of sypres to cary the Sacrament in.'[5] An unavailing attempt to restore the status quo was made in the time of Queen Mary, and shortly before her death the churchwardens of St. Peter's, Sheffield, included in their accounts: 'Paid for a cloth to the sepulchre-house containing 12 yards at 8d the yard, 8s' 'Paid to Hugh the painter, for painting the sepulchre-cloth, 4s'; 'Paid for setting up of the Resurrection, 7d.'[6] The last

[1] *Ibid.*, p. 144. [2] Bridgett, *op. cit.*, vol. II, p. 252.
[3] Feasey, *op. cit.*, p. 154.
[4] Walcott, *Inventories at Westminster Abbey at the Dissolution* (n.d.), p. 2.
[5] Feasey, *op. cit.*, p. 154.
[6] Hunter, *History of Hallamshire* (1869), p. 246.

entry seems to indicate a change of scene on Holy Saturday evening or Easter Sunday morning.

It was customary for a continuous watch to be kept before the sepulchre throughout the *Triduum Sacrum*, and contemporary accounts give evidence of this. In 1538, the churchwardens of St. Margaret's, Westminster, 'paid for mats for the parishioners to kneel upon when they reverenced their maker, 4s 4d.'[1] The watchers would have been deputed in relays, as is evident from the entry in the accounts of All Hallows on the Wall, London, for 1531: 'for brede and dryncke for them that wachyd the sepucre, 1d.' Again in the same year, at St. Stephen's, Walbrook: 'It'm for bryde and alle for thym that wachys the sepulker, 6d.'[2] The watchers also were not infrequently paid for their services, as we learn from Walberswick in Suffolk in 1471: a small sum 'for watching of candle Estorne nytis.'[3] At St. Mary's, Devizes, also, in 1499: 'to four men for keeping of the sepulch. two nights, 1s 2d.'[4]

The fee for a priest to 'bury' the Sacrament would seem to have been 2d., as the accounts of St. Ewen, Bristol, in the 37th year of the reign of Henry VI show: 'For berying of the sepulchre iid.'[5] The price had not been augmented by 1517 and the churchwarden's accounts of St. Andrew Hubbard (London) say: 'Item, paid to a prest ffor berrying of the sakkerment, iid.'[6]

The many lighted candles intensified the danger of fire, and the Rule of St. Saviour and St. Bridget, observed by the Brigittines of Syon, stipulated that no more than two tapers were to burn during the nights of Friday and Saturday 'in a more syker place for eschewying of perelle.'[7] Precautions

[1] Bridgett, *op. cit.*, vol. II, p. 254; Feasey, *op. cit.*, p. 169. [2] Cook, *op. cit.*, p. 171.
[3] Bridgett, *op. cit.*, vol. II, p. 255. [4] *Ibid.* [5] Feasey, *op. cit.*, p. 166. [6] *Ibid.*
[7] *Rule of St. Saviour and St. Bridgett*, cap. XXXVII; Aungier, *The History and Antiquities of Syon Monastery* (1840), pp. 350–51.

of the kind were by no means taken at St. Edmund's, Salisbury, where, in addition to the great taper, a hundred candles on prickets burned before the sepulchre.[1] An official, known as the 'Alderman of the Sepulchre Light,' is mentioned in the accounts of Wagtoft in Lincolnshire in 1545. Probably his office was either to superintend the parish collections for providing the lights, or to regulate the burning of the tapers and the watching at the sepulchre.[2]

Bequests were frequently made to maintain these lights. A legacy of William Smyth to St. Mary's, Devizes, in 1436 provided 'for the maintenance of three sepulchre tapers,'[3] and in 1528 Richard Nethersole bequeathed a cow to Wymynswold in Kent to maintain 'a taper of 4 lbs of wax at the least to the honour of the holy Resurrection of our Lord';[4] while Robert Curteys left 3s 4d for the 'sepulchre light' at Castor, Northamptonshire, in 1544.[5] The young men and women of the parish of Heybridge in Essex supplied the lights in the 21st year of King Henry VIII, as the churchwarden's accounts show: 'The bachelors of the parish of Heybridge have delivered the nine tapers, belonging to the sepulchre, at the feast of Easter, each containing five pounds of wax, and they have above all charges 5s 10d; and so remaineth in the stock clearly above all forty-three pounds of wax which resteth in . . . the hands of Richard Langore, wax chandler. Also in the said year, the maidens of the said parish have delivered in the nine tapers belonging to the said sepulchre, at the feast of Easter, every taper containing five pounds of wax, and they have above all

[1] Cook, *op. cit.*, p. 171. [2] Bridgett, *op. cit.*, vol. II, p. 254.
[3] *Ibid.*; *Wiltshire Archaeological Magazine*, vol. II, p. 252. [4] Cook, *op. cit.*, p. 171.
[5] *Ibid.*

charges 2s 10d.'[1] The cathedral chapter of Rochester in 1545 granted a priest by the name of Nicholas Arnold lodgings by Gundulf's Tower at a rent of 'one pound of wax to be offered on Good Friday to the sepulchre of our Lord' in the choir.[2] The tenancy must have been of short duration—three years at the most—unless the rental was radically altered.

The permanent and structural part of the Easter sepulchre in England was a recess in the north chancel wall, reaching to the ground, and covered by a cusped and crocketed arch. Many of these sepulchres were enriched with tracery and appropriate sculptured figures. The majority that remain are of the late Decorated period. One of the finest, though not one of the most ornate, is in Lincoln cathedral (thirteenth century): three divisions, each consisting of a trefoil-headed open niche, canopied and crocketed, with sculptured panels at the base representing the sleeping soldiers. Lincolnshire and the neighbouring counties provide most of the sculptured sepulchres. They generally consist of three stages: a base, on the front of which are panels or niches containing carved figures of sleeping soldiers; an arched recess in which the receptacle containing the Eucharist was deposited; and a canopy adorned with sculpture representing the risen Christ.[3]

The structure still to be seen at Twywell in Northamptonshire would seem to combine both aumbry and sepulchre: a low segmented arch on filleted shafts, and, above it, two aumbry doors, beneath a pitched roof-like shrine, but in relief and hence only half.[4] One of the finest of these sepulchres is at Heckington, five miles from Sleaford.

[1] Bridgett, *op. cit.*, vol. II, p. 254.
[2] Cook, *English Cathedrals through the Centuries*, p. 123.
[3] Cook, *English Mediaeval Parish Church*, p. 172.
[4] Pevsner, *Buildings of England: Northamptonshire*, p. 435, 1961.

It is divided into three bays, with the wall surfaces covered with foliage carved in low relief. The lower portion of the central division shows the recess in which the Sacrament was placed. A splendid specimen is found also at Hawton in Nottinghamshire, in which a small niche to contain the Eucharist has been hollowed out of the wall at the back of the left-hand compartment. The tomb of the donor, Sir Robert de Compton (d. 1330) adjoins the sepulchre. At Sibthorpe in the same county, two soldiers crouch on either side of the niche for the Sacrament. The sepulchre erected at Tarrant Hinton in Dorset by the rector, Thomas Trotes-well, in 1530 bears the inscription: '*Venite et videte locum ubi positus erat Dominus.*'

Tombs were sometimes made to serve the double purpose of providing a memorial to the deceased and at the same time serving as the Easter sepulchre. Thomas Windsor (d. 1486) of Stanwell in Middlesex by his will (1479) ordered 'a plain tomb of marble of a competent height, to the intent that it may bear the blessed body of our Lord at the time of Easter, to stand upon the same; and mine arms and a convenient scripture to be set about the tomb.' The tomb was to be erected 'in the north side of the choir of the church of our Lady of Stanwell, before the image of our Lady, where the sepulture of our Lord standeth.'[1] Eleanor, widow of Sir Roger Townsend, left instructions in her will (1499) that a new tomb be made in the chancel of Rainham St. Mary (Norfolk) for her husband and herself, upon which tomb to be 'cunningly graven a sepulchre for Easter-day, if a chapel be not made at her decease.'[2]

[1] *Testamenta Vetusta*, p. 352; Bridgett, *op. cit.*, vol. II, p. 253; Cook, *op. cit.*, p. 172.
[2] Blomefield, *History of Norfolk* (London, 1807), vol. VII, p. 132; Rock, *op. cit.*, vol. III, p. 79, n. 86; Cook, *op. cit.*, p. 172.

In 1531, Thomas Fiennes, Lord Dacre, directed that his tomb should be made ready in the church of Hurstmonceaux (Sussex), on the north side of the high altar: 'to be there made for placing the sepulchre of our Lord, with all fitting furniture thereto in honour of the most blessed Sacrament; also, I will that 100 l. be employed towards the lights about the said sepulchre, in wax tapers of ten pounds weight each, to burn about it.'[1]

A structure in the form of a chest tomb was sometimes erected to serve as an Easter sepulchre: on the north side of the chancel, with one end against the east wall. Several of these are found in the churches of West Somerset (e.g. Porlock) and in St. John's, Winchester.[2]

Corpus Christi: *Procession*

There is evidence from the first half of the fourteenth century for a procession with the Sacrament at St. Augustine's Abbey, Canterbury, on Ascension Day, but this choice of day would appear to have been unusual.[3]

The feast of Corpus Christi on the Thursday after Trinity Sunday was first officially authorized by Pope Urban IV in 1264, but the solemnity had been already observed at Fosses in the diocese of Liège in 1246. It was indeed at Liège that Juliana of Mont Cornillon had envisaged the idea of a specific feast in honour of the Sacrament of the Altar, although the synod of 1287 had prescribed a no more dignified position for the reserved Eucharist than 'under the altar' or in a 'cupboard.'

[1] *Test. Vet.*, p. 653; Rock, *op. cit.*, vol. III, p. 79, n. 85; Cox and Harvey, *op. cit.*, p. 76.

[2] Cox and Harvey, *op. cit.*, pp. 76–77.

[3] Thompson, *Customary of the Benedictine Monasteries of St. Augustine, Canterbury, and Saint Peter, Westminster*, vol. I, p. 115; vol. II, p. 285.

The solemnity was not at first generally observed, and it required Clement V in 1311 to renew the promulgation of the feast. Still, however, it was not customary to have a procession with the Sacrament, although we find one at St. Gereon in Cologne sometime between 1264 and 1279.[1] By the fifteenth century a procession of the kind had become popular in Germany and elsewhere, especially since the Eucharist was carried in a monstrance, and consequently visible to the faithful.

It was not, however, always visible, and a very elaborate 'solempnitie of array for the fest of Corpus Christi' was bequeathed in 1449 by William Bruges, Garter King of Arms, to St. George's, Stamford. The Sacrament was placed in a little silver box inside a 'cup' of the same material.[2]

[1] Köster, *op. cit.*, p. 50. [2] Oman, *op. cit.*, p. 82, n. 2.

21: ENGLISH EUCHARISTIC RESERVATION AT THE REFORMATION

THE sixteenth century was essentially a time of religious changes, when, with each successive ruler, the people were compelled to alter and adjust their beliefs and devotions. An old man in the reign of Queen Elizabeth might well have despaired of finding the truth, when he was asked to execrate what he had been previously commanded to worship and adore.

Henry VIII (1509–47) had separated from Rome, destroyed the religious houses and desecrated the shrines of the saints, but, as long as he lived, the honour due to the Blessed Sacrament was secure. The hanging pyx remained suspended in all the churches of the realm and the ceremonies connected with the Easter sepulchre continued as heretofore. In 1538, the second of the royal Injunctions had directed: 'The light before the Sacrament of the altar, and the light about the sepulchre, which for the adorning of the church and divine service ye shall suffer to remain.'[1] The king's commands were naturally supported by the bishops, and in the same year the archbishop of York, Edward Lee, said in the Instructions to the clergy of his diocese: 'Nevertheless they may still use lights in the rood-loft, and afore the Sacrament, and at the sepulchre at Easter, according to the King's Injunctions.'[2] Similar regulations were issued for the diocese of Ely by Thomas Goodrich in 1541: 'That no offering or setting of lights or candles

[1] Frere, *Visitation Articles and Injunctions of the Period of the Reformation, Alcuin Club* (1910), vol. II, p. 38.
[2] *Ibid.*, p. 48.

should be suffered in any church, but only to the blessed Sacrament of the altar.'[1]

The faithful also were exhorted to pray before the sepulchre. Thus Roger Edgeworth, canon of Salisbury, said in a sermon: 'The devout ceremonies of Palm Sundays in processions and on Good Fridays about the laying of the cross and Sacrament into the sepulchre, gloriously arrayed, be so necessary to succour the lability of man's remembrance, that if they were not used once every year, it is to be feared the Christ's Passion would soon be forgotten.'[2] Again, on Good Friday, 1538, when the bishop of Lincoln, John Longland, preached before Henry VIII, the sermon was concluded with an exhortation to his hearers to pay a visit to the sepulchre: 'In the mean season I shall exhort you all in our Lord God, as of old custom hath here this day been used, every one of you, ere you depart, with most entire devotion, kneeling before our Saviour Lord God, this our Jesus Christ which hath suffered so much for us, to whom we are so much bounden, who lieth in yonder sepulchre, in honour of him, of his passion and death, and of his five wounds, to say five Pater Nosters, five Aves, and one Creed, that it may please his merciful goodness to make us partners of the merits of his most glorious passion, blood and death.'[3] This interim period, as it might be called, came to an end on the death of Henry, and under his son, Edward VI (1547–53), the last vestiges of devotion to the reserved Eucharist were successively swept away.

The Royal Injunctions of 1547 had authorized 'only the two lights upon the holy altar, before the Sacrament, which for the signification that Christ is the very true light

[1] *Ibid.*, p. 67.
[2] *Edgeworth's Sermons*, fol. 94, edit. 1557; Bridgett, *op. cit.*, vol. II, p. 249.
[3] Sermon printed by Petyt; *ibid.*, p. 250.

of the world they shall suffer to remain still.'[1] The lights, as we have seen, appear to have been the altar candles. The reformers, however, had no intention of continuing the Henrician compromise, and by 1549 the hanging pyxes had been removed, and the Eucharist was no longer reserved in the churches. This is evident from the fourth of the fifteen demands of the Devonshire rebels, which insisted that they should be put back. Cranmer, in his reply to these 'ignorant people in things pertaining to God,' laid stress on the fact that this method of reservation had never been authorized by Rome: a somewhat *non sequitur* reply under the circumstances, as these poor yokels had never said it had, but they knew no mode of reserving the Sacrament other than in a hanging pyx, and it was the removal of the Eucharist that was so bitterly resented.[2]

In the previous year (1548), one of the articles of Thomas Cranmer for the diocese of Canterbury had inquired of the clergy 'whether they had upon Good Friday last past the sepulchres with their lights, having the Sacrament therein?'[3] The required answer would certainly have been in the negative, as may be judged from the views of his chaplain, Thomas Becon: 'Christ was buried in a poor monument, sepulchre or grave, without any funeral pomp. Antichrist is buried in a glorious tomb, well gilt and very gorgeously set out with many torches, and with great solemnity, and with angels gloriously postured that bear his soul to heaven.'[4] In 1550, the bishop of London, Nicholas Ridley, demanded of the clergy of his diocese: 'Whether the minister or any other doth reserve the Sacrament, and not immediately

[1] Frere, *op. cit.*, vol. II, p. 116.
[2] Cranmer, *Miscellaneous Writings and Letters, Parker Society*, vol. II, pp. 172–73.
[3] Frere, *op. cit.*, vol. II, p. 183.
[4] Becon, *Acts of Christ and Antichrist* (1564); Feasey, *op. cit.*, p. 134.

receive it?'[1] Also, 'Whether there be any . . . tabernacles?'[2] The course of events in Worcester may be seen from a manuscript of Bishop Blandford: '1548, March 15 being Palm Sunday, no palms hallowed, no cross borne on Easter Eve, no fire hallowed, but the Paschal taper and the font. On Easter day the pix, with the Sacrament in it, was taken out of the sepulchre, they singing, "Christ is risen," without procession. On Good Friday, no creeping to the cross.' 'Also on October 20th was taken away the cup with the body of Christ from the altar of St. Mary's church (cathedral) and in other churches and chapels.' '1549. No sepulchre or service of sepulchre on Good Friday. On Easter Even no Paschal hallowed, nor fire, nor incense, nor font.'[3]

With the accession of Mary in 1553, a concerted effort was made by the bishops once again to reserve the Sacrament in all the cathedrals and parish churches. It would seem from an injunction of Cardinal Pole that a tabernacle 'raised and fixed in the middle of the high altar' was now to be the preferred mode of reservation, 'so that it cannot easily be moved; otherwise in the most convenient and honourable place and nearest to the altar which can be found.' The Eucharist was forbidden to be reserved '*in bursa vel in loculo*,' but rather in a pyx furnished with linen.[4] Ordinaries were to begin with their own churches, and then see that the regulations were carried out elsewhere.[5] A lamp or candle was to burn continuously before the reserved Sacrament, 'as was the ancient and laudable custom of the English Church (*ecclesiae Anglicanae*) and of other provinces.'[6] The Cardinal in his injunctions for the University

[1] Frere, *op. cit.*, vol. II, p. 237. [2] *Ibid.*, p. 240.
[3] Green, *History of Worcester*, vol. I, p. 127; Bridgett, *op. cit.*, vol. II, pp. 250–51.
[4] Wilkins, *op. cit.*, t. IV, pp. 121–22; Frere, *op. cit.*, vol. II, 393, n. 1.
[5] Wilkins, *ibid.* [6] *Ibid.*, t. IV, pp. 121–22, 797.

.C.L., *Bruxelles*

PLATE 13

SACRAMENT HOUSE

St. Pierre, Louvain, 1450. The earliest extant example in Belgium

Facing page 162

A.C.L., Bruxelles

PLATE 14

SACRAMENT HOUSE
St. Leonard, Léau, Belgium, 1552

of Cambridge in 1557 prescribed a silver-gilt pyx which had been consecrated by a bishop, stressing the care with which the Eucharist should be reserved, 'lest it might fall into sacrilegious hands,' and issuing a warning against keeping the sacred species longer than fifteen days.[1] Among the articles issued in the same year for the diocese of Canterbury was one directing the clergy to provide a light and a small sacring bell when taking the Sacrament to the sick.[2]

Pole would have been influenced in favour of a tabernacle on the high altar by the custom introduced at Verona by Matteo Giberti (1524–43), which the then pope, Paul IV (1555–59), was recommending. On the other hand, the bishop of London, Edmund Bonner, was clearly envisaging a restoration of the hanging pyx in his Injunctions for 1554 and 1555: 'A pyx with an honest and decent cover,' to be provided by the churchwardens and parishoners.[3] He enquired also 'whether the said archdeacons do foresee and provide that the blessed Sacrament of the altar be reverently preserved and kept in a pix, and hanged upon the altar, or otherwise decently and safely kept and placed; and that the host so reserved in the pix be once in the week taken and received of the priest, or such person for whom the same is reserved, and another consecrated host put in the place thereof; and the same not be suffered there long to continue, but changed and renewed according to the old custom and usage of the Church?'[4]

The regulations enjoined by Pole came to be prescribed by the bishops in their several dioceses. Richard Pate, bishop of Hereford, said: 'You shall provide, with as convenient speed as you can, a comely tabernacle, in a fair

[1] Frere, *op. cit.*, vol. II, p. 416.
[2] *Ibid.*, vol. II, p. 425.
[3] *Ibid.*, vol. II, pp. 345, 366.
[4] *Ibid.*, vol. II, p. 341.

pyx to keep the blessed Sacrament upon the high altar or in some convenient place nigh thereunto, and cause a light continually to be kept burning before it.'[1] The 'tabernacle set in the midst of the high altar' in the cathedral church of Gloucester, according to the visitation charge of the bishop, James Brooke (1556), was to serve as an exemplar for 'every parish, as nigh as their ability shall extend unto.' The churchwardens throughout the diocese were to see that these tabernacles were 'provided and bought, at the parish charge.'[2] A tabernacle of stone or one of wood and iron was among the recommendations of the bishop, Cuthbert Tunstall, to the dean and chapter of Durham. The visitation document (June 17th, 1556) stressed the need for greater security in reserving the Sacrament, as in the late reign the Eucharist had not only been spurned, but thrown on the ground and trampled under foot.[3] The Catholic restoration, however, was of short duration, and in 1558 Protestantism returned with the accession of Elizabeth.

It is doubtful whether it had been possible during the brief Marian interlude for all the parish churches of the country to have restored the hanging pyx or tabernacle. That would have very largely depended upon the promptitude with which the churchwardens had carried out the instructions of the bishops.

A return to Protestantism was by no means certain in the first few months of Elizabeth's reign. Queen Mary had died on November 17th, 1558, and yet in March 1559 we find the Lord Mayor of London severely rebuked by the Order in Council for doing nothing about a sacrilege which had been committed in the church of St. Mary-le-Bow (London), when the Sacrament had been pulled down,

[1] *Ibid.*, vol. II, p. 393. [2] *Ibid.*, vol. II, p. 408. [3] *Ibid.*, vol. II, p. 414.

and the images, vestments and books defaced. The mayor was ordered to discover and punish the culprits.[1] The doubt, however was dispelled by the Interpretation of the Bishops, 1560–61, and the 'Order of Articles prescribed to Ministers' made it clear that the Sacrament was no longer to be reserved in the churches of this country.[2]

In 1565, Bentham, bishop of Coventry and Lichfield, issued an Injunction for his diocese: 'See that you set up the table of the Commandments in the place where the Sacrament did hang, with other godly sentences which be lately set forth.'[3] Grindal's articles for the province of York were ruthlessly iconoclastic, 'Whether . . . all . . . pixes . . . and such other relics and monuments of superstition and idolatry be utterly defaced, broken and destroyed. And if not, where, and in whose custody they remain?'[4] 'On the reverent hanging-up of the Sacrament under a canopy' was the ninth of the articles in the controversy between Thomas Harding and Bishop Jewel of Salisbury (1564).[5]

The fate of these 'monuments of superstition' at the hands of the churchwardens in certain of the parish churches of Lincolnshire in 1566 has been recorded in the *Inventarium Monumentorum Superstitionis*, preserved in the Lincoln episcopal register.[6] They comprise one hundred and fifty-three churches, and explicitly mention fifty Easter sepulchres as defaced and destroyed. At Aswardby: 'One sepulchre broken in peces and defaced and burnte';[7] Belton: 'A sepulker with little Jack, broken inpeces one year ago,

[1] Privy Council, Acts, VII, 77.
[2] Frere, *op. cit.*, vol. III, p. 65.
[3] *Ibid.*, vol. III, p. 165.
[4] *Ibid.*, vol. III, p. 255.
[5] Bridgett, *op. cit.*, vol. II, p. 92.
[6] Peacock, *English Church Furniture, Ornaments and Decorations at the Period of the Reformation, as exhibited in a list of the goods destroyed in certain Lincolnshire churches, A.D.* 1566, London, 1866.
[7] *Ibid.*, p. 34.

but little Jack was broken in peces this year.'[1] 'Jack in a box' was a contemporary blasphemous reference to the Eucharist, and here 'little Jack' would probably have been the pyx for the sepulchre. The sepulchre at Billingborough 'was burnte in melting lead for to mend or churche.'[2]

After 'true religion was established,' the sepulchres were put to a variety of uses by the Lincolnshire churchwardens. The most respectable use was at Castle Bytham and Owmby, where they were employed as 'communion tables.'[3] At Croxton: 'whearof is made a shelf for to set dishes on';[4] Denton: 'sold to Johnne Orson and he haith made a presse therof to laie clothes therein';[5] Dowsby: 'given to a poore woman fyve years ago who brent it';[6] Dorrington: 'was broke and sold to the said William Storre and Robert Cappe who have made a henne penne of it';[7] Horbling: 'was sold to Robert Lond, and he saith he haith made a presse therof';[8] Markby: 'sold to William Badge the said tyme, who haithe made necessaries thereof for his house';[9] Stallingborough: 'defacid whearof wee made a bear (bier) to carie the dead corps and other thinges';[10] Thurlby: 'bre't for the glasier, by churchwardens, since this lent';[11] North Witham: 'sold to ffrauncis flower by the whole consent of the whole parish (1560) . . . wch haithe made a presse thereof.'[12]

A similar desecration and destruction of pyxes is recorded. At Bonby: 'defacid and broken in peces and thereof is made a salt celler for salt';[13] Broughton: 'ii pixes—ar defacid and geven awaie by churchwardens unto a child to

[1] *Ibid.*, pp. 46–47.
[2] *Ibid.*, p. 50.
[3] *Ibid.*, pp. 60, 120.
[4] *Ibid.*, p. 65.
[5] *Ibid.*, p. 67.
[6] *Ibid.*, p. 72.
[7] *Ibid.*, p. 73.
[8] *Ibid.*, p. 108.
[9] *Ibid.*, p. 117.
[10] *Ibid.*, p. 144.
[11] *Ibid.*, p. 152.
[12] *Ibid.*, p. 167.
[13] *Ibid.*, p. 53.

plaie wt all';[1] Branston: 'The covering of the pix sold to John Storr and his wief occupieth yt in wiping her eies';[2] Edenham: 'The pixe defaced and sold to Thomas Clepole in presence of parishioners, 1564';[3] Harlaxton: 'One pixe broken in peces and defaced';[4] Stallingborough: 'A pixe and a crismatorie—sold and defacid and melted to make a bell bouldr, the 1st yr. Eliz.';[5] Waddingham St. Peter: 'One pix of yvorie broken in peces';[6] Wilsford: 'Pix sold to a pewterer in 4 an. Eliz.'[7]

A number of entries in the inventory record the disappearance of ornaments from the churches, which suggests that they may have been taken by well-wishers of the old religion, in the vain hope that Catholicism would one day be restored. Thus at Blyton: 'A sepulker of wainscot—taken from the church by the vicar and remayneth in his house as wee suppose';[8] Ewerby: 'Canapie and pix the old viccar had in beginning of Elizabeth's reign, and he is dead and what is become of them we cannot tell';[9] Stallingborough: 'A pix—gone we knowe not howe nor who was churchwardens, but as we thinck in the said fyrst yeare';[10] Waddingham St. Mary: 'One pixe gone we knowe not howe';[11] South Willingham: 'One pixe and one hallywater fatte gone and conveighed awaie we knowe not howe.'[12]

The above list concerns a comparatively small number of country churches in a single county of England, but the eucharistic ornaments were similarly disposed of throughout the land. The magnificent and costly pyxes and monstrances, given by generous donors over the centuries to cathedrals, religious houses, collegiate and parish churches were all broken up or sold for profane purposes.

[1] *Ibid.*, p. 55.
[2] *Ibid.*, p. 57.
[3] *Ibid.*, p. 74.
[4] *Ibid.*, p. 99.
[5] *Ibid.*, p. 144.
[6] *Ibid.*, p. 157.
[7] *Ibid.*, p. 163.
[8] *Ibid.*, p. 52.
[9] *Ibid.*, p. 80.
[10] *Ibid.*, p. 144
[11] *Ibid.*, p. 156.
[12] *Ibid.*, p. 163.

PART III

RESERVATION FROM THE REFORMATION TO THE CODIFICATION OF CANON LAW

22: PURPOSE OF RESERVATION

(*a*) Communion of the Sick and Viaticum

THE primary purpose for reserving the Eucharist was repeated in the decree of the council of Trent enjoining such reservation in churches. The practice, which is found in many of the councils and was a most ancient custom of the Catholic Church, was referred to as both 'salutary and necessary.'[1] Later, in the same session, an anathema was imposed on anyone who should say that it was not lawful for the Eucharist to be reserved *in sacrario*, and that after Communion it ought to be distributed to the bystanders, rather than fittingly (*honorifice*) be taken to the sick.[2] The council spoke of reservation *in sacrario*, without any further regulation as to where or in what manner.

(*b*) Communion of the Faithful in Church

The practice of giving Communion after Mass, as we have seen, was customary in some churches, at least on certain occasions, in the later middle ages. It was, however, greatly extended by the reform legislation following the council of Trent, as conducive to more frequent Communion.

The reception of Communion at a time entirely unconnected with Mass would seem to have originated with the religious orders: Barnabites, Capuchins and Jesuits. The usage was not at first very general, and was regarded by the secular clergy as a ruse on the part of the religious

[1] Counc. Trent, 2 October, 1551, sess. XIII, cap. VI, can. 7; Denzinger-Schönmetzer, *op. cit.*, no. 1645, p. 388.
[2] *Ibid.*, can. 7; *ibid.*, no. 1657, p. 390.

to attract people to their churches. Later, it became an accepted practice at Easter and the great festivals,[1] although, according to the mind of the Church, as Benedict XIV pointed out in the constitution *Certiores* (13 November, 1742), it was desirable that Communion should be given *in* the Mass. If, however, circumstances should make it necessary, the reception of preconsecrated hosts was permissible.[2]

St. Charles Borromeo would seem to have been one of the first to permit the giving of Holy Communion divorced from the Mass, as appears from the fifth provincial council of Milan (1579). It is admitted that the 'most ancient rite' is for the faithful to receive Communion in the solemn Mass, but, the council goes on to say, it is not forbidden, should occasion arise, to receive at some other time.[3]

A permission of the kind, though not so explicitly worded, is found in the synods of St. Omer (1583), Prague (1605), and Antwerp (1610), and also in the rituals of Augsburg and Constance (1597).[4] The synod of Tournai in 1600 and again in 1643 directed that Holy Communion could be given out of Mass until noon in large churches on Christmas Day, Palm Sunday and Easter.[5] An almost similar authorization for Easter in cathedral and collegiate churches occurs in the *Caeremoniale Episcoporum* (1600).[6] It was therefore no new regulation for the Roman ritual of 1614 to direct the parish priest to reserve enough particles both for the sick and others of the faithful.[7]

[1] Köster, *op. cit.*, pp. 101–02.
[2] *Ibid.*, p. 102.
[3] Ratti, *Acta Ecclesiae Mediolanensis*, vol. 2, p. 548.
[4] Köster, *op. cit.*, p. 102.
[5] Hartzheim, *op. cit.*, t. VIII, p. 484; t. IX, p. 625.
[6] *Caerem. Episc.*, lib. 2, cap. XXX.
[7] *Rit. Rom.*, 1614, *SS. Euch. Sacr.*, p. 48, edit. 1925, tit. 4, cap. I, n. 2–5, p. 122.

The custom of receiving Holy Communion from the tabernacle outside the time of Mass became increasingly common in the succeeding centuries, and was still further extended by the decree of St. Pius X on frequent Communion (20 December, 1905). In recent years, however, with the general advance in liturgical studies, the practice has been discouraged, when there is no immediate necessity.

(*c*) Worship of the Reserved Sacrament

The Protestant denial of the Catholic doctrine of the Eucharist led the council of Trent solemnly to anathematize those who rejected the legitimacy of adoring the sacred species, at the same time approving the 'laudable and universal rite' of carrying the Sacrament in procession.[1]

Organized devotion to the Blessed Sacrament existed in Milan some years before Trent, and in 1527 the *Quarant'Ore* was instituted in the church of S. Sepolcro, and prayers of forty hours' duration before the Eucharist were prescribed four times in the year. Two years later, the devotion was held in all the churches of the city, on account of a severe drought. The practice was finally established for the various churches of the city of Milan through the instrumentality of the Barnabite St. Antonio Zaccaria in 1537, from whence it spread throughout Latin Christendom.

'When we first hear of the devotion, the forty hours of our Lord's resting in the tomb are cited as the reason for that particular span of time. The fact that the devotion started in a church dedicated to the Holy Sepulchre is relevant.' The connection, however, soon faded into the background.[2]

[1] Counc. Trent, 2 October, 1551, sess. XIII, can. 6; Denzinger-Schönmetzer, *op. cit.*, n. 1656, p. 390.

[2] Jungmann, *Pastoral Liturgy*, pp. 223–24.

A use of the Sacrament, which might well lead to superstition, was discouraged by St. Charles Borromeo in the provincial council of 1573: 'When storm-clouds, tempests, whirlwinds or hail storms arise, the priest must not, in order to dispel the storm, make use of the little vessel (*vasculum*) in which the most holy Sacrament of the Eucharist is reserved. But the tabernacle in which it is kept upon the altar may be opened, and then he may piously and devoutly recite in its presence (*in ejus conspectu*) such litanies and other religious prayers as may have been drawn up for this purpose.'[1]

Benediction with the Sacrament was prescribed in one of the constitutions of the Confraternity of the Blessed Sacrament at Mantua in 1576: 'Then let him give them the benediction with the tabernacle of the Sacrament.'[2]

There was, however, still a feeling in some churches that an excessive frequency of eucharistic manifestations lessened the veneration that was due to the Sacrament. This was the opinion of the provincial council of Malines in 1617, whose decrees were approved by Pope Paul V: '*ne nimia frequentia minuat reverentiam*.'[3] The practice of blessing the faithful with the Eucharist, however, became very general in the seventeenth and subsequent centuries.

Jean-Baptiste Thiers says in his *Traité de l'exposition du saint sacrement de l'autel*[4]: The custom of blessing the people with the Sacrament after a procession would seem to be of recent origin, since he has 'not found any ritual or ceremonial more than a hundred years old which makes mention of it.'[5]

[1] Ratti, *Acta Eccles. Mediol.*, vol. I, p. 98.

[2] *Poi egli dia la benedittione col Tabernacolo del Sacramento.* Thurston, *op. cit.*, August 1901, pp. 188–89.

[3] Mansi, *op. cit.*, t. XXXIV, col. 1450. [4] First edition in 1673.

[5] Thiers, *Traité de l'exposition du saint sacrement de l'autel*, edit. 1679, bk. V, chap. VII, p. 752.

The primary purpose of reservation became more and more subordinated to the idea of worship, and Congregations came to be founded for this end. Visits to the reserved Sacrament were encouraged in devotional manuals, as we find in St. Alphonsus Liguori (d. 1787), and in the nineteenth-century Eucharistic Congresses were held in various countries. From the second half of the sixteenth century, synods had admitted that one of the reasons for the reserved Sacrament was that it might be venerated by the faithful. We find this at Tournai (1574), Ypres (1577), Prague (1605), Antwerp (1610), and Osnabruck (1628). The synod of Metz (1699) said that there should always be a host in the tabernacle for the adoration of those who come into the church (*ab introeuntibus in templum*).[1]

[1] Hartzheim, *op. cit.*, t. X, p. 236.

23: PLACE OF RESERVATION

(*a*) Outside a Church

In Private Houses

THE reservation of the Eucharist in private houses had been forbidden for many centuries, but the decrees of two seventeenth-century German synods show that the practice was not altogether extinct. In 1662, the synod of Cologne had said that the Sacrament was only to be reserved in church (*in loco sacro*), even though the pretext for keeping it elsewhere was to adore the sacred species or to comfort the sick (*infirmis succurendi*).[1] A similar injunction is found in the synod of Paderborn (1688), with the additional proviso forbidding the Eucharist to be used as a kind of medicine (*specie medicinae*) or as a remedy against evil practices (*tollendi maleficii*).[2] If, however, there was any likelihood of profanation, bishops and nuncios could sanction reservation in the house of the parish priest, or, if necessary, elsewhere.[3]

On a Journey

In 1677, the Congregation of Cardinals, who acted as interpreters of the council of Trent, condemned the detestable practice (*detestabilem usum*) of regulars carrying about the holy Eucharist in a 'purse' (*crumena*). It was grossly irreverent and contrary to the canons.[4]

Since the fifteenth century, the popes had been accustomed to carry the Sacrament with them on a journey. Benedict XIII (1727–29) was the last to avail himself of the practice, although two later popes had, in troublous times,

[1] *Ibid.*, t. IX, p. 986. [2] *Ibid.*, t. X, p. 146.
[3] Köster, *op. cit.*, p. 106. [4] *Ibid.*, p. 107.

secretly carried the Eucharist on their persons as a safeguard in peril and, if necessary, as viaticum: Pius VI on his enforced exile from Rome (1798–99), and Pius IX on his flight to Gaeta (1848).

(*b*) Inside a Church

In Cathedral, Collegiate and Parish Churches

The right to reserve the Blessed Sacrament in cathedral churches, though they were so often no longer parochial, was clearly presupposed both by the Congregation of Bishops and Regulars in 1579 and the Congregation of Rites in 1593.[1]

There was no doubt as to the obligation of reserving the Eucharist in all parish churches, but, owing to a possible lack of security, the first provincial council of Lima (Peru) in 1582 directed that reservation in a parish church depended on the judgement of the bishop.[2]

The increase in devotion to the reserved Sacrament led inevitably to reservation in subsidiary churches, as we find recommended in the synod of Paderborn[3] (1688), and prescribed in those of Ratisbon (1588), Trent (1593) and Cologne (1660).[4] It was, however, only under certain circumstances that this was permitted by the nineteenth-century provincial councils of Rouen (1850) and Prague (1860).[5]

In 1614, the Congregation of Cardinals suggested that if there were three or four very poor neighbouring parishes in the diocese of Spoleto it might be advisable for only one of them to reserve the Eucharist.[6]

[1] *Ibid.*, p. 108. [2] *Ibid.*, pp. 109–10.
[3] Hartzheim, *op. cit.*, t. X, p. 150.
[4] *Ibid.*, t. VII, p. 1063; t. VIII, p. 411; t. IX, p. 989.
[5] Köster, *op. cit.*, p. iii. [6] *Ibid.*, p. 112.

Particular legislation at least presupposed that the Sacrament would be reserved in collegiate churches: Milan I (1565), Compostella (1565), Toledo (1582–83), Hildesheim (1652) and Naples (1699). The obligation was imposed by the provincial synod of Ravenna (1855).[1]

Among Regulars

The constitution (*Licet debitum*) of Paul III to the Society of Jesus in 1540, made it clear that the Eucharist was normally reserved in churches of the Order: '*Eucharistiae sacramentum quod in suis ecclesiis decenter tenere socios praefatis volumus.*'[2]

Reservation in private oratories was for long the exception rather than the rule, and, although it had never been specifically forbidden, it nevertheless required a special concession from Rome, as appears from a decree of the Congregation of Cardinals to Mexico in 1700. The same Congregation, seven years later, forbade the Sacrament to be reserved in the granges and country houses of regulars.[3]

Reservation within the choir or enclosure of a convent was proscribed by the council of Trent, notwithstanding any indult or privilege to the contrary.[4] The prohibition was clear and definite, yet in 1582 the Congregation of Cardinals made an exception at Innsbruck 'for the consolation of the nuns.'[5]

[1] *Ibid.*, p. 116.
[2] *Ibid.*, p. 113.
[3] *Ibid.*, pp. 114–15.
[4] Counc. Trent, 1563, sess. XXV, cap. X.
[5] Köster, *op. cit.*, p. 114.

A.C.L., Bruxelles

PLATE 15

SACRAMENT HOUSE

St. Jacques, Louvain, 1539. Note railing with prickets for candles

PLATE 16

MONSTRANCE

Monastery of the Jerónimos, Belem, Portugal, 1506

24: MODE OF RESERVATION

Where within the Church the Eucharist should be reserved

Italy

THE first serious movement in favour of a tabernacle on the altar originated with the bishop of Verona, Matteo Giberti (1524–43), and his constitutions had a great influence with Pope Paul IV (1555–58) and St. Charles Borromeo (d. 1584). This mode of reservation was prescribed by the first provincial council of Milan[1] (1565) and the older and traditional methods were forbidden: aumbries (*custodiae in pariete*) were either to be removed or diverted to other uses (*ad alios scopos*).[2] A tabernacle on the altar was ordered also in the *Instructio fabricae et suppelectilis ecclesiasticae* of St. Charles and in the diocesan statutes of Pavia (1576; 1612). Paul IV had advocated the use of a tabernacle, but in 1573 Gregory XIII, in a letter to the Confraternity of the Blessed Sacrament at the church of S. Maria sopra Minerva, affirmed that it was not possible to prescribe one fixed place for the reserved Sacrament in all churches.[3] The *Sacerdotale Romanum* (1564) had come to a similar conclusion. The first definitive Roman directive '*in altari*' is found in 1584 in a ritual for the diocese of Rome, followed in 1614 by a ritual for the Universal Church.

Synods and councils throughout Italy issued decrees for the carrying out of the regulation respecting the tabernacle, and about the year 1600 the archbishop of Trent (Cosentinus) was able to say of the traditional practice: '*morem in armario*

[1] Ratti, *op. cit.*, vol 2, p. 46; Mansi, *op. cit.*, t. XXXIV, col. 17.
[2] *Ibid.*, vol. 2, p. 548. [3] *Bullar. Rom.* VIII, 52.

murali asservandi jam evanuisse,' although, so late as 1593, the diocesan synod had for the first time forbidden aumbries.[1] The council of Aquileia (1596) authorized these 'small openings in the wall' (*fenestellae*) to be used in future for the holy oils, which were to be kept in silver vessels under lock and key.[2] About the same time, the archbishop of Cosenza in Calabria wrote that the use of aumbries in his diocese had ceased altogether, since the old usage was no longer approved by the Holy See.[3] The tabernacle had become well-nigh universal in Italy in the space of a decade, although 'some other seemly place' had been permitted as an alternative by a council at Amalfi in 1597.[4] Even the *Caeremoniale Episcoporum* (1600), if the whole text is carefully examined, did not exclude reservation either outside or above the altar, while giving the preference to '*in altari*.'[5]

The tabernacle received various forms, and at the end of the sixteenth century it sometimes appeared as part of the gradine of the altar: '*tabernacle à la théatine*,' as it came to be called. Orsini in a visitation report speaks of a 'marble tabernacle set in the gradine, after the manner of the Theatine fathers, as is commonly said.'[6] In some churches, the tabernacle proper was no more than an obscure little cupboard underneath the base of a large domical structure: *antrum* or 'cave,' as it was termed by the Neapolitan priest Sebastian Paoli in the middle of the eighteenth century.[7] The synod of Pistoia (1786) directed that the tabernacle should be in a more elevated position than heretofore, in

[1] Braun, *Altar*, vol. 2, p. 592.
[2] Thiers, *op. cit.*, t. I, bk. i, chap. V, p. 37.
[3] *Ibid.*, p. 38.
[4] Mansi, *op. cit.*, t. XXXV, col. 1109–10.
[5] *Caerem. Episc.*, lib. i, cap. XII, para. 8.
[6] Maffei, *op. cit.*, p. 126. The Order of Clerks Regular (Theatines) dates from 1524, and owes its name to Giovanni Caraffa, who was bishop of Theati (Chieti) and later Pope Paul IV.
[7] Bishop, *op. cit.*, p. 35.

order to attract the attention and reverence of the faithful. This tabernacle, high up above the altar, was in a position which is often occupied by the throne for exposition, and is in fact used for that purpose in at least two of the churches of Florence: S. Maria del Fiore (cathedral) and Ssma. Annunziata.

Spain

Reservation on the altar was prescribed by the provincial council of Compostella (1565) and the council of Toledo (1582–83), although as Braun has pointed out, the construction of altars in sixteenth-century Spain would not appear to have favoured this mode of reservation. However, in the following century there was scarcely any other.[1] The provincial council of Mexico (1555) did no more than refer to the reservation of the Sacrament in general terms.[2]

A distinctive mode of reservation appeared in Aragon in the late fifteenth and early sixteenth century: a circular or oval cavity, sheltered by glass, high up above the sculptures of the lofty and massive retable. Examples of the kind are met with in the two cathedral churches of Saragossa: *La Seo* and *El Pilar*. The *sagrario* in the old cathedral has a surround decorated with the heads of little winged cherubim, while overshadowing the cavity, as a canopy, is a group of six angels holding a heavy cloth which falls in folds. It was the work of Gil Morlanes in 1488.[3] That of *El Pilar* is later: the oval of the cavity, pointed at either end, is surrounded by a double fringe decorated with leaves and heads of cherubim. Four angelic singers, bearing musical instruments, hold it up: a theme

[1] Braun, *op. cit.*, vol. 2, p. 592. [2] *Ibid.*
[3] F. Abbad Rios, *La Seo y el Pilar de Zaragoza*, p. 36.

dear to the Italian *Quattrocento* and charmingly interpreted by Filippo Lippi and Melozzo da Forli. The eternal Father and the Holy Ghost in the form of a dove look down upon the eucharistic receptacle—a work of Damián Forment, owing much to Florentine influence.[1]

Portugal

William Lyndwood, as we have seen, referred to Portugal as a country in which the Eucharist was normally reserved in an aumbry, but in the centuries following the Tridentine reform the use of a tabernacle on the altar has become well-nigh universal. The hanging pyx, however, had not been altogether unknown. It was enjoined in the fifteenth-century in the Benedictine abbey of Paço de Sousa, at least for the *Triduum Sacrum*,[2] and its legality was affirmed by the Congregation of Rites in a letter to the bishop of Guarda, dated 10 June, 1602.[3]

Already in 1519, an inconspicuous chapel for the Sacrament had been erected near the sacristy in the Cistercian abbey of Alcobaça.

The large gilded and profusely ornamented retablos of the *talha* type, which became prevalent in the time of John V (1706–50), were all provided with a tabernacle. The example at Tarouca occupies the entire east wall, soaring up to the roof in a series of steps, and terminating in a throne for exposition.

[1] *Ibid.*, p. 118.

[2] *Memorias do Mosteiro de Paço de Sousa e Index dos Documentos do Arquivo compostos por Frei António de Assuncão Meireles, Publicacão e prefacio do Academico Titular Fundador Alfredo Pimenta, Lisboa*, 1942, *Academia Portuguesa de História, Publicacoẽs Comemerativas do Duplo Centenario da Fundacão e Restauracão de Portugal*, doc. 2, 9, pp. 126–27. The notes on the fifteenth-century liturgical reform at Paço de Sousa were kindly supplied by Mgr. de Azevedo, master of ceremonies at the primatial church of Braga.

[3] 'The method of reserving the Eucharist in a vessel hanging over the altar is recognized as lawful.' Köster, *op. cit.*, p. 126, n. 41.

France

The use of a tabernacle on the altar was advocated by a number of the post-Tridentine councils and synods, but France, with its vaunted 'Gallican Liberties,' was by no means always prepared to abandon its traditional modes of reservation at the behest of Rome. In 1550, the synod of Cambrai had permitted an alternative: either 'in a fitting (*honesto*) place over the altar or in an aumbry securely locked,' but in 1567 the words '*super altare*' were omitted.[1] The bishop of Grenoble, John (d. 1561), prescribed '*in altari*' in his visitation decrees, as also did the provincial council of Aix en Provence in 1585, although here the bishop, for some serious reason, was authorized to direct otherwise.[2]

In 1583, the synods of Rheims and Bordeaux required no more than a '*locus honestus*,' but in 1609 we find Narbonne counselling '*in altari*,' while admitting the propriety of '*in alio eminentiori et decentiori loco*.'[3] Toulouse in 1590 wholeheartedly approved the post-Tridentine legislation, ordering a wooden tabernacle to be placed on the altar, and forbidding 'suspension' or any other mode of reserving the Sacrament.[4] A tabernacle was prescribed also by the bishop of Nantes in his visitation decrees in 1638, as the hanging pyx was held to be too dangerous a form of reservation: '*Mond. Sgr. visitant le saint ciboire . . . et ayant veu une corde qui le tient laquelle, si elle cassoit, il tomberait par terre, ordonne que, sur l'autel, il sera fait un tabernacle pour mettre led saint ciboire*.'[5] Accidents certainly had occurred, as we have shown, but

[1] Hartzheim, *op. cit.*, t. VI, p. 700; t. VII, p. 225.
[2] Köster, *op. cit.*, p. 121. [3] *Ibid.*, pp. 121–22. [4] *Ibid.*
[5] *Rég. des Visites épisc. des églises de Nantes*; *Mémoire de la Société Archéologique de Nantes*, IV, p. 98.

they seem to have been exceedingly rare, and decrees ordering a tabernacle to be placed on the altar were unusual in France before the Revolution.

'*In altari*,' as one permissible use, is found, however, in the Lyons ritual (1614), the statutes of the bishop of Noyon, Francis de Clermont (1661–1701), the Toulon ritual (1780), and at Beauvais in 1783.[1] The ritual of Soissons (1753) said specifically that the use '*in ipso altari*' had not been adopted in any of the ancient churches.[2] Thiers, writing in 1688, said that it was only recently that tabernacles had been introduced in France,[3] and in 1745 Dom Chardon admitted that many of the churches still continued to reserve either in the sanctuary or in an aumbry.[4] Chardon mentions also the use of a little 'coffer' suspended over the altar.[5] The liturgical travels of De Moléon at the beginning of the eighteenth century cite some twenty churches in which the Eucharist was reserved in some form of suspension, and the Benedictine abbey of St. Maur des Fossez had a gold dove.[6] The ritual of Lisieux, which appeared in 1744 and had been largely adopted from that of Rouen (1742), offered a choice as to the place of reservation: 'that the Eucharistic Bread may be worthily reserved, the *ciborium* in which it is placed shall either be suspended over the high altar under a decorated canopy or locked away in a tabernacle.'[7] The *Caerimoniale Parisiense* of 1703 has an illustration of an altar with a hanging pyx in the form of a dove. The old Gothic ornaments have been retained as

[1] Köster, *op. cit.*, p. 124. [2] *Ibid.*
[3] Thiers, *Dissertations sur les principaux autels* (Paris, 1688), chap. XXIV, p. 195.
[4] Chardon, *op. cit.*, t. II, p. 253. [5] *Ibid.*, t. II, p. 250.
[6] Moléon, *Voyages Liturgiques de France* (Paris, 1718), p. 179.
[7] Dix, *op. cit.*, pp. 70–71.

regards essentials, though every detail had been clothed in the latest classical forms.[1]

The restoration of religious worship in France, authorized by the Concordat of 1801, introduced tabernacles into many of the churches, but they were by no means universal, and many of the hanging pyxes remained well on into the nineteenth century.

In 1878, the Congregation of Rites approved the restoration of the eucharistic dove in the cathedral church of Amiens, and a like privilege was granted later to the Bendictine abbey of Solesmes, where it is still in use. A hanging pyx is found today in the Cistercian abbeys of Boquen (Brittany) and Hauterive (Switzerland). In 1951 the Sacrament was reserved at Pontorson in an aumbry in the east wall to the left of the high altar.

Cistercian Baroque Suspension

A distinctive mode of reservation especially favoured in the French Cistercian churches in the seventeenth and eighteenth centuries is said by Dom Chardon to have owed its origin to Cîteaux.[2] Lebrun spoke of it as a 'Gallican usage, which originated in the East,' but there does not seem to be any evidence for this.[3] The vessel containing the Eucharist was in the form of an open cup, under a little tent-shaped canopy and suspended from a statue, crown or pastoral staff. It was, however, found in churches other than Cistercian, and the cathedral church of St. Pol de Léon (Britanny) has a wooden crozier representing a palm tree, which was used for the eucharistic suspension.

[1] Comper, *Practical Considerations on the Gothic or English Altar and Certain Dependent Ornaments*; *Transactions of St. Paul's Ecclesiological Society*, vol. III (1895), p. 197.
[2] Chardon, *op. cit.*, vol. II, p. 267.
[3] Lebrun, *Explication . . . de la Messe* (Paris, 1726), t. II, pp. 270–71.

Something similar was observed by Moléon in the cathedral of St. Gatian at Tours.[1]

The Cistercian general chapter of 1601 in directing that the tabernacle should, if possible, be in the most prominent place on or over (*super*) the high altar was attempting to standardize the mode of reservation in accordance with post-Tridentine regulations and may well have had the modern form of tabernacle in mind, but the term '*tabernaculum*' could have been equally applied to 'suspension.'[2] The baroque form of suspension was clearly preferred by the Cisterican ritual of 1689, which, in a manner of speaking, 'gathered up the fragments that remained' of the traditional rite: *si Sacramentum fuerit suspensum, ut debet.*[3] The revised ritual of 1721 still envisaged this mode of reservation: 'On the gradine of this altar and in the middle is the crozier serving for the suspension of the holy Sacrament.'[4] A choice was given by the French ritual designed for the nuns of the Order (1715): '*Il sera suspendu sur le grand autel ou bien ce vase sera mis dans une armoire fermant à clef.*'[5] There was a further ritual, proper to the Mother House (1724), which indicated that 'the crozier from which the holy Sacrament is hung stood in the middle of the gradine of the high altar.'[6] This suspension was noted by Joseph Hahn in his *Reflexions on Cîteaux on the occasion of the general chapter of* 1699. The vessel for the Eucharist, he says, was attached to a bracket in the form of a crozier fixed to the cross, and thus suspended over the altar: *De crucifixo majoris altaris eminet baculus ferreus incurvatus super locum calicis, pendulum*

[1] Moléon, *op. cit.*, p. 114.
[2] *Cap.Gen.* 1601, cap. VII, n. 28; Canivez, *op. cit.*, t. VII, pp. 207–08.
[3] *Rit. Cist.*, 1689, lib. II, cap. VIII, n. 34.
[4] *Rit. Cist.*, 1721, lib. I, chap. III, n. 3.
[5] *Rituel françois des Réligieuses de l'Ordre de Cisteaux*, 1715, liv. I, chap. III, n. 8, 9.
[6] *Rituel propre de l'Abbaye de Cisteaux de* 1724, liv. I, chap. III, n. 3.

habens vitream capsam pro cibario, ad instar lucernae.[1] The glass vessel for the Eucharist had been exchanged for one of gold by 1724.[2] The ritual proper to the mother house, which appeared in that year, referred to this mode of suspension as a 'modern rite': 'Nostre rit moderne est de conserver les hosties pour les communions dans un ciboire doré mis en suspension sous un pavillon sur l'autel, y ayant dedans un linge fin et très propre entre les plis duquel elles sont enveloppées comme entre deux suaires.'[3] The sacristan is directed to take the greatest care in lowering and raising the eucharistic vessel, in order to avoid an accident.[4]

A copy of an act drawn up by two notaries at Dijon (3 January, 1590), describing the damage caused by the Protestants in 1589, suggests that the modern form of tabernacle may have been in use at Cîteaux at that time.[5]

Baroque suspension for eucharistic reservation in Cistercian churches assumed a number of forms. At Bohéries, for example, the tabernacle was in the form of a wooden angel painted in white, holding a globe in his hand, in which the hosts were kept. A cord was affixed to the globe for the purpose of lowering and raising it.[6] Dom Martène said that at La Ferté the 'Blessed Sacrament is raised up in a ciborium sustained by the holy Virgin taken up into heaven by angels.'[7] A figure of the Virgin at Boquen held a bell-shaped ornament from which was suspended the vessel containing the Eucharist. The 'bell' has long since

[1] *Cistercienser Chronik*, 1909, p. 174.
[2] *Rituel . . . de* 1724, liv. I, chap. III, n. 3.
[3] *Ibid.*, part I, liv. i, chap. XVIII, n. i. [4] *Ibid.*
[5] 'A tabernacle of admirable workmanship and immense size was placed on (over) the high altar, in which the ciborium of the Blessed Sacrament was kept.' MS., library, Abbaye des Dombes.
[6] MS. *Mémoires de Nicolas-Joseph Grain*, from information supplied by Fr. Anselme Dimier, monk of Scourmont.
[7] Martène, *op. cit.*, part I, p. 226; Beaunier, *Receuil Historique des Abbayes et Prieurez de France*, t. II, pp. 463–64.

disappeared, but the figure, which was taken to Lambelle at the Revolution to serve as the goddess of reason, is found today above the interior of the west door in the former collegiate church of Notre Dame.[1] A number of writers have also mentioned the statue of the Virgin which held the suspension of the Eucharist over the high altar at La Trappe.[2] Louis du Bois in his history of the abbey said that the high altar had been reconstructed in 1720, but that the suspension was older. The Sacrament was hung below a small flag, which the Virgin held in her right hand; while the single word *θεοτόκω* was inscribed under the figure.[3] An explanation of the figure was given by Armand de Rancé:

> Si quaeras natum cur matris dextera gestat,
> Sola fuit tanto munere digna parens;
> Non poterat fungi majori munere mater,
> Nec poterat major dextera ferre Deum.

A description of the method of reservation in the house of the French exiles at Val Sainte has been left to us by a traveller who visited the house in 1812: 'The tabernacle,' he said, 'took the form of a royal crown, held up near the roof by two badly sculptured angels: not to say hideous. When a religious wanted Holy Communion, the ciborium, hidden in the crown, was lowered by means of a cord, and then pulled up again.'[4]

An example of this Cistercian baroque suspension is found today at Valloires near Montreuil sur Mer (1741–56), although no longer serving as a receptacle for the Eucharist. A great palm tree of iron, curving into a magnificent

[1] It would be a gracious act to restore the figure to Boquen, which is again in Cistercian hands, and where the Eucharist is reserved in a hanging pyx.

[2] Martène, *op. cit.*, part I, p. 75; Moléon, *Voyages Liturgiques de France* (Paris, 1718), p. 225.

[3] Louis du Bois, *Histoire civile, religieuse, et littéraire de l'abbaye de la Trappe* (Paris, 1824), pp. 214–15.

[4] Tarenne, *Voyage à la Val-Sainte* (1812), p. 26.

crozier adorned with foliage, rises above the rococo tabernacle of the high altar. Little cupids flutter round the base of the trunk, which is entwined with branches of olive and lilies. A fringed canopy is suspended from the crozier, beneath which hangs the eucharistic dove. The dove is lowered by means of a small wheel concealed in the trunk of the palm tree, letting down a cord which passes over a pulley hanging from the top. It is held by two little white angels with outstretched limbs.[1] The suspension was largely the work of the Austrian exile, Simon Georges, Baron von Pfaffenhofen ('Pfaff'), and is more Austrian or Bavarian in style than French.

Germany

Several of the post-Tridentine councils and synods in Germany gave little or no indication as to where the Eucharist should be reserved, saying no more than the decrees of Innocent III and Honorius III in respect to security measures.

About the end of the sixteenth century, the administrator of the diocese of Ratisbon, James Myller, in his book *Ornatus ecclesiasticus* (1591), agreed that the Sacrament might be reserved *in altari*, as well as in sacrament houses.[2] The synods of Brixen (1603) and Constance (1609) prescribed *aut in altari aut modo consueto in armario fieri posse*,[3] as did also those of Cologne (1622) and Paderborn (1688).[4] Others again recommended *in altari*, while admitting the possibility of other modes of reservation: Osnabruck (1628), Münster (1655), Hildesheim (1652), and Trier (1678).[5] No alternative

[1] Pierre Dubois, *L'Abbaye de Valloires*, pp. 47-49, n.d.
[2] Köster, *op. cit.*, p. 122.
[3] Hartzheim, *op. cit.*, t. VIII, p. 564; t. VIII, p. 858.
[4] Köster, *op. cit.*, p. 125, n. 36. [5] *Ibid.*, n. 37.

to *in altari* was offered by the provincial synod of Salzburg (1616) and the diocesan synod of Freising, nor yet in the rituals of Strasburg (1742) and Constance (1766).[1] Warmia[2] in the synod of 1610 had the distinction of being the first diocese of German language to prescribe *in altari*, though adding by way of a rider: 'in so far as it is possible and able to be carried out fittingly.'[3]

Aumbries and sacrament houses (*domuncula sacramentaria*) were in some cases ordered to be destroyed, 'lest the faithful be led into error,' whatever that might have meant; but the traditional modes of reserving the Eucharist were by no means abrogated.[4] So late as 1860 the provincial council of Cologne, while deferring to the canons and the Congregation of Rites, admitted that the tabernacle or *scrinium* for reserving the Sacrament might be either on the altar or away from it in a sacramental tower.[5] In the same year also, the council of Prague (Bohemia) decreed that reservation *in armariolis seu pastophoriis columnae* was not to be discontinued, and those existing should be retained, on account of the reverence paid to them by their ancestors, as well as for their artistic value.[6] Yet so long ago as 1605 a synod of Prague had said that, although the traditional place for the reserved Sacrament was on the right side of the altar, it was more seemly (*decentius*) for the Eucharist to be on the high altar itself or, possibly, in some chapel outside the choir, so long as it was conspicuous.[7] In 1863, the Congregation of Rites prohibited the bishop of Limburg from reintroducing sacrament houses in his diocese, without, however, forbidding their use where it was already the custom.[8]

[1] *Ibid.*, n. 38. [2] Ermland, now Poland.
[3] Hartzheim, *op. cit.*, t. IX, p. 146.
[4] Köster, *op. cit.*, p. 125. [5] *Ibid.* [6] *Ibid.*, n. 39.
[7] Hartzheim, *op. cit.*, t. VIII, pp. 701, 752; Köster, *op. cit.*, pp. 122–23.
[8] Köster, *op. cit.*, pp. 125–26.

Still today, there are churches in Germany which reserve in a sacrament house, as we find in the former Cistercian churches of Altenberg and Salem. Permission for the use of a hanging pyx was granted to the Benedictine abbey of Maria Laach in 1954,[1] but no advantage has yet been taken of the indult. A similar privilege has been conceded to Montserrat in Catalonia.

It is sometimes said that a particular mode of reserving the Eucharist was traditional in a diocese, but this has by no means always been the case. In Münster, for example, *in altari* was prescribed in 1279; *locus singularis, mundus et signatus* in 1536; *locus dignus* in 1652; *in medio altaris* as 'desirable' in 1655; *locus dignus* again in 1668; *in turriculis sacramentalibus* as permissible in 1860.[2]

Belgium

The post-Tridentine regulations regarding the reservation of the Eucharist would seem to have been met with a somewhat feeble response in the baroque centuries. An attempt to enforce them was made at Namur in 1639, with directions that the venerable Sacrament should be reserved 'in the middle of the high altar,'[3] but there would not seem to have been any very general response. Several of the Belgian synods, however, admitted the prescription as a legitimate alternative. This was the case at Ypres in 1609, where a choice of sacrament house (*a dextro latere summi altaris*), aumbry (*in muro*), or altar (*in ipso altari*) was given.[4] Antwerp, also, in the following year (1610) permitted either altar (*in medio altaris*) or aumbry (*in pariete a septemtrione juxta*

[1] *Reinische Merkur*, 15 October, 1954.
[2] Köster, *op. cit.*, p. 127. [3] Maffei, *op. cit.*, p. 100, n. i.
[4] Syn. Ypres, 1609, tit. V, cap. V; Hartzheim, *op. cit.*, t. VIII, p. 806.

altare) reservation.[1] Yet a tabernacle on the altar was the exception, and churches vied with one another in erecting or restoring wall tabernacles or sacrament houses.

A wall tabernacle, savouring of the Flemish renaissance, was set up at Termonde in 1629, while at Minderhout in the province of Antwerp there is one dating from 1738, on the epistle side of the sanctuary.[2] A number of sacrament houses were restored in the early years of the seventeenth century, as a result of their destruction by the Iconoclasts. This was the case at St. Martin's, Alost, in 1604 and St. Sulpice, Diest, in 1615.[3] It is, however, remarkable that the aumbry in Notre Dame, Bruges, was restored so lately as 1863,[4] and a sacrament house was erected in Notre-Dame au-dela de la Dyle at Malines in 1902.[5] Yet sacrament houses were not always retained, even in Belgium, and they were destroyed at St. Gertrude, Louvain, in *c.* 1712 and St. Quentin, Hasselt, in 1818.[6]

Still today the Eucharist is reserved in a number of churches away from the altar, and in the Cistercian abbey of Orval, there is a highly decorative aumbry in the north wall of the presbytery. This was not, however, the mode of reservation in the eighteenth century, and at the apostolic visitation of the house in 1725 the Premonstratensian abbot of Grimbergen, spoke of 'a silver dove under a little canopy': *supra mensam altaris sub parva umbella.*[7] Elsewhere, also, modes of reservation other than in a tabernacle have been introduced of recent years. At Pontorson, an aumbry is in use, to the left of the high altar, built into the east wall. More remarkable still is the aumbry recently constructed

[1] Syn. Antwerp, 1610; *Ibid.*, p. 991.
[2] Maffei, *op. cit.*, p. 81.
[3] *Ibid.*, pp. 113–14.
[4] *Ibid.*, p. 115.
[5] *Ibid.*, pp. 115–16.
[6] *Ibid.*, pp. 119–20.
[7] *Archief. van het Aartsbisdom*, Utrecht, XV, 420.

in the chapel of the sisters, living under the Benedictine rule, above the catacombs of S. Priscilla in Rome. The altar stands away from the wall. Pope John XXIII paid a visit to the chapel and was expressly shown the aumbry, at which the pontiff gave no sign of disapproval. In this present year (1964), the new church of St. Martin of Tours at Aycliffe, Dover, has been provided with an aumbry for the Eucharist. It is, however, clear that the present mind of the Holy See is that there should be a tabernacle fixed to the middle of the altar, and that the more ancient modes of reserving the Eucharist are no longer permissible, apart from exceptional circumstances.[1]

A decree of the Congregation of Rites, issued in 1957 on the question of 'other modes,' strictly forbade an eucharistic tabernacle that was not on the altar itself, and proceeded to give examples: in the wall (*in pariete*), or at the side or behind the altar, or in sacrament houses (*in aediculis*) or pillars (*in columnis*) separated from the altar. Yet, even here, exceptions were envisaged, and sacrament houses were permitted, if their use was an 'immemorial custom.'[2] The decree recalls also the thirteenth-century injunctions of popes and councils as to the paramount importance of security measures, so that there may be no danger of profanation.[3] In the previous year (1956), a 'tabernacle away from the altar' had been condemned by Pope Pius XII in his address to the participants of the Assisi liturgical congress. It was, said the pontiff, a separation of two things that ought to be united, either as regards their origin or nature.[4]

[1] *Cod. Jur. Canon*, 1918, lib. 3, pars 3, tit. XV, can. 1269, i.
[2] *S.R.C.*, 1 June, 1957, n. 8. [3] *Ibid.*, n. 5.
[4] *Acta Apost. Sedis*, XLVIII (1956), p. 722.

25: ALTAR OF RESERVATION

At the beginning of the Reformation period, Paris de Grassis (d. 1528), in a book on ceremonial, advised that the Sacrament should be removed from the altar before a pontifical Mass, as it was unfitting for the bishop either to sit down or to wear a mitre in the presence of the Eucharist.[1] The *Caeremoniale Episcoporum* of Clement VIII (1600) directed that what remained of the sacred species after Communion on Easter Day might either stay on the altar or be taken '*in locum repositionis*' by another priest, but the edition of Innocent X (1651) had no such alternative, and ordered the removal immediately after Communion. Decrees of the Congregation of Bishops and Regulars in 1579 and 1594, had forestalled the *Caeremoniale Episcoporum* in directing the Eucharist to be reserved on a side altar in cathedral churches, as the pontifical ceremonies might cause unintentional irreverence. A side altar was prescribed also in the *Rituale Sacramentorum* (1584) and the *Rituale Romanum* (1614). However, in answer to queries in 1579 and again in 1594 (twice), Rome left the choice of the altar on which to reserve the Sacrament to the bishops of the respective dioceses.[2]

It had been the wish of the Grand Duke of Tuscany at the council of Pistoia (1786) that the picture over an altar should represent the titular of the church, but an exception was made for the altar of the Blessed Sacrament, which should have only the cross.[3]

[1] Peter de Grassis, *Caerem. Card. et Episc.*, lib. i, cap. XVIII (Rome, 1569), p. 34.
[2] Köster, *op. cit.*, p. 123. [3] Counc. Pistoia, 1786, art. XXVIII.

'inari

PLATE 17

HIGH ALTAR, SS. ANNUNZIATA, FLORENCE
With Sixteenth-century Tabernacle behind and above the Altar

ıg page 194

PLATE 18

A Spanish Pyx

A renaissance pyx in silver. Parcel-gilt of the Sixteenth century. Designed for the reservation of the Blessed Sacrament when enclosed in a tabernacle

Canon Law, following the directions of the *Caeremoniale Episcoporum*, requires churches in which the choir office is recited before the high altar to reserve the Eucharist elsewhere.[1]

[1] *Cod. Jur. Canon.* (1918), lib. 3, pars 3, tit. XV, can. 1268, 3, 4.

26: MULTIPLICITY OF PLACES OF RESERVATION

IN 1597, a decree of the Congregation of Rites forbade the Sacrament to be reserved in several places in the same church at the same time, as also did the Congregation of Bishops and Regulars in 1620. In spite of this, however, a decree of the Congregation of Rites to the archbishop of Santiago (Chile) in 1861, failed to condemn the practice, although it was very usual in the country, especially among the regulars.[1] Seven years later (1868), the same Congregation recognized the usage of the cathedral church of Urgel, where for more than sixty years the Eucharist had been reserved on the high altar and also in a side chapel, which had its own separate door.[2]

In the baroque centuries, churches which had retained the hanging pyx frequently reserved in two places, as suspension was an inconvenient mode for the Communion of the faithful. Instances of this were recorded by Moléon in his *Voyages Liturgiques*, as, for example, at Angers, where in the collegiate churches the chapter had one method of reservation and the parishioners another.[3] There had indeed been legislation authorizing dual reservation, and in 1565 the provincial council of Compostella had directed that cathedral churches, which have a care of souls, must see that the Eucharist is also reserved in another chapel, appointed by the bishop.[4] The synod of Tournai (1574) prescribed that the Sacrament should be kept in one place '*pro adoratione*' and in another '*pro viatico infirmorum*.'[5]

[1] Köster, *op. cit.*, p. 132.
[2] *Ibid.*
[3] Moléon, *op. cit.*, p. 103.
[4] Köster, *op. cit.*, p. 133.
[5] *Ibid.*

In the nineteenth century, the practice was forbidden by the provincial council of Bordeaux (1850) and the plenary council of Baltimore (1866), but other synodical decrees made no mention of any prohibition, and the custom had occurred in past centuries in both France and North America.[1] The provincial council of Vienna (1858) only permitted it if the church was very large (*perampla*) or there was some pressing necessity (*evidentem necessitatem*). Stefansdom in Vienna reserves today at an altar near the entrance to the cathedral church and also at the east end of the north aisle. *Perampla* may well be the reason, but a spokesman said that the size of the building presupposed two churches. The more ancient Franciscan houses in several of the German provinces were accustomed to reserve on the altar of the choir for the community and on another altar for the Communion of the faithful, and the custom was confirmed by St. Pius X, although it was not continued in the houses founded after the *Kulturkampf*.[2]

The code of Canon Law in Canon 1268 forbids the Eucharist to be habitually reserved on more than one altar in the same church.[3]

[1] *Ibid.* [2] *Ibid.* [3] *Cod. Jur. Canon.* (1918), lib. III, pars 3, tit. XV, can. 1268.

27: MATERIAL OF THE TABERNACLE

In 1575, the Congregation of Bishops and Regulars directed that the tabernacle should be made of wood, although it was rather in the nature of a recommendation than a strict obligation.[1] Marble or brass was preferred in the Roman Ritual of the Sacraments (1584), but wood was permitted.[2] A number of synods were of a like mind, if it was impossible to obtain marble or some precious metal. A similar choice of material was prescribed in an instruction of the Congregation of the Discipline of the Sacraments in 1938, advising, in the following year, the use of an iron coffer (*vera arca ferrea*).[3]

Risk of fire motivated the demand of visitors in the diocese of Breslau (1687–88) that the tabernacle should be 'walled' (*murata*) and furnished with an 'iron door' (*porta ferrea*).[4] St. Charles Borromeo issued instructions that wooden tabernacles must be of such a quality that they were proof against damp.[5] The fourth provincial council of Milan (1576), also, directed that tabernacles must be so disposed that the Sacrament can be easily taken out, and it should never be necessary to climb on the altar.[6] A bronze tabernacle in the form of a tower was given to the cathedral church of Milan by Pius IV, a Milanese by birth.

Wooden tabernacles were normally gilded, and a decree to that effect was issued by the Congregation of Bishops and Regulars in 1575. The interior was to be lined with

[1] Köster, *op. cit.*, p. 136. [2] *Ibid.*
[3] *Ibid.*, pp. 216–17. [4] *Ibid.*, p. 137.
[5] *Instruct. Fabr. Eccles.*; Ratti, *op. cit.*, vol. II, p. 1425.
[6] Provinc. Counc. Milan, 1576; Mansi, *op. cit.*, t. XXXIV, col. 221–22.

silk.[1] A fine specimen of an eighteenth-century gilded wooden tabernacle, formerly in the Cistercian abbey of Morimond, is found today in the neighbouring parish church of Fresnoy.

[1] Maffei, *op. cit.*, p. 127.

28: FORM OF THE TABERNACLE

IN the time of the Renaissance, tabernacles often had the appearance of temples, adorned with columns, pediments and domes, and such accessories as were proper to constructions of the kind. Thus an inventory of the papal chapel in 1547 says: '*Un tabernacolo d'argento, in modo di tempio*.'[1]

Rome has never given a positive norm as to the form of a tabernacle; while the first provincial council of Milan (1565) and the *Instructio Fabricae Ecclesiae* were chiefly concerned with its security and general appearance.[2] The Roman Ritual of the Sacraments (1584) forbade any perforation in the tabernacle, for fear that mice, flies, gnats or ants might get inside.[3] A possible intrusion of insects or dust was the concern also of the synods of Brixen (1603), Namur (1625), Ypres (1629) and Paderborn (1688).[4] The provincial council of Prague in 1860 prescribed a covering of some precious metal on the inside, if the door of the tabernacle should be perforated.[5] In reply to an inquiry from the General Master of Ceremonies (*Magister Caeremoniarum Generalis*) for the kingdom of Spain, the Congregation of Rites in 1806 forbade apertures in the tabernacle, whereby the eucharistic vessel could be seen, and a similarly negative reply was given to the archbishop of Valladolid respecting the reservation of the host on Holy Thursday for the Mass of the Presanctified on the following day.[6]

[1] Barbier de Montault, *Œuvres Complètes*, t. I (Poitiers, 1889), p. 315.
[2] Ratti, *op. cit.*, vol. 2, pp. 46, 1425. [3] Köster, *op. cit.*, p. 139.
[4] Hartzheim, *op. cit.*, t. VIII, p. 564; t. IX, p. 340; t. IX, p. 499; t. X, p. 150.
[5] Köster, *op. cit.*, p. 139. [6] *Ibid.*, pp. 139–40.

It would seem probable that the diocesan statutes of the bishop of Verona, Matteo Giberti (1524–43), would have been the first to require the tabernacle to be firmly fixed to the altar (*bene et firmiter stabiliatur*), that sacrilegious hands might be unable to remove it.[1] The regulation was repeated by St. Charles Borromeo in the *Instructio Fabricae Ecclesiae*, the diocesan synod of 1582 and the *Sacramentale Ambrosianum*.[2] It was not, however, prescribed in the liturgical books of Rome, nor, at first, by any decree of the Holy See, although its suitability had been expressed by a number of councils and synods: Aix (1585), Toulouse (1590), Aquileia (1596), Antwerp (1610), and Paderborn (1688).[3] An immovable tabernacle, as we have seen, is expressly enjoined in the Codex of Canon Law.

[1] *Constit.*, tit. V, cap. II; Köster, *op. cit.*, p. 140.
[2] Ratti, *op. cit.*, vol. 2, pp. 1425, 1047; *Sacram. Ambros.*, I, cap. 1295.
[3] Köster, *op. cit.*, p. 140, n. 108.

29: ORNAMENTATION OF THE TABERNACLE

St. Charles Borromeo recommended tabernacles to be gilded and ornamented with symbols of the Passion. The choice of subject might well have been designed to exclude anything that savoured of the profane. We must remember that it was the age of the renaissance when classical imagery was much in vogue. In 1570, the council of Malines had forbidden the portrayal of satyrs, fauns, sirens or nymphs, as unsuitable for the decoration of tabernacles and sacrament houses.[1]

The gilding of tabernacles was enjoined in the pastoral instruction of the bishop of Ypres (1768), as well as in the provincial councils of Embrun (1727) and Ravenna (1855). A suitable (*decens*) picture on the door was authorized by the provincial council of Avignon (1725), to serve as a substitute for gilding in poor churches.[2]

A lining of silk was prescribed for the interior of the tabernacle by the fourth provincial council of Milan (1576).[3]

The use of a corporal inside the tabernacle was not ordered in Roman legislation prior to the Code of Canon Law (1918), and there was no mention of it in the regulations of St. Charles. It was, however, enjoined in a number of synods as, for example, Narbonne in 1609.[4] A similar injunction is found in the Cistercian general chapter of 1601[5] and also in the ritual proper to the mother house of Cîteaux

[1] Mansi, *op. cit.*, t. XXXIV, col. 589–90. [2] Köster, *op. cit.*, pp. 141–42.
[3] Mansi, *op. cit.*, t. XXXIV, col. 221–22. A similar ruling occurs in the pastoral instruction of the bishop of Ypres in 1768.
[4] Köster, *op. cit.*, p. 144.
[5] *Cap. Gen.* 1601, cap. VII, 28; Canivez, *op. cit.*, t. VII, p. 207.

(1724): 'Sous le pied du ciboire il y aura un petit corporalier de forme convenable.'[1]

A baroque variation of canopy (*conopeo*, *padiglione*) over the tabernacle was recommended by St. Charles Borromeo: an ample veil surmounted by a crown and open at the sides, the extremities of which are fixed to the wall. It was to be wrapped completely round the tabernacle on ferias in the form of a tower; be slightly open in front, so as to make the tabernacle visible, on feasts; and be fully open on solemnities. Recent synodical decrees have continued to prescribe red as the normal colour, with *morello* in Advent and Lent.[2] Red is the colour for the Eucharist in the Ambrosian rite, even for the cover of the pyx or monstrance. This *conopeo*[3] is the successor of the drapery (*drapperia*, *velum*) that in the middle ages hung as a kind of 'tent' before the wall tabernacles and other eucharistic structures, or of that covering (*opertorium*) for the sacred vessels which reverence demanded.[4] A *conopaeum* was enjoined in the Roman ritual of 1614,[5] and accepted in a number of dioceses, although there remained a certain freedom in the matter.[6] Councils and synods determined the material, which was generally silk.[7] St. Charles advised silk interwoven with gold or silver, when this was possible.[8]

[1] *Rit. propre de l'Abbaye de Cisteaux*, 1724, part I, liv. i, chap. XVIII, n.i.

[2] *Morello*, 'blackish': a darker colour than ordinary violet.

[3] *Conopeo*, *χωνοπεῖον*, *zanzariera*, *velo*. [4] Righetti, *op. cit.*, vol. I, p. 440.

[5] *Rit. Rom.*, 1614, *De SS. Euch. Sacr.*, p. 49; edit. 1925, tit. IV, cap. I, n. 6, pp. 122–23.

[6] Köster, *op. cit.*, pp. 144–45. [7] *Ibid.*, pp. 145–46. [8] Ratti, *op. cit.*, vol. 2, 1575.

30: WHAT MAY BE IN THE TABERNACLE

THE tabernacle at the time of the Reformation still frequently contained both the Eucharist and the holy oil. The fourth provincial council of Milan (1576) and also the Ambrosian sacramentary, authorized by St. Charles, said that there must only be the Sacrament in the tabernacle: *ab alia re vacuum*;[1] but the *Sacerdotale Romanum*, which appeared in 1579, clearly envisaged a reservation of the two together.[2] Several of the synods in the latter part of the sixteenth century and the beginning of the seventeenth had equally permitted this dual reservation, although sometimes with a qualification: *ubi commode alio loco fieri non posset*, as we find in the synods of Olmütz (1591), Brixen (1603), and Metz (1604).[3] In 1580, the synod of Breslau expressly authorized a single locked receptacle for the Eucharist, chrism and holy oils.[4] Joint reservation was prescribed also by the synods of Haarlem (1564), Prague (1565), and Augsburg (1567),[5] and in the first provincial council of Mexico (1555). Gradually, however, the example set by St. Charles came to be the general custom, but so late as 1766 the ritual of Constance permitted the older practice under certain conditions.[6]

Sometimes the monstrance was kept in the tabernacle, and the possibility of this was taken into account in a new construction: provincial council of Aix (1585) and synods of Prague (1606), Ghent (1650), Cologne (1662), Chelmo (1745), Westminster (1852), and Vienna (1858).[7]

[1] *Ibid.*, p. 349. [2] *Sacerdot. Roman.*, 1579, pp. 105r–105v.
[3] Hartzheim, *op. cit.*, t. VIII, pp. 337, 542; t. IX, p. 765.
[4] *Ibid.*, t. VII, p. 893. [5] *Ibid.*, t. VII, pp. 15, 32, 166.
[6] Dold, *Die Konstanzer Ritualientexte*, p. 55.
[7] Köster, *op. cit.*, pp. 148, 148, n. 148.

31: CARE IN RESERVING THE EUCHARIST

THE safety of the sacred species had always been of paramount importance in any consideration of reservation, and to this end a resident priest was required. A *motu proprio* of Gregory XVI (1833) had granted permission for the Daughters of Charity to reserve the Eucharist, so long as there was a resident priest.[1] Thirty years later, however, in reply to a request of the bishop of Orihuela (Spain), the Congregation of Rites had permitted the Eucharist to be reserved in the private oratory of these sisters, even if there was no resident priest, and indults were granted to the vicar apostolic of Hong Kong in 1874, and to the bishop of Fulda in 1883, although permissions of the kind were far from numerous.[2]

Reservation of the Eucharist in the choir or enclosure of a convent is forbidden by canon 1267 of the Codex of Canon Law (1918).

The key of the tabernacle is normally in the custody of the priest, and this has been expressly enjoined in a number of councils and synods: Salzburg (1569) and Olmütz (1591) among others.[3] An exception existed in Spain and the Kingdom of Naples, where the key was held by a layman.[4] A subdeacon was permitted to open the tabernacle by a synod of Cologne in 1622 and a provincial council in 1860.[5] The *motu proprio* of Gregory XVI to the Daughters of Charity in 1833 stipulated that the key should be in the safe possession of the sister sacristan.[6]

[1] *Ibid.*, pp. 149–50.
[2] *Ibid.*, p. 150.
[3] Hartzheim, *op. cit.*, t. VII, p. 353; t. VIII, p. 339.
[4] Köster, *op. cit.*, p. 152.
[5] *Ibid.*
[6] *Ibid.*, p. 154.

32: PYX

SYNODS continued to insist that there should be two pyxes in the tabernacle, so that one of them could be taken to the sick. The synod of Metz (1699) added the warning that if a church failed to comply with this regulation within three months the culprits would be severely punished.[1] The growing number of communicants necessitated a larger pyx. The hosts for Communion were normally placed on the corporal and distributed from the paten, but a pyx was used if there were many communicants.[2]

[1] Hartzheim, *op. cit.*, t. X, p. 236.

[2] Cf. provincial councils of Aix 1585) and Toulouse (1590); synod of Pavia (1612). Köster, *op. cit.*, p. 157.

33: MATERIAL OF THE PYX

THE *Sacerdotale Romanum* (1579) gave no indication as to the material suitable for the pyx, but intimated that it should be of such a kind that it was impossible to be gnawed through by mice.[1] St. Charles, on the other hand, enjoined precious metal in his *Instructio Fabricae Ecclesiae*: gold or silver.[2] Silver was ordered by the Congregation of Rites (1588), with a prohibition of the use of ivory,[3] and the same metal was prescribed in the *Rituale Sacramentorum Romanum* (1584) and the *Caeremoniale Episcoporum* (1600).[4] The Roman ritual of 1614, mindful of poor churches, said no more than: *ex solida decentique materia*,[5] and the Codex of Canon Law (1918) has reaffirmed this.[6] Many of the synods approved the use of silver, with the interior of the pyx gilded.

A certain amount of doubt has attended the use of ivory. It had been permitted by the synods of Cambrai (1550) and St. Omer (1583),[7] but the Congregation of Rites (1588) and several of the synods considered the material to be too inferior. Ivory is not mentioned by many of the synods in their care for the eucharistic vessels, although this may have been on account of its comparative rarity.

In 1625, the synodal statutes of Namur prohibited the use of pyxes of copper and tin,[8] although they had been

[1] *Sacerdot. Rom.*, 1579, tract. IV, cap. LXXXII.
[2] Ratti, *op. cit.*, vol. 2, pp. 1576–77.
[3] The interior of the pyx was to be gilded. Köster, *op. cit.*, p. 158.
[4] *Rit. Sacr. Rom.*, p. 299; *Caerem. Episc.*, lib. 2, cap. XXIX, n. 2 and cap. XXX, n. 2.
[5] *Rit. Rom.*, 1614, p. 48; edit. 1925, tit. IV, cap. I, n. 5t, p. 122.
[6] *Cod. Jur. Canon*, 1918, lib. 3, pars 3, tit. XV, can. 1270.
[7] Hartzheim, *op. cit.*, t. VI, p. 900; t. VII, p. 922.
[8] *Ibid.*, t. VII, p. 913.

admitted as suitable in the previous century. Copper, without any restriction as to its use, was approved by the synods of Cambrai (1550) and St. Omer (1583), but, following a decree of the Congregation of Rites, a later synod of Cambrai (1661), permitted its use with certain limitations.[1] It was, however, definitely excluded by the synods of Namur (1637), Cologne (1662), and Besançon (1707).[2] Cologne gave a 'liability to rust' (*quia aeruginem causabat*) as the reason for its prohibition.[3]

Tin was envisaged as a possibility by the synods of St. Omer (1583) and Cologne (1662), and, with a certain restriction, by the synod of Cambrai (1661).[4] St. Charles permitted its use in a case of extreme poverty,[5] as also did the synod of Paderborn (1688).[6] It was, however, forbidden as a material for the 'cup' (*cuppa*) by the synods of Namur (1639) and Besançon (1707).[7]

Pyxes fashioned from yellow copper ore (*aurichalcea deaurata*) were admitted in the diocese of Pavia until 1619, when the permission, except for the base, was revoked.[8] Its use for the base and lid of the pyx was approved by the synod of Prague (1605);[9] while the synod of Manfredonia (1567)[10] and the *Instructio Fabricae Ecclesiae* of St. Charles[11] permitted *aurichalcea*, without any restriction, if a church was too poor to afford silver.

Brass (*aes*) was altogether prohibited by the synods of Cologne (1662) and Paderborn (1688), as the 'rust, which it brings about, causes vomiting.'[12]

Pyxes of wood were not originally forbidden, and the visitation decrees at Pavia in 1576 said that the 'ciborium'

[1] *Ibid.*, t. IX, p. 889.
[2] *Ibid.*, t. IX, pp. 573, 986; t. X, p. 316.
[3] *Ibid.*, t. IX, p. 986.
[4] *Ibid.*, t. IX, p. 889.
[5] Ratti, *op. cit.*, vol. 2, pp. 1576–77.
[6] Hartzheim, *op. cit.*, t. X, p. 151.
[7] *Ibid.*, t. IX, p. 573, t. X; pp. 316–17.
[8] Köster, *op. cit.*, p. 160.
[9] Hartzheim, *op. cit.*, t. VIII, p. 702.
[10] Mansi, *op. cit.*, t. XXXV, col. 837.
[11] Ratti, *op. cit.*, vol. 2, pp. 1576–77.
[12] Köster, *op. cit.*, p. 160.

must be at least of 'gilded wood' (*rameum deauratum*), although the use of wood was proscribed shortly afterwards.[1] It was specifically forbidden in 1591 in the visitations in the diocese of Benevento,[2] and, in the following century, in the diocese of Breslau (1651–52[3]), as well as by the synods of Cologne (1662) and Paderborn (1688), as there was a danger of a wooden pyx breaking (*ob periculum fractionis*[4]). They were, however, countenanced by the ritual of Beauvais as late as 1783, covered with silk (*bombyce*). Towards the end of the century, both the cathedral and the church of St. Stephen in Beauvais, still used a wooden pyx, transferring the sacred species to a silver ciborium for distributing Holy Communion.[5]

There is no direct evidence for the use of glass or earthenware (*testacea*) pyxes, but they were forbidden, *ob periculum fractionis*, in the synods of Cologne (1662) and Paderborn (1688), as also were pyxes of stone, *ob humiditatem et gravitatem*.[6] Pyxes of glass under any circumstances whatsoever were proscribed by the Congregation of Rites in reply to a petition from the bishop of Mandoñedo (Spain) in 1880.[7]

Agate, jasper or crystal pyxes are rare, but in 1861, on the occasion of the beatification of Benedict Joseph Labre, Pius IX gave a crystal pyx to the church of S. Maria ai Monti in Rome.[8]

More frequent Communion necessitated a larger form of pyx, which became more like our actual ciborium.

The earliest post-Reformation English ciborium is at Danby Hall, near Middleham in Yorkshire, where it was used in the chapel of the Scropes. It dates from the time of Charles I.[9]

[1] *Ibid.* [2] Mansi, *op. cit.*, t. XXXVI, col. 502–03. [3] Köster, *op. cit.*, p. 160.
[4] Hartzheim, *op. cit.*, t. IX, p. 986; t. X, p. 151.
[5] Köster, *op. cit.*, pp. 160–61; Corblet, *op. cit.*, vol. II, p. 290.
[6] *Ibid.*, p. 161. [7] *Ibid.* [8] *Ibid.* [9] Oman, *op. cit.*, pp. 281–82.

34: MANNER OF PLACING THE EUCHARIST IN THE PYX

It was customary in the middle ages for the Eucharist to be reserved in a small pyx within a larger one, and this was enjoined in the visitation decrees for the diocese of Breslau in 1561, 1567–68, 1670 and 1687.[1] The *Ornatus Ecclesiasticus* and the synod of Cambrai (1661) concurred in this, if the larger pyx was not silver.[2] There was, however, no reference to the practice in the Roman liturgical books and decrees, and it was not mentioned by St. Charles. In any case, the custom soon fell into desuetude, as the two receptacles were inconvenient now that reservation was for the Communion of the faithful, rather than specifically for the sick. In the sixteenth and seventeenth centuries, a number of synods advocated the placing of the Sacrament within the pyx on a piece of material (*aliquis pannus*), and so late as 1707 it had been prescribed by the synod of Besançon.[3] It was by no means universally approved. The Roman ritual of 1614 had made no mention of it, and it was specifically forbidden by the synods of Constance (1616) and Antwerp (1643).[4] The cleansing of the pyx would be easier without any linen or cloth, and insertions of the kind were thought by some to attract insects.

[1] Köster, *op. cit.*, p. 163.
[2] *Ornat. Eccles.*, pars 2, cap. XVIII, p. 40; Hartzheim, *op. cit.*, t. IX, p. 40.
[3] Hartzheim, *op. cit.*, t. X, p. 316.
[4] *Ibid.*, t. IX, pp. 642, 670.

John R. Freeman

PLATE 19

COMBINED PYX AND MONSTRANCE

Silver-gilt, the two angels partly coloured. Spanish (Saragossa), about 1525

John R. Freeman

PLATE 20

GERMAN MONSTRANCE

Silver, parcel-gilt, set with pastes. Made at Augsburg, mark of Johann Zeckel. About 1700.

In the scene of the Last Supper the Consecrated Host is intended to fill the place of the figure of Christ in the midst of the disciples.

35: VEIL OF THE PYX

A VEIL ornamented with fringes of silk was enjoined by the synods of Cambrai (1550) and Chelmo (1583),[1] but many of the synods and St. Charles Borromeo, while approving a veil, spoke of it in more general terms, which the Roman ritual followed, in directing that it should be white in colour.

[1] *Ibid.*, t. VI, p. 700; t. VII, p. 976.

36: NUMBER OF HOSTS RESERVED

THE practice of giving Communion out of Mass necessitated the reservation of a larger number of particles than formerly, although both the *Sacerdotale Romanum* and the *Rituale Sacramentorum Romanum* caution against the consecration of too many hosts. A number of synods, especially in the first decades after the council of Trent, said that the particles should not exceed what might reasonably be sufficient for a month's Communions.[1] Churches in which it was not yet customary to give Communion out of Mass would have continued to reserve no more than were necessary for the sick. The Cistercian Congregation of Castile explicitly states in the *Usos* of 1568 and 1798 that the Sacrament was reserved for no other purpose.

The Codex of Canon Law, following the text of the Roman ritual, says merely that a sufficient number of particles should be reserved for the Communion of the sick and others of the faithful.[2]

[1] Köster, *op. cit.*, p. 165, n. 263.

[2] *Cod. Jur. Canon.*, can. 1270.

37: RENEWAL OF THE RESERVED SACRAMENT

THE Roman liturgical books immediately following Trent enjoined a frequent renewal of the reserved Sacrament, without specifying the exact time, but the *Caeremoniale Episcoporum* (1600) advised 'at least once a week.'[1] There was, however, no insistence upon a weekly renewal, and the regulations varied in the different dioceses: every week, every fortnight or, especially in Germany, once a month. Six weeks was the allotted span in the diocese of Chur in 1605, while the provincial council of Naples (1699) decided on once or twice in the week. The season of the year affected the time for renewal according to the provincial council of Avignon (1725) and the synod of Chelmo (1745): after fifteen days in winter and eight days in summer.[2]

No fixed time is given in the Codex of Canon Law, which says that the particles for reservation must be fresh and frequently renewed, with the old ones consumed, so that there may not be any fear of corruption. In spite of this, the norm for renewal is unquestionably a week.

Nothing has been stipulated *in jure communi* as to the precise day for the renewal of the Eucharist. Sunday, however, is the usual day, for the practical reason that there are more communicants on this day and a renewal is more easily carried out. Several synods[3] proposed Thursday, as it was the day of the institution of the Blessed Sacrament: a choice enjoined by St. Charles Borromeo.[4]

[1] *Caerem. Episc.*, 1606, lib. I, cap. VI, n. 2.
[2] Köster, *op. cit.*, p. 168.
[3] e.g., Prague (1605). Hartzheim, *op. cit.*. t. VIII, p. 702.
[4] *Sacram. Ambros.*; Ratti, *op. cit.*, vol. II, p. 1296. *Rituale Sacramentorum ad usum Mediolanensis*, 1815, p. 72.

38: LIGHT BEFORE THE RESERVED SACRAMENT

THE obligation for a light to burn continuously before the reserved Sacrament already existed here and there towards the end of the middle ages, which in the post-Tridentine era was extended by synods more or less universally, except in those churches where extreme poverty made it necessary to restrict the light to certain times and days. The synod of Cambrai (1550), before the close of the council, had directed that a light should burn before the reserved Sacrament in the churches of the diocese, as 'he is present, who dwells in inaccessible light and lightens our darkness.'[1] The Roman ritual of 1614 ordered 'many lights' (*lampades*), or 'at least one,' to burn continuously day and night.[2] Canon 1271 in the Codex of Canon Law (1918) has been taken from this ritual. The light has become a perpetual reminder of the Eucharistic presence, and its absence would lead one to suppose that the Sacrament was no longer in the tabernacle. Nothing, however, has been prescribed as to how the lamps are to be fixed, nor yet as to their colour or material. A council of Amalfi (1597) required the light to burn in front of the tabernacle, and not at the side,[3] but Canon Law says no more than *coram tabernaculo*.[4] For some grave reason, a bishop may authorize the removal of the Eucharist from the tabernacle to a safer and more secure place during the night, but the light must never be omitted.[5]

[1] Hartzheim, *op. cit.*, t. VI, p. 756.
[2] *Rit. Rom.*, 1614, p. 49; edit. 1917, tit. IV, cap. I, n. 6.
[3] Mansi, *op. cit.*, t. XXXV, col. 1109–10.
[4] *Cod. Jur. Can.*, can. 1271. [5] *Ibid.*, can. 1269, 3.

39: MONSTRANCE

THE form, as well as the material, of the monstrance has varied over the years: gold, silver, silver-gilt, copper, tin and pewter have all been employed. Wood even seems to have been used on occasions, as the synod of Namur (1639) directed the removal of wooden monstrances: '*remonstrantiae ligneae, penitus removeantur*.'[1]

The appearance of the monstrance was outlined by the fourth provincial council of Milan (1576): 'The tabernacle which serves for processions or exposition may be encircled with transparent glass or crystal, and it should have a lunette of the form prescribed by the instructions regarding ecclesiastical furniture, of such a kind that it can open easily and that particles, should there be any, can be easily gathered up. The lunette and its support at least should be of silver.'[2]

The monstrance was known sometimes as a 'melkisedech.'[3]

By the second half of the seventeenth century, the 'sun' form of monstrance had supplanted that of the 'little tower,' although it was already in existence in the time of Louis XII (1499–1515), and Raphael had depicted just such a one in his famous fresco in the *Stanza della Segnatura* of the Vatican (1509), known to subsequent ages as *La Disputa* ('The Discussion').[4]

[1] Maffei, *op. cit.*, p. 132. [2] Mansi, *op. cit.*, t. XXXIV, col. 222.
[3] Maffei, *op. cit.*, p. 133.
[4] The fresco is rather a 'Glorification of the Christian Faith.'

40: RITUAL RESERVATION

Triduum Sacrum

WITH the gradual disappearance of the Easter sepulchre, the importance of the 'altar of repose' for the reservation of the Eucharist on Holy Thursday, in readiness for the Mass of the Presanctified on the following day, was greatly enhanced. The 'altar' had come to be known as the 'sepulchre,' and, adorned with masses of flowers and countless lights, was attended by worshippers, often throughout the night. At the end of the Mass, the Blessed Sacrament was carried to the place of repose by the celebrant, as the hymn *Pange lingua* was sung. Then, on the following day, the Sacrament was brought to the altar for the Presanctified rite, after the Veneration of the Cross, and the hymn of Venantius Fortunatus, *Vexilla Regis*, was sung.

Now, with the 'Restored Order of Holy Week,' which became obligatory in the Roman rite by the decree *Maxima Redemptionis* of 16 November, 1955, the exterior splendour of the 'altar of repose' has been somewhat curtailed. It should be adorned austerely, as it is not an altar of exposition, but a place of reservation with hangings and lights. The visits of the faithful must be 'prudently linked with the liturgy,' and not protracted after midnight. The procession on Holy Thursday, which now takes place in the evening at the close of the Mass of the Last Supper, remains much as it was before, but on Good Friday the hosts for the Communion of the clergy and laity are brought to the altar by the deacon, attended by two taperers and an acolyte with an *ombrellino*, and three antiphons have taken the place of the hymn.[1]

The 'restored order' has been introduced also at Lyons, although the diocese has retained its own distinctive rite for the Mass. Four *induti*[2] had been directed in the Neo-Gallican missal of Montazet (1768) to carry the canopy over the Sacrament in the procession. Benediction was given at the 'altar of repose,' after a collect (*Respice, quaesumus, Domine*) and the singing of *O Salutaris hostia*.

Mass of the Presanctified has never figured in the Good Friday liturgy of the Ambrosian rite, but already in the time of St. Charles Borromeo a number of churches had introduced adoration of the Eucharist in the 'sepulchre' (*scurolo*) on Holy Thursday. The custom, which in 1576 was no more than optional devotion, was for the first time incorporated in the Ambrosian missal of 1594, with the function of the Blessed Sacrament copied from the Roman rite.[3] At the conclusion of the Mass on Holy Thursday, a procession to the *scurolo* is enjoined, with the singing of *Pange lingua*.[4] The Eucharist remains in this place of repose until Holy Saturday, when, after the blessing of the font in the liturgy of the Easter Vigil, the celebrant in white vestments goes processionally to the *scurolo* and takes the Sacrament to the altar, where it is replaced in the tabernacle. The rubric directs a '*lampada accesa*' to be carried, as it is ostensibly night-time.[5]

Triduum Sacrum: Rite of Braga

Alone of all the Churches of Western Christendom, Braga has retained the ceremony of the Easter sepulchre

[1] *Adoremus te, Christe*; *Per lignum servi facti sumus*; *Salvator mundi, salva nos.*

[2] *Induti* in the rite of Lyons are assistants vested as priests, deacons or subdeacons: known also as *symmistae* (*symmuses*) or *revestiti.*

[3] *Ufficio della Settimana Santa secondo il Rito Ambrosiano* (Milan, 1935), pp. 347–48, n. 2.

[4] *Ibid.*, pp. 347–50. [5] *Ibid.*, pp. 672–73.

in its medieval setting, with processions of 'burial' and 'resurrection,' although the actual ceremony in the primatial church cannot be traced back earlier than the second half of the sixteenth century.

Origin in Portugal

It is found in the Braga missal of Balthasar Limpo[1] (1558) for the first time in the cathedral church, and, probably in imitation of this usage, it appears in the first printed ceremonial of the Benedictine Congregation of Tibães in 1647. It is not, however, in the missal of the Spanish Congregation of Valladolid, which was published in 1568.

From whence did Braga derive the ceremony?

The first allusion to a procession of the kind is found in the *Leal Conselheiro* of King Duarte (1433–38), where in chapter ninety-seven, treating of the offices in the royal chapel, it is said that the liturgy on Good Friday lasted three and a half hours, and that in the course of it the Host was transferred from the high altar, after the Mass of the Presanctified, to the sepulchre: *mudamento do sagramento do altar pequeno do altar principal, e o oficio do altar e mudamento do sagramento do altar do muymento.*[2] It is significant that the ceremony should appear in the time of Duarte, who was the son of an English princess, who came to Portugal with her suite and chaplains. England, as we have seen, was a country in which the Easter sepulchre was a universal feature, and if, through the marriage of John I, some elements of the English liturgy were introduced into Portugal, it is not surprising that this usage should have been included.[3]

[1] *Missal. Bracen.*, 1558, pp. 305–08.
[2] *Leal Conselheiro*, edit. J. M. Piel (Lisbon, 1942), p. 356.
[3] Corbin, *Essai sur la Musique Religieuse Portugaise au Moyen Age* (1100–1385), chap. VIII, p. 314. Paris, 1952.

The role attributed to Paul de Portalegre (1510) may possibly have had a similar origin. A 'procession of burial' (*enterrão*) with the Sacrament carried on a bier, and a ceremonial identical with that observed today in the primatial church of Braga has been described by Campello de Macedo, grand treasurer of the Chapel Royal in the time of John IV (1640–56), in the *Thesouro de Ceremonías*.[1] It originated in Portugal, he says, with the secular canons of St. John the Evangelist (*Lóios*) in the convent of Vilar de Frades, near Barcelos, in the diocese of Braga, from whence the ceremony was extended to the cathedrals of the country.[2] The statement was confirmed by the chronicler of the canons, Francisco de Santa Maria, in *O Céu aberto na Terra* ('Heaven opened on earth'), who said further that the ceremony was introduced after a visit to Jerusalem by Paul de Portalegre, a member of the Congregation and the author of *Flos Sanctorum* and an 'Itinerary to the Holy Land,' who died in 1510. It has been concluded from this that the introduction of the procession was a direct result of the Palestinian visit, but it would be unlikely that the Eucharist would figure in an Orthodox commemoration of the burial.

A more probable explanation of its appearance in Portugal is that it was taken from the mother house of the Congregation, St. George in Alga (Venice), where it is known that a ceremony of the kind existed.[3]

Not many years after the adoption of the procession at Vilar de Frades, it is found in the Benedictine abbey of St.

[1] Campello de Macedo was master of ceremonies in the Benedictine abbey of Tibães in 1637. *Thesouro de Ceremonías de Tibães* (1637), p. 379.

[2] The canons of St. John were founded in Lisbon in 1420, and approved by Eugenius IV, receiving the constitutions of the canons of St. George in Alga, Venice.

[3] The church of St. Mark in Venice had a similar ceremony.

Saviour, at Paço de Sousa, in the diocese of Oporto. The abbot, John Álvares, who had been installed in 1461, introduced a liturgical reform, and in a letter to his community, dated from '*Bruxelas*' on 24 December, 1467, described in some detail the ceremonies for eight days in the year. Among these, 'Thursday of the Washing of the Feet' and 'Friday of the Passion' were included, when the Eucharist was directed to be reserved in a '*custodia*' above the altar, covered by a veil. On the Friday, the procession, the 'burial of our Lord,' and the singing of the Lamentations were to take place, after which the Eucharist and the wood of the cross were to be placed in the sepulchre (*moimento*), where they were to remain until the morning of Easter. Before the *Te Deum* of the Resurrection, the community, with candles in their hands and preceded by the crucifer and thurifer, were directed to go to the sepulchre. There the officiant censed the inside of the sepulchre and removed the cross, giving it to the deacon who carried it in the procession. Then the priest took out the Blessed Sacrament, intoning *Christus resurgens ex mortuis* as he did so, while the community continued: *Jam non moritur*, etc. The procession visited the cloisters, nave and adjacent church of Santa Maria do Corporal,[1] where the *Te Deum* was sung, at the conclusion of which the Eucharist and the cross were placed over the altar. The ceremony concluded with the gospel *Maria Magdalena et Maria Jacobi*, the *Te decet laus*, and a prayer.[2]

[1] The church was on the north side of the abbey church, and served as a cemetery chapel. It was demolished at the beginning of the seventeenth century.

[2] *Memorias de Mosteiro de Paço de Sousa e Index dos Documentos do Arquivo compostos por Frei António de Assuncão Meireles, publicacão e prefacio do Academico Titular Fundador Alfredo Pimenta, Lisboa*, 1942. *Academia Portuguesa de História, Publicoês Comemerativas do Duplo Centenario da Fundãcão e Restauração de Portugal*, doc. 2, 9, pp. 126–27. Notes given to the author by the master of ceremonies of the primatial church of Braga, Mgr. de Azevedo.

The 'burial' ceremonies in a developed form are found in a processional, printed at Lisbon in 1607,[1] and they are again met with in a processional of 1728, which was discovered by chance in the organ tribune of the cathedral church of Lamego in 1942.

Notwithstanding this, however, a decree of the Congregation of Rites, designed primarily for the diocese of Leiria, condemned the practice of taking the body of the Lord on a bier to the tomb as an 'abuse.'

The custom has survived in the diocese of Braga, where a distinctive liturgy is in use.

[1] *Cimelios*, Univ. Coimbra, MSI, 89.

41: THE RITE OF BRAGA

Altar of Repose at Braga

Two hosts for reservation are consecrated in the Mass of Holy Thursday, and taken to the 'altar of repose' after the *communio*. The celebrant, holding the *custodia*[1] or chalice containing the Eucharist, intones the antiphon for vespers (*Calicem salutaris accipiam*) and, to the accompaniment of organ and bells, takes the Sacrament to the place of repose, while the choir continues the office. In the primatial church, a small chapel in the north transept serves for both *reposoir* and sepulchre.

After the veneration of the cross on Good Friday, the Eucharist is brought back to the high altar for the Presanctified rite. The procession to the chapel is made in silence. The archbishop,[2] taking the *custodia* from the *capsula*, intones: *Corpus quod pro vobis tradetur*, which is continued by the choir as the procession returns to the high altar. A subdeacon in a folded chasuble carries the processional cross, accompanied by two taperers and two thurifers in girded albs, while six clerics in black copes carry a cloth of gold canopy over the Sacrament.

Easter Sepulchre at Braga: Processions of 'Burial' and 'Resurrection'

The unique ceremonies witnessed today in the primatial church of Braga and certain other churches of the diocese on Good Friday and Easter Day deserve a detailed commentary.

[1] The *custodia* is a eucharistic vessel peculiar to the Church of Braga.

[2] In the primatial church, the Eucharist is always carried by the archbishop, even when he is not the celebrant.

Good Friday. When the celebrant has made his Communion, he turns to the people with the *custodia*[1] containing the Eucharist and intones the vesper antiphon: *Calicem salutaris*. Then, replacing the Sacrament on the corporal, the choir continue vespers on their knees. In the meanwhile, four priests in albs and black chasubles, with, as a sign of mourning, amices on their heads, bring a bier (*feretrum*) covered with a black and gold pall to the altar. Inside the bier are four folded cloths, on which are an altar stone, corporal, missal empty cruets and keys. Two woodcuts in a work on papal ceremonial by Christopher Marcel (1516), which appeared in Venice in 1582, depict the carrying of the bier to the sepulchre in a fashion almost identical to that of Braga, although there is no mention of a procession in the text.[2] The bier is laid on the altar: the *custodia* or chalice placed inside it and the key hung round the neck of the celebrant. The Sacrament is then censed, and the two thurifers continue to swing their censers until the conclusion of vespers.

The 'procession of burial' (*procissão de enterrão*), which follows the office, proceeds slowly round the cathedral to the chapel which is to serve as the sepulchre; closed by a violet curtain (lenten veil). The participants in the procession, carrying candles, have their heads covered as 'a sign of mourning' (*in signum luctus*): seminarists turning up the back of their surplices, the clerics with amices or hoods of choir dress. (The oldest ceremonial of the convent of the Holy Cross at Poitiers directed two priests with amices on their heads, after the veneration of the cross on Good Friday, to place a small particle in a corporal, in readiness for the ceremony of the '*depositio*.'[3]) At Braga, the bier

[1] If there is no *custodia*, the cleansed chalice of the Presanctified rite is used.
[2] *Sacr. Caerem. sive Rit Eccles.* (Venice, 1582), lib. II, cap. XLIV, p. 157; cap. XLVIII, p. 160.
[3] Martène, *De antiq. eccles rit.*, t. III, lib. 4, cap. XXIII.

is carried by four priests under a black canopy, but in 1700, in the episcopate of João de Sousa (1696–1703), the pall over the bier was white and the canopy cloth of silver with fringe and tassels.[1]

The chants sung during the procession are taken from the liturgy of the *Triduum Sacrum*. Two youthful clerics plaintively sing: 'Heu, heu, our Lord and Saviour,'[2] and a station is made as the choir respond: 'We are become orphans without a father: our mothers are as widows.'[3] The *heu* theme is a kind of *planctus*, borrowed from the Lamentations of Jeremiah.[4] It is repeated each time with a different response: 'The crown is fallen from our head: woe to us, because we have sinned'; 'The Spirit of our heart, Christ the Lord, condemned to a most shameful death'; 'The joy of our heart is ceased: our lute (*cithera*) is turned into mourning.'[5] Until the procession reaches the sepulchre, cries of *Heu*, *heu* are repeated by the cantors and choir alternately. The Braga text was followed in a Cistercian processional, which appeared in Lisbon in 1757. The verses were in polyphony, arranged for four voices.

On arrival at the sepulchre, the bier is placed on the altar, and censed. It is interesting to note the similarity of the versicles and responses which follow with those found in the English liturgical books for the *depositio* ceremony:

℣. For a dwelling place he has chosen peace.

℟. He may be found in Sion.

[1] *Fastos Episcopães*, t. III, cap VIII, p 222.

[2] *Heu, heu, Domine, Salvator noster.*

[3] *Pupilli facti sumus absque Patre*: *Mater nostra vidua. Lament. Jerem.*, V, 3

[4] *Lament. Jerem.* (*Threni*), V, 3, 16, 15.

[5] *Cecedit corona capitis nostri*: *vae nobis quia peccavimus*; *Spiritus cordis nostri, Christus Dominus, morte turpissima condemnatus*; *Defecit gaudium cordis*: *versa est in luctum cithera nostra. Chorus*, in place of *cithera*, in the Vulgate. *Lament. Jerem.*, V, 16 . . . *Lament. Jerem.*, V, 15.

℣. My body.
℟. Shall rest in peace.
℣. In very peace.
℟. I will sleep and take my rest.[1]

Then the curtain before the door of the chapel is withdrawn, revealing the bier containing the Eucharist at the top of a long flight of 'steps' (gradines), with a statue of Our Lady of Sorrows at its foot. The choir sings the responsary *Sepulto Domino*, which figures in so many of the medieval 'burial' ceremonies:[2] At the Lord's burial, the tomb (*monumentum*) is made secure, rolling a stone to the door of the monument. ℣. Placing soldiers to guard it. ℣. The chief priests coming to Pilate, besought him to order a guard for the sepulchre: Go, he said, guard it as you know: then, going away, they made it secure. ℣. Placing. . . .[3] The procession then returns to the sacristy: the participants with their heads covered as before.

The text of the actual missal (1924) follows closely that of the missal of 1558, in which it appeared for the first time. A detailed description of these ceremonies is found in *Methodo da Liturgia Bracharense o modo de celebrar com a devida perfeicão o Sacrosancto Sacrificio da Missa*, a work compiled by António Tomás dos Reis in 1837. The rubric is longer than in the missal, but, with the exception of two small points, the texts are identical: (1) The bier contains nothing besides the Host; (2) The manner in which *Heu, heu* should be sung is explained minutely.

[1] ℣. *In pace factus est locus ejus.* ℟. *Et habitatio ejus in Sion.* ℣. *Caro mea.* ℟. *Requiescet in spe.* ℣. *In pace in idipsum.* ℟. *Dormiam et requiescam.*

[2] e.g., Brit. Mus. Harl. MS. 2983, fo. 30a.

[3] *Sepulto Domino, signatum est monumentum, volventes lapidem ad ostium monumenti.* ℣. *Ponentes milites, qui custodirent illud.* ℣. *Accedentes principes sacerdotum ad Pilatum, petierunt, ut juberet custodiri sepulchrum: Ite, inquit, custodite sicut scitis: illi autem abeuntes munierunt illud.* ℣. *Ponentes . . . Accedentes principes*, with a shorter verse, is the ninth responsary for matins of Holy Saturday.

The current use of Braga follows exactly the 'procession of burial' as portrayed by Alberto Castellani in the *Liber Sacerdotalis* (1523), except that in the primatial church there is no blessing with the Sacrament before it is placed in the sepulchre.

Easter Day. The Sacrament has remained in the sepulchre since Good Friday, awaiting the 'resurrection' on the third day: the black pall exchanged for one of cloth of gold; the figure of Our Lady of Sorrows removed. The archbishop, when he has prayed before the bier and high altar, is vested at the throne in amice, alb, stole and cope. The procession moves to the sepulchre: crucifer with primatial cross, taperers, thurifers, deacons of the throne, two canons in copes. The heads of the participants are no longer covered, although an ancient *ordinarium* of the church of St. Aper, Toul, directed the community (Benedictine) to veil their heads with amices in the procession to the place of 'burial' on Easter morning.[1] The Eucharist is taken from the bier and placed in a monstrance: *depositio* has given place to *elevatio*; 'burial' to 'resurrection.' Then, having censed the *Sanctissimum* and recited a versicle and collect, the archbishop carries the monstrance round the cathedral to the chapel of the Blessed Sacrament in the south transept. The cloth of gold canopy is borne by two canons in copes; while two other canons, in choir dress, carry a recumbent plain wooden cross under a white gauze veil.

The chant in the 'Procession of the Resurrection' (*Procissão do Resurreicão*) is confined to *Regina Coeli laetare*, which is twice sung to a plainchant setting and several times with an

[1] Martène, *De Antiq. Eccles. Rit.*, t. IV, lib. III, cap. XVI, ii, col. 419–20.

PLATE 21

OFFERTORY PROCESSION

Over the altar the Sacrament is reserved under a trumpet-shaped canopy. Frontispiece, Auxerre Missal, 1738

Facing page 226

PLATE 22

CHURCH OF OUR LADY OF PEACE, BRAINTREE, ESSEX

Designed by Geoffrey Webb. The tabernacle for the reservation of the Blessed Sacrament is completely enveloped with the tent-like veil.

elaborate musical rendering. Benediction is given before replacing the Sacrament in the tabernacle. The procession then returns to the choir, as the Easter hymn *O filii et filiae* is sung. Terce follows, as the archbishop vests for the Mass of the 'Solemnity of Solemnities.'

NOTE

THE purpose of this Supplement is to indicate something of the history of the reservation of the Blessed Sacrament in the Church of England and the Anglican Communion, as it was and as it subsequently developed, since the time when Papal authority was repudiated under Henry VIII, and the Latin Mass abolished under Edward VI.

The author of this chapter is an Anglican priest: the author of the main work is a Roman Catholic layman. There are no contradictions in matters of fact, where the two works overlap; but the reader is asked to make allowance for any seeming difference of approach which may appear in dealing with the question in hand.

I am indebted to a number of people who have kindly searched in parish records and particularly to Mr. A. W. Kewin of Liverpool, and also to the Superiors of a number of Anglican Communities who have kindly supplied me with precise information about the date when Reservation was first started in their chapels.

C. E. POCKNEE.

SUPPLEMENT

By Cyril E. Pocknee

RESERVATION IN THE CHURCH OF ENGLAND AND THE ANGLICAN COMMUNION SINCE 1549 UNTIL THE PRESENT CENTURY

1549–1662

Although Archbishop Cranmer and the English Reformers sought to recover the ideals of the Primitive Church, and thereby abolished any extra-liturgical cultus of the Reserved Sacrament, to which the Latin West had become accustomed since the twelfth century, they did not abolish the idea that the Sacrament of the Altar might be reserved at the Communion Service in church and conveyed to a sick person. Cranmer and his associates were probably unfamiliar with Justin Martyr's Apology, written about A.D. 150 (see page 3), in which the Consecrated Species were conveyed by the deacons to those who were prevented from being present at the Eucharist on Sunday mornings. Nevertheless, the English Reformers in the First English Prayer Book of 1549, in the Office for the Communion of the Sick, made provision for the Eucharistic elements to be brought from the service in church to the sick person, in a manner that resembles the custom mentioned by Justin thus:

'If the same day there be a celebration of the Holy Communion in the Church, then shall the priest reserve (at the open Communion) so much of the Sacrament of the Body and Blood as shall serve the sick person, and so many as shall communicate with him (if there be any). And so soon as he conveniently may, after the open Communion ended in the Church, shall go and minister the same, first to those that are appointed to communicate with the sick (if there be any), and last of all to the sick person himself.' (The spelling has been modernized.)

It was further directed that the sick man should give notice overnight, or early in the morning, of his desire to communicate, and of the number proposing to communicate with him. This method of communicating the sick is mentioned first in order in the 1549 Office and is obviously regarded as the more usual one in the case of notice being given. But a further rubric adds: 'But if the day be not appointed for the open Communion in the Church, then (upon convenient warning given) the curate shall come and visit the sick person afore noon. And having a convenient place in the sick man's house (where he may reverently celebrate) . . . he shall there celebrate the Holy Communion' and a proper Collect, Epistle and Gospel follows for use in such a contingency. But even here the idea of reserving the Sacrament is not entirely abandoned for a further rubric adds: 'And if there be more sick persons to be visited the same day that the curate doth celebrate in any sick man's house, then shall the curate (there) reserve so much of the Sacrament of the Body and Blood: as shall serve the other sick persons, and such as be appointed to communicate with them (if there be any). And immediately carry it, and minister it unto them.' So that we see the priest was expected to consecrate the elements once only and not to officiate at several full celebrations in the houses of the sick on one day. As we shall see, the custom of reserving the consecrated elements from the service in church and taking them directly to the sick was to persist in the Church of England down to the nineteenth century. It is probable that the English Reformers thought, however, that the custom of celebrating the Eucharist at the bedside of a sick person could be traced back to primitive origins; but when the learned Bingham came to treat of this matter in the first part of the eighteenth century in his *Origines Ecclesiasticae* he was hard put to it to find any primitive evidence for the consecration of the bread and wine in the sick room.

The method of taking the Consecrated Elements direct from the service in church to the sick person was suitable in towns where the chalice could be carried a short distance to the house. But in country districts and more scattered parishes where the priest would have to cross fields and stiles, and possibly unbridged streams, such a method would prove impossible. It is not surprising, therefore, that the pre-Reformation version of *viaticum* must have continued in some places whereby the Sacrament was continuously reserved in a pyx in church and taken to the sick person when required. The evidence from the King's Commissioners shows us that in two instances the pyx contained the Blessed Sacrament during their inspection of church ornaments in 1552 at Edlesborough, Bucks., and at Flintham, Notts.[1] While at Saffron Walden, Essex, their visitation to the church there on October 5th, 1552, records: 'Goods delivered for the ministration of divine service. To James Cowle and Thomas Marten, churchwardens, a chalice of silver and gilt, of xv ounces, a cope of red velvet, a carpet of blue velvet for the communion table, and vii linen cloths for the same, a little round box to carry the Sacrament in, with a purse to put it in, and all the surplices.'[2] This pyx would scarcely have been permitted to be retained if the Sacrament was not to be reserved in some manner in church

[1] Public Record Office, *Ex. Q.R. Miscel. Ch. Goods*, 1/37 and 7/82.
[2] *Proceedings of Essex Archaeological Society*, n.s. III, p. 62.

during the period from 1549–1552. Indeed, this example was recorded less than a month before the Second English Prayer Book was to be authorized on November 1st.

In the Second Prayer Book of 1552 the directions for reservation given in the 1549 rite were omitted and also the instruction to celebrate in the sick man's house. But the Collect, Epistle and Gospel of 1549 were retained, prefaced by this rubric: 'But if the sick person be not able to come to the church, and yet is desirous to receive the Communion in his house, then he must give knowledge overnight, or else early in the morning to the Curate, signifying also how many be appointed to communicate with him. And having a convenient place in the sick man's house, where the Curate may reverently minister, and a good number to receive the Communion with the sick person, with the things necessary for the same, he shall there minister the Holy Communion.' Thus the individual priest might reserve the Sacrament, but no method was prescribed, and he might carry it to the sick man and those who were to communicate with him, but he was not sufficiently instructed what service he was to use in administering it. It can be argued, therefore, from the expression 'minister' in the 1552 rubric that the parish priest was not required to have a full celebration in the sick person's room.

From 1553 to 1558 the Latin rite and its ceremonies had a temporary revival under Queen Mary and we know that continuous reservation was restored in many parishes.

With the accession of Queen Elizabeth I to the throne of England on November 17th, 1558, a policy of extreme caution was pursued by the Sovereign in religious matters; and she endeavoured to strike a balance between the views which were a legacy from Queen Mary's reign and the new views which the more extreme reformers were burning to proclaim. Nowhere is this more in evidence than in the question of the reservation of the Eucharist for the sick.

A revision of the 1552 Prayer Book was authorized in 1559 and it contained some interesting changes. There are two versions of the Elizabethan Prayer Book, one in English and one in Latin. The English version repeats the rubric from 1552 in regard to the curate 'ministering' the Holy Communion in the house of the sick person; but nothing is explicitly stated about the Sacrament being consecrated there, although this might be inferred from the instruction that 'the Priest shall first receive the Communion himself.'

The Latin Prayer Book appeared in 1560 and was intended for use at the Universities of Oxford and Cambridge and the Colleges of Eton and Winchester. The book was also recommended for the private use by all the clergy when they did not read the prayers publicly in church. The Latin book contains the propers for a Requiem on the day of a funeral and also a method of reserving the Sacrament for the sick, which we translate as follows: 'But if the sick man cannot come to church, and asks to receive Communion in his own house, then he shall signify to the parish priest at least the day before, or early in the morning, how many intend to communicate with him. And if it happen that on the same day the Lord's Supper is celebrated, then the priest at the Supper shall reserve so much of the Sacrament as suffices for the sick man, and soon after the end of the service shall go to the sick man with some of those present, and shall first communicate (with)[1] those who stand by the sick man and have been present at the Supper, and last with the sick man. But first let the General Confession and absolution with the Collect be recited, as has previously

[1] The Latin here reads, *communicabit cum illis.*

been directed.'[1] It is certain, therefore, that Elizabeth and Archbishop Parker did not regard Reservation of the 1549 type as inconsistent with the Elizabethan settlement of religion. That reservation for the sick was practised in Elizabeth's reign seems to be the only reasonable interpretation of a letter of Calvin, which Strype (1643–1737) reproduces in substance thus: 'The mention of Calvin must bring in a remarkable letter which he wrote in the month of August this year (1561) concerning ecclesiastical rites used in our office of private prayer newly established, which were scrupled by some of the English exiles upon their return, chiefly because not used by the reformed church in Geneva, concerning which they had sent to Calvin for his resolution and judgment. . . . The fourth query was, whether it were convenient to communicate the sick? And if so with what number and company? And whether in this private communion the public office should be used, or no office, but the consecrated bread only brought from the church unto the party home to his house? To which Calvin gave in substance the answer. That the sick should not be denied the sacrament, many weighty causes moved him; for should they not be communicated it would be a very blameworthy neglect of Christ's institution. . . . He liked not carrying the sacrament up and down promiscuously; for the avoiding of superstition in some and ambition and vain ostentation in others; many for such ends being apt in those days to come to these private sacraments. Which he esteemed a very difficult thing to prevent. And therefore the greater judgment and care should be used to whom they gave it. And lastly, he looked upon it as a preposterous thing to bring bread as holy

[1] *Liturgical Services of the reign of Queen Elizabeth* (*Parker Soc.* 1847), p. 404.

from the church; but to carry it in pomp, by no means tolerable.'[1]

It is of interest to note that Convocation in 1640 decided unanimously 'to petition the Royal Majesty that the Latin Version of the Public Prayers be again imprinted,'[2] the reference being to the Latin book of 1560. This Book, therefore, and the method of Reservation which it prescribed, were given the approval of the Convocation of Canterbury, in the reign of Charles I.

Bishop Lancelot Andrewes (d. 1626), defending the Anglican position against the Roman Cardinal Perron, wrote: 'It cannot be denied but reserving the Sacrament was suffered a long time in the Primitive Church. . . . But for the sick, it was always sent them home, were the distance never so great. And against the time of extremity it was thought not amiss to have it *reserved*; that, if the priest should not then be in a state to go to the sick party, and there to consecrate it for him yet at least it might be sent him, as in the case of Serapion. For it is sure they made far greater account of the receiving it as their *viaticum* than some do now. But neither doth this touch us, who desire of any that is in that case may not refuse but go to him, and minister it him. So that *Reservation* needeth not; the intent is had without it.'[3]

From the 1662 *Prayer Book until the Oxford Movement*

Anthony Sparrow, successively Bishop of Exeter and Norwich, commenting in 1657 on the Office for the Sick in the Prayer Book of 1604, gives it as his judgment that reservation is still permitted: 'The rubric at the Communion

[1] Strype, *Annals of the Reformation* (Oxford 1824), vol. 1, p. 387.
[2] E. Cardwell, *Synodalia*, vol. 2, p. 628.
[3] *Minor Works* in *Library of Anglo-Catholic Théology*, pp. 17–19.

of the sick, directs the priest to deliver the Communion to the sick; but does not there set down how much of the Communion service shall be used at the delivering of the Communion to the sick; and therefore seems to me, to refer us to former directions in times past. Now the direction formerly was this: "If the same day (that the sick is to receive the Communion) there be a celebration of the Holy Communion in church, then shall the priest reserve (at the open Communion) so much of the Sacrament, etc." '[1] The testimony of Sparrow is important as he was present at the Savoy Conference in 1661 and was one of those who helped to frame the 1662 Prayer Book. At the time of the Offertory in the Communion Service in the 1662 Book a new rubric was introduced, 'The Priest shall place upon the Table so much Bread and Wine, as he shall think sufficient.' While another rubric at the conclusion of the Service was enlarged to read: 'And if any of the Bread and Wine remain unconsecrated the Curate shall have it to his own use, *but if any remain of that which was consecrated, it shall not be carried out of the church, but the Priest and such other of the communicants as he shall call unto him, shall, immediately after the Blessing, reverently eat and drink the same.*'

The words we have italicized were an addition in 1662 to the original form of the rubric as set out in the Prayer Books of 1559 and 1604. This enlarged rubric, together with the one inserted at the offertory, have been interpreted by some commentators as precluding the reservation of the Consecrated Species for the sick. But historically it can be demonstrated that these rubrics have nothing to do with the question of reservation; and the point is never raised by the compilers of the 1662 rites or the commentators of

[1] Anthony Sparrow, *A Rationale or Practical Exposition of the Book of Common Prayer* (Ed. S. Downes, 1722), p. 223.

that period. It is surprising how closely these rubrics agree with the pseudo-Clement writing in the seventh century: 'Let so many Hosts be offered on the altar as ought to suffice for the people. But if any remain let them not be reserved until the morrow, but be carefully consumed by the clerks with fear and trembling.'[1] As the pseudo-Clement included those who would be communicated with the reserved Sacrament among those for whom the elements were to suffice, there seems no reason why the 1662 rubrics, from the literary point of view as the direct descendants, should not do the same.

There can be no doubt that the framers of the 1662 rite were familiar with the pseudo-Clementine rubric as it is expressly mentioned by Cosin in his comments on 'If any of the Bread and Wine remain.'[2] Also Cosin, writing before 1662, had remarked: 'It is likewise here ordered, "that if any of the bread and wine remain, the curate shall have it to his own use." Which words some curates have abused and extended so far, that they suppose they may take all that remains of the consecrated bread and wine itself, home to their houses, and there eat and drink the same with their other common meats . . . whereas the rubric only intends it of such bread and wine as remains unconsecrate of that which was provided for the parish, (as appeareth by the articles of enquiry hereabouts in the visitations of divers bishops). And therefore for the better clearing of this particular, some words are needful here to be added, whereby the priest may be enjoined to consider the number of them which are to receive the Sacrament, and to consecrate the bread and wine in such a proportion as shall be sufficient for them; but if any of the consecrated elements be left, that he and others with him shall decently eat and

[1] P.G., Tome 1, col. 484. [2] Cosin, Works, vol. 5 (*Lib. Ang. Cath. Theol.*, p. 132).

drink them in church before all the people depart from it.'[1] These words of Cosin explain why the addition to the original rubric was made; and this was to prevent the misuse and profanation of the Consecrated remains and their treatment as though they were unconsecrated.

Anthony Sparrow, whose writings we have already cited, interprets the rubric in the same manner as Cosin: '*If any of the Bread and Wine remain the curate shall have it to his own use.* This is if it were not consecrated; for if it be consecrated, it is all to be spent with fear and reverence by the communicants in the church.'[2] Yet, as we have already seen, Sparrow had advocated the Communion of the sick from the Sacrament reserved.

Another of the compilers of the 1662 rite was Herbert Thorndike, a Prebendary of Westminster. In his *Reformation of the Church of England better than that of the Council of Trent*, written about 1670, he even advocates perpetual reservation: 'And thus far I will particularize, as concerning the Eucharist that the Church is to endeavour the celebrating of it so frequently that it may be reserved to the next Communion. For in the meantime it ought to be so ready for them, that pass into the other world, that they need not stay for the consecrating it on purpose for every one. The reason of the necessity of it for all, which hath been delivered, aggravates it very much in danger of death. And the practice of the church attests it to the utmost. Neither will there be any necessity of giving it in one kind only, as by some passages of antiquity may be collected if common reason could deceive in a subject of this nature.'[3]

Hamon L'Estrange in the second edition of his *Alliance of Divine Offices*, published in 1690, commenting on the

[1] *Ibid.*, p. 519. [2] Sparrow, *Rationale* (Ed. Downes, 1722), p. 180.
[3] Thorndike, *Works*, vol. 5 (L.A.C.T., p. 578).

Communion of the sick in the 1662 Book says: 'Upon this account the primitive fathers, though passionately indulgent towards, and tender of their sick brethren, in granting them their spiritual *viaticum*; yet always took a care that the elements should be consecrated in church. And, indeed, if consecration be of any import, if with God it prevaileth anything effectual towards the making those elements the Body and Blood of Christ, if in us it createth any greater reverence to those dreadful mysteries, then certainly that congregation must needs excel others which is made in the full congregation, "where there is such a concourse of reverend saints, plying the throne of grace so ardently, and so unanimously for a blessing upon those elements" (Chrysost.). This rubric therefore being so consonant to antiquity, and passing the censure of Bucer without the least reproof, had a fair plea for its continuation, had not the Eucharist so reserved been abused by superstitions carrying it about in solemn procession; and the habitual adoration frequented in the Romish practice, moved our reformers to expunge it. This notwithstanding, I observe in a Latin translation of our liturgy, anno 2 Elizabeth, this rubric exactly set down according to the first liturgy of Edw. VI, enjoining the minister to reserve "sufficient for the sick person." . . . Whereby it is most evident the translation was made peculiarly for the service of the universities, and two colleges of Winchester and Eton. . . . Now this translation being framed particularly for those learned societies, they might be the better trusted with the elements reserved, upon a rational presumption that the greater light they enjoyed, the less prone and disposed would they be to error and superstition.'[1]

[1] L'Estrange's *Alliance of Divine Offices* in L.A.C.T., pp. 451–2.

Joseph Bingham in his celebrated work, *Origines Ecclesiasticae* or *The Antiquities of the Christian Church*, written between 1708 and 1722, argued in Book 15, chap. 4, for the full celebration of the Eucharist in the sick room as a custom of the primitive Church. But a careful reading of the early sources, which he cites, will show they are not examples of a clinical Celebration at the bedside. They are rather examples of bishops or priests in prison celebrating the Eucharist, or else of Masses in private oratories belonging to persons of some standing. These latter were what Jungmann has termed the Mass in a domestic oratory, where there would be a whole family with the servants gathered together.[1]

The Church of England was seriously impoverished by the secession of those bishops and priests who declined to take the oath of allegiance to William III, and who became known as the Non-Jurors. Nevertheless, freed from the trammels of the establishment and the Act of Uniformity, they produced a series of remarkable liturgical rites. It is when we turn to the English Non-Jurors' rite of the Holy Communion published in 1718, that we find the following amended and expanded form of the 1662 rubric regarding the disposal of the Consecrated Elements: 'If there be any persons who through sickness or any other urgent cause are under a necessity of communicating at their houses, then the Priest shall reserve at the open Communion so much of the Sacrament of the Body and Blood, as shall serve those who are to receive at home. And if after that, or if, when none are to communicate at their houses, any of the Consecrated Elements remain, then it shall not be carried out of the Church; but the Priest, and such other of the

[1] J. A. Jungmann, *The Mass of the Roman Rite*, vol. 1, pp. 212–18.

communicants as he shall then call unto him, shall immediately after the Blessing reverently eat and drink the same.'[1]

In the Liturgy of 1734, commonly called 'Deacon's Liturgy' after its compiler, the priest is not simply to reserve if there are sick persons to be communicated immediately after the Service, but also, 'always observing that some of the consecrated elements be constantly reserved in the vestry or some other convenient place in the Church under a safe lock, of which both the Priest and the Deacon are to have a key.'[2]

But the Liturgy of the Scottish Non-Jurors compiled by Thomas Rattray in 1734 seems to have had the most influence as it was to be copied in some respects by the Scottish Prayer Book of 1764. Rattray's liturgy states, 'Always observing that some of the Consecrated Elements be constantly reserved in the Vestry, or some other convenient place in the Church, under a safe lock, in case of any sudden emergency, wherein they may be wanted. But he shall take care that they never be kept too long, but renewed from Time to Time.'[3]

The Scottish Liturgy of 1764 was without rubrics after the Blessing, so that nothing was said in regard to the disposal of the remains of the Consecrated Elements. But it is a well-established and testified fact[4] that continuous reservation has been practised by Episcopalians in Scotland during the eighteenth and nineteenth centuries and the rubric which appears in the 1929 Scottish Prayer Book: 'According to long-existing custom in the Scottish Church,

[1] W. J. Grisbrooke, *Anglican Liturgies in the Seventeenth and Eighteenth Centuries*, p. 296.
[2] *Ibid.*, p. 316. [3] *Ibid.*, p. 332.
[4] See V. Staley, *Hierurgia Anglicana*, vol. 2, pp. 166–68, also J. Dowden, *The Annotated Scottish Communion Office* (1884), pp. 279 and 328.

the Presbyter may reserve so much of the Consecrated Gifts as may be required for the Communion of the Sick and others who could not be present at the celebration in church. All that remaineth of the Holy Sacrament, and is not so required, the Presbyter and such other of the communicants as he shall then call unto him shall, after the Blessing, reverently eat and drink' was but a confirmation and perpetuation of long established custom.[1]

It is certain, however, that Reservation of the 1549 or 'Justinian' type had never been entirely abandoned in the Church of England. The Reverend T. Keble writing in 1897 stated: 'I was told yesterday by a lady of ninety-one years old, that she remembered that her father, a very conscientious country clergyman, was in the habit of taking the Blessed Sacrament from the altar to a sick person who lived near the church, while the communicants waited in their places until his return.'[2]

John Wordsworth, Bishop of Salisbury, writing in 1901 also said: 'I am inclined to think that something like the custom of the first Prayer-book, which is really nothing but a slight extension on one side and restriction on the other of the primitive custom described by Justin Martyr in the second century, viz. that of sending Communion by the Deacons to the absent (*Apol.* i. 67), has had greater traditional continuance among us than is perhaps generally supposed. I have heard of a case of the sacrament being taken to a sick woman directly after a public celebration at Corfe Castle, fifty years ago, and I am told that the like tradition exists at Pentridge. I shall be glad to know if it can be traced elsewhere.'[3]

[1] F. C. Eeles, *Traditional Ceremonial and Customs connected with the Scottish Liturgy* (Alcuin Club, 1910), pp. 95–103.
[2] M. MacColl, *The Reformation Settlement* (1900), p. 167.
[3] J. Wordsworth, *Further considerations on Public Worship* (1901), p. 65.

H. E. Jones

PLATE 23

HANGING PYX

Holy Trinity Cathedral, Gloucester, Twentieth century

H. E. Jones

PLATE 24
HANGING PYX
Detail of Plate 23

But even more conclusive than the foregoing evidence is that of the former assistant priest of St. Oswald's, Durham, J. W. Kempe, who has left on record the fact that he communicated John Bacchus Dykes, the celebrated priest-musician and former Vicar of St. Oswald's, several times with the pre-Consecrated Elements from the altar in the months before Dykes died in 1876.[1]

Mr. Kempe has also drawn attention to the fact that it was customary in the earlier decades of the nineteenth century for the Eucharist to be 'carried from the Altar of Durham Cathedral for the communion of sick persons in the "College," or Cathedral Close.'[2] The same writer also states that he had observed this manner of communicating the sick in a Yorkshire parish (unnamed) where he stayed when on vacation as a student.

From the Oxford Movement until the present time

After the leisurely and latitudinarian atmosphere of the late Hanoverian era in England, the Oxford Movement brought new vigour and life into the Church of England. The sacramental life was stressed and weekly and even more frequent celebrations of the Holy Communion became customary. It was inevitable that in the second phase of the movement from 1845 onwards, when it became pastoral as well as theological, that the question of continuous reservation of the Sacrament of the Altar for the Communion of the sick should have come to the fore. Nevertheless, the revival of perpetual Reservation in the Church of England was not exclusively connected with its use as a means of *viaticum* for the sick, and it is evident that the

[1] J. W. Kempe, *Reservation of the Blessed Sacrament* (1887), p. 100.
[2] *Ibid.*, pp. 100–1.

cultus of the Sacrament Reserved was also in the minds of some who advocated continuous Reservation after 1845.

There can be little doubt that it was Dr. John Mason Neale who first revived perpetual Reservation in the Church of England in the oratory of the Sisterhood of St. Margaret at East Grinstead, Sussex, which he founded in 1854. The community records show that in 1857 the Sisters were making daily visits to the Sacrament reserved in their oratory, and that in 1859 Benediction of the Blessed Sacrament was in use. This oratory was not the present convent chapel as that was not built until 1865.

Most other Anglican Communities in England did not have continuous Reservation until the present century. But a notable exception was the Community of the Reparation to Jesus in the Blessed Sacrament, Rushworth Street, London, S.E. (now in the Southwark diocese), where the Community log-book for May 1873 reads as follows: 'An Altar was presented to the order for the Sisters' chapel. It was built for the Reservation of the Blessed Sacrament. The Father Superior (the Reverend Father Alfred Benjamin Goulden) celebrated the Holy Mass for the first time and the Blessed Sacrament was reserved in the Tabernacle. This was sanctioned by the Bishop of Winchester, Bishop Wilberforce.'

Some of the more obscure, and in some instances now defunct, communities had Reservation in the 1860's and 1870's. Information regarding these is given by P. F. Anson in *The Call of the Cloister* (1964 ed.), pp. 361–64.

Of the better known Anglican Communities, some had occasional Reservation before continuous Reservation became the practice. The following dates for perpetual

Reservation have been taken from the records of the Communities named:

Community of St. Peter the Apostle, Horbury, 1871.
Sisters of Bethany, Lloyd Square, 1900.
Society of the Most Holy Trinity, Ascot, 1914.
Community of St. Mary the Virgin, Wantage, 1914.
Sisters of the Church, Kilburn, 1916.
Convent of the Holy Rood, North Ormesby, 1917.
Community of St. John the Baptist, Clewer, 1920.
Society of St. John the Evangelist, Cowley, 1923.
Community of the Resurrection, Mirfield, 1928.

When we turn to consider the evidence for the revival of continuous Reservation since the Oxford Movement in English parish churches the matter becomes more complex and difficult to trace. Many parishes have no records which make reference to these things. In the middle of the nineteenth century many Anglican bishops[1] and their legal advisers considered the custom to be prohibited by the rubric at the end of the 1662 Communion Service 'none shall remain,' although, as we have pointed out, the custom of taking the Consecrated Elements from the altar to the sick room persisted in some places. It was not until 1920 with the publication of W. Lockton's *The Remains at the Eucharist* that the historical and theological background of this rubric came to be properly understood and appreciated.

Where continuous Reservation was revived in many parishes it was done without undue attention being drawn to its revival because of the alleged illegality of the practice. Sometimes it was in sacristies and sometimes even in parsonages and clergy houses. Churches such as St.

[1] *Memoirs of Archbishop Temple*, ed. E. G. Sandford (1906), vol. 2, pp. 307–8.

Matthew's, Westminster; The Ascension, Lavender Hill, and St. Bartholomew's, Brighton, had perpetual Reservation in a crypt chapel or in a chapel apart from the main church building which was approached by a staircase and was known only to the more faithful and devout members of the congregation. It would be true to state that up to the period of the first Great War of 1914–18 continuous Reservation was seldom or never on or near the High Altar.

The first conclusive evidence for perpetual Reservation is to be found in the records of St. James-the-Less, Liverpool, and this was in 1875 in the Brocklebank chapel of that church.

From 1866 under Father Lowder at St. Peter's, London Docks, there was occasional Reservation because of a cholera epidemic of that year; and this was sanctioned by the Bishop of London, Dr. Tait. Nevertheless, we may think that this 'occasional' Reservation was fairly frequent as in the period 1873–79 'the Father used to carry the Blessed Sacrament from the chapel to the High Altar, and in Its Presence a hymn or two would be sung, not necessarily the hymns usually associated with Benediction, after which the Father would give the Blessing, saying the words while holding the ciborium towards the congregation.' But the parish records at St. Peter's show that permanent Reservation was not started until December 16th, 1898.

Other churches associated with the Catholic Revival introduced perpetual Reservation as follows:

St. Margaret's, Princes Road, Liverpool, 1878 (in the sacristy).

All Saints', Plymouth, 1882.

All Saints', Middlesbrough, 1884.

St. Barnabas', Pimlico, 1887.[1]
St. John's, Tuebrook, Liverpool, 1896.
Freeland, Oxford, 1899.

In the pro-Cathedral of St. Peter's, Liverpool, a service of Benediction and Procession of the Blessed Sacrament was held at nine in the evening in 1875 in connexion with the Feast of Corpus Christi. The facts were published in the *Manchester Guardian* and they were substantiated by the priest who conducted the service. It is perhaps a little ironical that one of the most 'Protestant' dioceses in the Church of England should have been in the van of the revival of a cultus of the Sacrament Reserved.

The Report of the Royal Commission on Ecclesiastical Discipline published in three volumes in 1906 contains numerous references to alleged illegalities, both in rite and ceremonial. But it would be unwise to place too much reliance on, or give too much credence to, the references to Reservation that are to be found in these documents. Many of the witnesses were amateurs, unversed in liturgical and ecclesiological history and studies; and all too often they tended to see something illegal and 'ritualistic.' Thus at Holy Trinity, Reading, a witness reported there was a tabernacle on the altar. The incumbent was able to show that this was merely a wooden structure at the back of the altar upon which the altar cross stood.

The period between 1906 and 1927 was a time of controversy. But it was also the time of Prayer Book revision, pursued in a rather leisurely manner, and interrupted by the War of 1914–18. During that war there was an increasing demand for Reservation for the sick, especially in the large towns and cities. Some bishops were prepared to

[1] No exact record is available as to when perpetual Reservation was started at St. Alban's, Holborn.

sanction this provided the place of reservation was in a chapel with a screen and gates that could be locked, and that no extra-liturgical devotions were held in connexion with the Sacrament Reserved.

But not all bishops were prepared to sanction even this arrangement. As late as 1929 the Bishop of Liverpool attempted to suppress continuous Reservation throughout the diocese. When an impasse was reached between the bishop, Dr. A. A. David, and the incumbents of St. Thomas's, Warwick Road, St. Stephen's and St. Margaret's, Princes Road, because of their refusal to give up continuous Reservation, it was suggested that a synod should be held to try and resolve the matter. The records of this synod make interesting and strange reading. For while the synod was invoking the guidance of the Holy Spirit upon its deliberations the postman had *already* delivered at the three vicarages concerned the decision of the synod. This stated that the three parishes were under an episcopal ban and out of fellowship with the diocese.

In 1927 proposals to revise the Prayer Book of 1662 were presented to Parliament. It should be underlined that these proposals had been discussed and approved by considerable majorites in both the Convocations of Canterbury and York as well as the Church Assembly. Nevertheless, there was a militant section of Evangelical Churchmen who were prepared to resist any revision or changes in the 1662 Book; and they found an outspoken champion in the Home Secretary, the Right Hon. Sir William Joynson Hicks, Member of Parliament for Twickenham.[1] Although the proposed Book of 1927 was approved by the House of Lords it suffered a resounding defeat in the House of

[1] See G. K. A. Bell, *Randall Davidson, Archbishop of Canterbury* (1935), vol. 2, pp. 1325–60.

Commons. There can be little doubt that the matter of Reservation for the sick was one of the controversial issues as the correspondence between the Home Secretary and the Archbishop of Canterbury plainly shows.

In 1928 the Prayer Book measure was again presented to Parliament; and in order to meet the objections of Hicks and his associates the rubrics in connexion with Reservation were considerably altered and enlarged so that an incumbent could only reserve with a licence from his bishop. But this had to be preceded by the obtaining of a faculty to insert an aumbry in the north wall of a chapel or a similar place; and this faculty would only be granted if the Parochial Church Council had given a majority decision in favour of such a proposal. The late Dr. W. H. Frere, at that time Bishop of Truro and one of the supporters of the 1927 proposals, described this change of policy between the 1927 and 1928 proposals as follows: 'With regard to the Reservation of the Blessed Sacrament there has been a sad faltering in the spirit of generosity and trust, which once prevailed; this had led, step after step, to the accumulation of a mass of rigid restrictions . . . found to be impracticable.'[1]

Although the Proposed Prayer Book of 1928 was also rejected by the House of Commons its contents have been widely used throughout the Church of England in varying degrees, from Royal Weddings in Westminster Abbey and the Baptism of the infants of Members of the House of Commons to the more ordinary services of parochial churches. Most bishops have been guided by the rubrics relating to Reservation in the Communion of the sick in the 1928 Book and faculties have been granted for an aumbry to be built or inserted in the north wall of a chapel or some similar place.

[1] *Walter Howard Frere*, ed. R. C. D. Jasper (1954), p. 159.

The Cathedrals have followed rather more slowly in the revival of continuous Reservation. The first instance was at Truro in June 1927, when a hanging pyx was hung over the altar of the St. Mary's aisle. But as this aisle was used as a parish church there were objections that this ornament had been inserted without a faculty; and in 1931 the pyx was hung in another part of the cathedral which was not used parochially. Chichester and Wakefield Cathedrals started perpetual Reservation in 1930, and Winchester followed in 1933.

Because of the rubrics in the 1928 Book most bishops and their chancellors declined to permit reservation immediately over or on a high altar. A section of eminent Anglican churchmen led by Father W. H. Frere, C.R., and A. S. Duncan-Jones, Dean of Chichester, had long advocated the revival of the hanging pyx as a method of reservation as this was the traditional custom in England before the Reformation.

Since the War of 1939–45 a more comprehensive policy has gradually been pursued in regard to methods of reservation. A hanging pyx was installed in Ely Cathedral in 1954 and another at Gloucester Cathedral in 1958. In recent years faculties have been granted for hanging pyxes in the London, Southwark and Oxford dioceses.[1]

The present Bishop of Southwark, Dr. Stockwood, has a hanging pyx for continuous Reservation over the altar in his chapel.

It has commonly been supposed that a tabernacle standing on the altar for reservation was an illegal ornament in the Church of England. But as long ago as 1930 the late Bishop of Bradford, Dr. Blunt, had this method in his chapel. We have also quoted the fact that in 1873 Bishop

[1] See Pocknee, *The Christian Altar* (1963), pp. 104–5.

Wilberforce, of Winchester, authorized this method in the chapel of an Anglican community. On February 2nd, 1953, a faculty was granted for a tabernacle to stand on the altar at Shiplake, Henley-on-Thames (Oxford diocese). In the same year at St. Julian's, Norwich, after the restoration of war damage, a general faculty was issued for the restoration of the church, and the stone high altar had a tabernacle on it when it was consecrated by Bishop Herbert, the diocesan.

Elaborate Sacrament Houses have also been installed in several churches during the past decade, e.g. Mickleton, Gloucestershire; St. Philip and St. James, Oxford; St. Mary-le-Bow, London. These have all received a faculty.

The effects of the second phase of the Oxford Movement after 1845 soon made themselves felt in other parts of the Anglican Communion. Outside the Provinces of Canterbury and York the Anglican Churches not being part of the establishment and untrammelled by Acts of Parliament or Royal Commissions on Ecclesiastical Discipline, have introduced perpetual Reservation on a wide scale and this has been followed by extra-liturgical services to the Blessed Sacrament in some instances. As early as 1864 we find continuous Reservation had been instituted at St. Paul's, Baltimore, in the Episcopal Church of the United States under the incumbency of Dr. W. E. Wyatt.[1]

It is also true to state in general terms that in other parts of the Anglican Communion no attempt has been made to suppress continuous Reservation as sometimes happened in the first decades of the present century in England. We have already noted the longstanding tradition for continuous Reservation in the Scottish Episcopal Church,

[1] E. Clowes Chorley, *Men and Movements in the American Episcopal Church* (New York, 1946), p. 255.

which can be traced back long before the Oxford Movement in England. Official recognition was given to this custom in the rubrics of the Scottish Prayer Book of 1929. Other Anglican Prayer Books, e.g. the South African rite of 1929, have also given official recognition to perpetual Reservation as a method of communicating the sick.

SELECTED BIBLIOGRAPHY

ANDRIEU, Michel. *Immixtio et Consecratio*. Paris, 1924.

ANDRIEU, Michel. *Les Ordines Romani du haut moyen âge*, 5 vols. Louvain, 1931–61.

ATCHLEY, E. G. C. *Ordo Romanus Primus*. London, 1905.

BISHOP, Edmund. *Liturgica Historica*. Oxford, 1918.

BLOUET, Léon. *Le Chrismale de Mortain*. Coutances, n.d.

BRAUN, Joseph. *Der Christliche Altar in seiner geschichtlichen Entwicklung*, 2 vols. Munich, 1924.

BRAUN, Joseph. *Der Christliche Altargerät*. Munich, 1932.

BUCHWALD, Rudolf. *De Liturgia Gallicana: dissertatio*. Breslau, 1890.

CATTANEO, Enrico. *I Canti della Frazione e Communione nella Liturgia Ambrosiana. Miscell. Mohlberg*, vol. 2. Rome, 1949.

Codex Juris Canonici. Rome, 1918.

COMPER, J. N. *Practical Considerations on the Gothic or English Altar and certain dependent Ornaments. St. Paul's Ecclesiological Society*, 1895.

COMPER, J. N. *The Reasonableness of the Ornaments Rubric illustrated by a comparison of the German and English Altars. St. Paul's Ecclesiological Society*, 1900.

COOK, G. H. *The English Mediaeval Parish Church*. London, 1955.

COOK, G. H. *The English Cathedrals through the Centuries*. London, 1957.

Corpus Scriptorum Ecclesiasticorum Latinorum. Vienna, 1890, 1906.

COX, J. C. and HARVEY, A. *English Church Furniture*. London, 1907.

Dictionnaire de Théologie Catholique. Paris, 1903 seq.

Dictionnaire d'Archéologie Chrétienne et de Liturgie. Cabrol, F. and LECLERCQ, H. Paris, 1907 seq.

DIJK, S. J. P. van and WALKER, J. Hazelden. *The Myth of the Aumbry*. London, 1957.

DIX, Gregory. *A Detection of Aumbries*. London, 1942.

DUCHESNE, Louis. *Liber Pontificalis*, vol. I. Paris, 1855.

DUGDALE, William. *Monasticon Anglicanum*, 5 vols. London, 1846.

EELES, F. C. *King's College Chapel, Aberdeen*. Edinburgh, 1956.

FEASEY, H. J. *Ancient English Holy Week Ceremonial*. London, 1897

FREESTONE, W. H. *The Sacrament Reserved. Alcuin Club*. London, 1917.

FRERE, W. H. *Visitation Articles and Injunctions of the Period of the Reformation*, 3 vols. *Alcuin Club*. London, 1910.

HARTZHEIM, J. *Concilia Germaniae*, 11 vols. Cologne, 1759–90.

JUNGMANN, J. A. *Missarum Sollemnia*, vol. 3. Paris, 1954.

KÖSTER, L. *De Custodia Sanctissimae Eucharistiae*. Rome, 1940.

LABBE, Philip. *Sacrosancta Concilia*, 15 vols. Paris, 1671–72.

LAMBOT, C. *North Italian Services of the 11th Century*. *Henry Bradshaw Society*, 1931.

LEBRUN, Pierre. *Explication . . . des prières et des cérémonies de la Messe*, 4 vols. Paris, 1726.

LECLERCQ, H. *Colombe Eucharistique*. *Dict. d'Archéol. Chrét. et de Lit.*, t. 3, part 2.

LECLERCQ, H. *Réserve Eucharistique*. *D.A.C.L.*, t. 14, part 2.

LOCKTON, W. *The Treatment of the Remains at the Eucharist after Holy Communion and the Time of the Ablutions*. Cambridge, 1920.

LYNDWOOD, William. *Provinciale seu Constitutiones Angliae*. Oxford, 1679.

MABILLON, Jean. *De Liturgia Gallicana*, 3 books. *Pat. Lat.*, t. LXXII, cols. 99–382.

MAFFEI, E. *La Réservation Eucharistique jusqu'à la Renaissance*. Brussels, 1942.

MANSI, J. D. *Sacrorum Conciliorum nova et amplissima Collectio*. Venice, 1767 seq.

MANY, S. *Praelectiones de Missa, cum appendice de Sanctissimo Eucharistiae Sacramento*. Paris, 1903.

MARTÈNE, Edmond and DURAND, Ursin. *Voyage Littéraire de deux religieux bénédictins de la Congrégation de Saint-Maur*, 2 parts. Paris, 1717.

MICKLETHWAITE, J. T. *Ornaments of the Rubric*. *Alcuin Club*. London, 1897.

MIGNE, J. P. *Patrologia Latina*. Paris, 1844–55.

MOLÉON, Sieur de (Lebrun-Desmarettes). *Voyages liturgiques de France*. Paris, 1718.

MURRAY, D. L. *Reservation: Its Purpose and Method*. *Alcuin Club*. London, 1923.

Ordines Romani, I-XV. MIGNE, J. P. *Pat. Lat.*, t. LXXVIII. Paris, 1895.

Peacock, E. *English Church Furniture, Ornaments and Decorations at the period of the Reformation* as exhibited in a list of the goods *destroyed in certain Lincolnshire churches*, 1566. London, 1866.

Raible, F. *Der Tabernakel einst und jetst.* Freiburg i/ Breisgau, 1908.

Ratti, Achille. *Acta Ecclesiae Mediolanensis*, vols. 2 and 3. Milan, 1892.

Righetti, Mario. *Manuale di Storia Liturgica*, vol. I. Milan, 1945.

Rock, Daniel. *The Church of our Fathers* as seen in St. Osmund's Rite for the Cathedral of Salisbury, 4 vols. Edit. Hart, G. W. and Frere, W. H. London, 1905.

Stone, Darwell. *The Reserved Sacrament.* London, 1918.

Thurston, H. *Benediction of the Blessed Sacrament, The Month.* London, 1901.

Thurston, H. *Reservation of the Blessed Sacrament. Catholic Encyclopedia*, vol. XII.

Walters, J. B. *London Churches at the Reformation.* London, 1939.

Wilkins, David. *Concilia Magnae Britanniae et Hiberniae*, 4 vols. London, 1737.

Young, Karl. *The Drama of the Mediaeval Church*, 2 vols. Oxford, 1933.

INDEX